Letters to ONE

SUNY series in Queer Politics and Cultures
———————
Cynthia Burack and Jyl J. Josephson, editors

Letters to ONE

Gay and Lesbian Voices from the 1950s and 1960s

Edited and with an Introduction by
CRAIG M. LOFTIN

Published by State University of New York Press, Albany

© 2012 State University of New York

All rights reserved

Printed in the United States of America

No part of this book may be used or reproduced in any manner whatsoever without written permission. No part of this book may be stored in a retrieval system or transmitted in any form or by any means including electronic, electrostatic, magnetic tape, mechanical, photocopying, recording, or otherwise without the prior permission in writing of the publisher.

For information, contact State University of New York Press, Albany, NY
www.sunypress.edu

Production by Eileen Meehan
Marketing by Anne M. Valentine

Library of Congress Cataloging-in-Publication Data

Loftin, Craig M.
  Letters to One : gay and lesbian voices from the 1950s and 1960s / Craig M. Loftin.
      p. cm. — (SUNY series in queer politics and cultures)
  Includes bibliographical references and index.
  ISBN 978-1-4384-4298-3 (pbk. : alk. paper)
  ISBN 978-1-4384-4297-6 (hbk. : alk. paper)
    1. Homosexuality—United States. 2. One (Los Angeles, Calif.) 3. Gays—United States. 4. Lesbians—United States. 5. Gay liberation movement—United States. I. Title.

HQ76.3.U5L64 2012
306.76'60973—dc23   2011035852

10 9 8 7 6 5 4 3 2 1

For Daniel and Maggie

Contents

Acknowledgments	ix
Introduction	1
Chapter 1: Biography and Self-Analysis	13
Chapter 2: Love, Sex, and Relationships	65
Chapter 3: Repression and Defiance	103
Chapter 4: Incarceration	151
Chapter 5: Representations and Stereotypes	197
Notes	221
Index	229

Acknowledgments

Thank you Joseph Hawkins, Pat Allen, Misha Schutt, Stuart Timmons, and all of the volunteers and staff at the ONE National Gay and Lesbian Archives for providing me access to the letters and such a wonderful environment to learn about gay history. Thank you Steve Ross, Leila Zenderland, John Laslett, Frank Stricker, and Bob Slayton for useful feedback on the introduction. Thank you Lois Banner for your perpetual inspiration. Thank you Larin McLaughlin, Beth Bouloukos, Andrew Kenyon, Eileen Meehan, Cynthia Burack, and Jyl Josephson at SUNY Press. Thank you Leila Rupp. Thank you Daniel for all your help.

Introduction

Letter writing is a dying craft. Whether communicating to relatives back home, to a lover during a period of separation, or to the editor of a newspaper, the process of writing words manually on an actual piece of paper has mostly been replaced by the ease and convenience of email, instant messaging, Facebook posts, Tweets, and other new forms of electronic communication. Communication through electronic messaging favors spontaneity and impulsivity, whereas the rituals of formal letter writing require more planning and thought. These rituals include choosing paper (friendly small stationery tinted blue or businesslike white 8-1/2" x 11"?) and deciding whether to handwrite or type the letter (handwriting evokes intimacy, typing evokes cold professionalism). All of the senses are involved in formal letter writing. The paper has a physical texture in the hands. Ink and pencil lead have distinctive odors; scribbling and typing make distinctive sounds. The gluey taste of envelopes and (in the past) stamps lingers in the mouth. Rather than merely pushing a "send" button, letters require physical effort to mail, time during which an individual might decide to revise the letter once more, or perhaps not send it at all.

The letters you are about to read were written by gay men and lesbians during the 1950s and the early to mid-1960s. These letters were written to the editors of *ONE*, the first openly gay magazine in the United States. *ONE* reached several thousand readers every month from 1953 to 1967. Although *ONE* did edit and publish some letters in its monthly "Letters to the Editor" section, most of the letters in this book have never been published in any form.

Each issue of *ONE* offered a broad range of gay-related contents, including essays, fiction, poetry, satire, and crime reports, as well as reviews of books, movies, and plays. *ONE* was published by ONE, Inc., one of three major American "homophile" organizations of the 1950s and 1960s (gay activists described themselves as "homophiles" until the late 1960s). The two other major homophile organizations were the Mattachine Society, founded in Los Angeles in 1950, and the Daughters of Bilitis, founded in San Francisco in 1955. ONE, Inc., was founded in late 1952 when several Mattachine members in Los Angeles broke away from Mattachine because they believed that publishing a monthly magazine would mobilize gay men and lesbians across the country more effectively than Mattachine's secretive organizing strategies. *ONE*'s approach was highly influential because the Mattachine Society and the Daughters of Bilitis both began publishing their own magazines modeled after *ONE* in subsequent years. In addition to these American homophile organizations, at least a dozen other homophile organizations existed in Western Europe during the 1950s, many with their own publications. Some of the letters in this book provide interesting details about these American and European organizations that were at the forefront of early gay rights activism, but most of these letters were written by individuals whose only contact with homophile activism was reading *ONE* magazine and writing a letter to the editor. These individuals did not consider themselves "activists" in any formal sense, but they nonetheless represented a growing civil rights impulse that was permeating gay individuals and communities nationwide in the 1950s and 1960s. Academic scholarship on the homophile movement has tended to overlook this grass-roots dimension.[1]

Letters to *ONE* usually opened with a request to "please renew my subscription," and then diverged into a variety of topics. Some correspondents gave the magazine soaring praise; others, damning criticism. Some wrote to share news about themselves or their local communities; others wrote just to get a few things "off my chest," in the words of one correspondent.[2] Some people asked for advice, such as how to find a lawyer, how to handle family problems, or how to meet other gay people. These letters offer a unique window into the collective thoughts and experiences of gay people at a time when their sexual identities and communities were often camouflaged and shrouded in secrecy.

During and after *ONE*'s years of publication, Dorr Legg, *ONE*'s business manager, kept careful guard over the thousands of letters written to the magazine. After Legg's death in 1994, the letters became part of the ONE National Gay and Lesbian Archives in Los Angeles, where I found them in unlabeled boxes while working as a volunteer and researcher. The letters chosen for this book provide the richest descriptions of the writers' lives and feelings.[3] These letters tell detailed stories, reveal personal information, and describe the thoughts, fears, and hopes of their writers. I favored letters with distinct voices or unexpected observations. The 127 letters in this volume represent a broad range of viewpoints and experiences, but they are not a representative sample of gay people across the country and should not be interpreted this way. Each letter represents only the person who wrote it. Together, however, these letters provide a collective mosaic of post–World War II gay and lesbian identity.

ONE received letters from every region of the country. This book contains letters from 25 states and the District of Columbia. Of the 127 letters, 28 came from California; 21 from New York; 7 each from Texas, Illinois, and Pennsylvania; 5 from Florida; 3 from Kansas, New Jersey, and Washington, D.C.; 2 each from Delaware, Indiana, Maryland, Michigan, Missouri, Ohio, Oklahoma, and Tennessee; and one each from Connecticut, Georgia, Massachusetts, Montana, Nebraska, Nevada, North Carolina, Washington, and Wisconsin. The Midwest and Deep South are the least represented regions in the ONE correspondence. Internationally, 5 letters came from Canada and 9 from other countries. Four letters gave no address. The letters came disproportionately from large cities such as New York City (19 letters) and Los Angeles (13 letters). Slightly less than one-half of the letters came from midsize towns, suburbs, or small towns.[4]

One might expect these letters to be bleak and depressing. According to conventional wisdom, gay men and lesbians suffered relentlessly in the 1950s and 1960s because of the repressive practices of the federal government, police, medical profession, and churches. Some letters certainly conform to these expectations. In most letters written to ONE, however, the general tone is not despair, but rather resilience and strategic adaptation with a sense of irony and even humor despite the serious challenges many writers faced. Gay people were undoubtedly victimized in these years, but most ONE correspondents did not think of themselves as victims. Their letters are nuanced and complex. They defy many assumptions about gay life in the 1950s and 1960s. Many letters seem strikingly contemporary, as if they could have been written in 2012 rather than 1955 because so many of the problems described in these letters persist today. Gay people still routinely suffer from police harassment, job discrimination, and religious condemnation, as well as everyday harassment, ostracism, and violence.

The letters vividly capture the fears, anxieties, and disasters that befell gay people during these years of McCarthyite repression and institutionalized homophobia, but they also demonstrate a countervailing trend: the significant growth of gay and lesbian communities after World War II. The very existence of the letters reflects the developing sophistication of a national gay subculture in the 1950s and 1960s. No comparable body of correspondence from so many self-identified gay men and lesbians is known to exist from earlier decades. The letters represent an unprecedented national dialogue about the status of gay people in the United States, facilitated by the first American publication to declare itself on its cover a "homosexual magazine" with a "homosexual viewpoint." Gay people invented many new institutions and experimented with new methods of individual and collective visibility in these years.[5] Widespread police crackdowns against gay individuals and communities in the 1950s, ironically, reflected the growing scale and visibility of the national gay subculture. More antigay crackdowns occurred because there were more gay institutions and communities to crack down on.

Several large-scale historical events in the mid-twentieth century influenced the growth of gay communities and identities in the United States. The first event was World War II. The war's massive gender-segregated military mobilization brought persons with homosexual desires together from across the country. In the early years of the war, the presence of gay and lesbian soldiers was largely considered unproblematic, allowing a gay and lesbian subculture to flourish within the military. This tolerance (due to the increased need for soldiers) served to spread the notion of homosexuality as a discreet identity and subculture with its own folkways and history. In 1943 military branches began investigating and dishonorably discharging lesbian and gay soldiers by the thousands. These expelled soldiers and their gay friends were shocked by such contemptible treatment after risking death for their country. According to Allan Bérubé, "The generation of gay men and women who served in World War II grew into adulthood fighting one war for their country and another to protect themselves from their government's escalating mobilization against them. When they returned to civilian life, some fought for their right to be treated fairly as patients, veterans, and citizens."[6] World War II made gay people aware of their large numbers and raised expectations about how they should be treated.

The second event was the 1948 publication of Alfred Kinsey's *Sexual Behavior in the Human Male*, better known as the male Kinsey Report. Kinsey was a zoologist at Indiana University who compiled thousands of detailed sex histories during the 1930s and 1940s. His published results were a best-selling cultural bombshell that revealed a wide gap between prudish American sexual morality and actual sexual behavior. According to the report, homosexual behavior was surprisingly common among American men. More than one-third of Kinsey's surveyed men had had adult sexual experiences involving orgasms with other men. The report statistically demonstrated that homosexuality was not some exotic abnormality but rather a routine part of human behavior. Kinsey concluded from his research that social prohibitions against homosexuality had no rational basis.[7] Similar to World War II, the Kinsey Reports (a female volume came out in 1953) emboldened gay people's sense of collective identity, reminded them of their large numbers, and indirectly encouraged protest against antigay laws and attitudes. Fittingly, *ONE* correspondents revered Kinsey. A poem published in *ONE*'s December 1953 issue declared, "You just mark my word: one day it will be *Saint* Kinsey!"[8]

The third event was the cold war. As tensions mounted between the United States and Soviet Union in the late 1940s and early 1950s, many robustly anticommunist politicians (such as U.S. Senator Joseph McCarthy) claimed that gay and lesbian government employees weakened national security because homosexuals were allegedly mentally unstable and uniquely susceptible to blackmail, thus more likely to divulge sensitive government secrets to Soviet spies. In 1950 a Senate subcommittee conducted hearings into the employment of "homosexuals and other sex perverts" in government. Thousands of lesbian and gay federal employees lost their jobs and careers in the following decades.[9]

ONE catered to a disproportionately middle-class, white-collar demographic that was more likely to feel the impact of cold war–related job anxieties compared to blue-collar workers. Many *ONE* correspondents were government employees who feared discovery of their homosexuality by government investigators. Others worked as engineers or secretaries for government-contracted private companies in the military-industrial complex, and thus were subject to the same extensive background scrutiny and antigay policies as government workers. A high number of *ONE* correspondents worked in education, a profession noted for rampant political blacklisting and loyalty oaths during the peak years of cold war hysteria. According to a 1961 readers' survey, approximately 20 percent of *ONE*'s readership worked in education as teachers, professors, or librarians, or were college students, and about 40 percent worked in white-collar jobs outside of education (including many government and government-contracted workers). Approximately 27 percent were blue-collar or agricultural workers, and the remaining 13 percent worked in creative professions such as music or art, or were unemployed.[10]

The fourth major historical event to influence the rise of gay and lesbian communities and activism was the post–World War II black civil rights movement. The black civil rights movement provided inspiration for gay people to contemplate their own collective power and to think about similarities between society's treatment of gay people and black people. World War II brought each group's second class status into sharper focus and resulted in more organized and vocal demands for full inclusion into American society. Both the black civil rights movement and the homophile movement sought to challenge prevailing stereotypes by depicting their constituencies as respectable, dignified, hard-working, patriotic, and nonthreatening. Yet important historical differences existed between the two groups as well. The black civil rights movement was much older, dating back to abolitionism before the Civil War. Gay Americans had no comparable tradition of formal activism on which to draw. In addition, most gay people in these years were able to "pass as heterosexual," whereas most black Americans could not pass as white. Homophile activists (who were predominantly white, as were *ONE*'s contributors and correspondents) thus adopted cautious strategies for fear that too much sudden visibility or noisy protest might incite a cataclysmic backlash. Some *ONE* correspondents advocated more aggressive protest strategies, such as street marches and public demonstrations, but at least as many feared that *ONE* magazine might already be pushing the boundaries of tolerance and might get shut down, its mailing lists seized, and subscribers arrested. To the early homophile activists and *ONE* subscribers, one of the lessons of the black civil rights movement was that significant change took a long time. It had been a long journey from slavery to *Brown v. Board of Education* in 1954. Major changes in social attitudes about gay people would take a long time as well. But change was possible.

These four events—World War II, the Kinsey Reports, cold war national security hysteria, and the black civil rights movement—created a social context ripe for the widespread growth of a civil rights impulse among lesbians and gay men during the 1950s. These events brought gay people together, validated their identities as gay men and lesbians, and gave them courage to challenge (individually and collectively) many of the long-held biases and bigotries against same-sex attraction and behavior. These events also made them scapegoats and targets to a variety of repressive forces, particularly McCarthyites adept at exploiting national security anxieties. Under the shadow of these events, a generation of lesbians and gay men tried to make sense of their lives, their growing feeling of community, as well as their marginalization. In their letters to *ONE*, their civil rights impulse is reflected in their increased confidence to assert their right to live their lives as they saw fit in a manner that felt natural and right.

The letters in this book are organized into five chapters reflecting several major recurring themes. Their categorization is somewhat imprecise, however, because individual letters often discuss multiple themes.

The letters in chapter 1, "Biography and Self-Analysis," are autobiographical and self-analytical in nature. These letters include "coming out" stories as well as opinions about the role of homosexuality in biology, society, and history. During the years these letters were written, homosexuality was listed as a "mental illness" in the first *Diagnostic and Statistical Manual of Mental Disorders (DSM)*, published in 1952. In 1973, the American Psychiatric Association removed homosexuality from its list of mental illnesses, mainly because of protests by gay activists.[11] The letters show that most *ONE* correspondents rejected the "mental illness" diagnosis long before 1973. Furthermore, the letters show that many psychologists, doctors, and therapists in the 1950s and 1960s also rejected the belief that homosexuality was a disease. Many correspondents told *ONE* that medical professionals had helped them accept their homosexuality and live happier lives.

Some of the letters in chapter 1 discuss the complex relationship between gender and sexuality. Gay people had long used manifestations of "gender inversion" as a means of recognizing one another, and scientific theories proclaiming that homosexuals were persons trapped in the bodies of the opposite gender were common before World War II. After World War II, the belief that homosexuality was a form of gender inversion declined because of the Kinsey Reports, which rejected any biological association between sexual preference and gender behavior. In addition, a middle-class model of homosexual identity that emphasized gender conformity rather than gender inversion became more prominent after World War II (reflecting the broader growth of middle-class identity in American society after World War II).[12] This postwar gay emphasis on gender conformity is expressed in several letters, sometimes in the form of animosity and loathing toward effeminate gay male "swishes."

Several correspondents noted that gay men tended to dominate discussions of gay civil rights and that lesbian voices seemed marginalized within the homophile movement. Only 18 percent of the letters in this book came from women. This is an overrepresentation of the actual percentage of letters *ONE* received from women, which was somewhere between 5 percent and 10 percent.[13] *ONE*'s editors continually struggled to attract more female readers. Most of the magazine's contributors were men, however, so its contents emphasized gay male experiences.

Some of the autobiographical letters in chapter 1 also touch on religion. Several *ONE* correspondents suffered religious conflict and church ostracism over their homosexuality, but resolved these conflicts by accepting their homosexuality as God's will. Interestingly, several ministers wrote lengthy letters praising *ONE* magazine and condemning antigay bigotry. Christian churches, overall, were certainly not in favor of homosexuality in the 1950s and 1960s, but they were not very noisy about it until the rise of the political "religious right" in later decades.[14] African-American churches in particular tended to avoid the topic of homosexuality in the immediate post–World War II years.[15]

Chapter 2, "Love, Sex, and Relationships," contains letters discussing more intimate aspects of gay life. From the letters received, sexual gratification (for men, at least) was not difficult to find in these years, even in unlikely places such as small towns. But finding relationships more substantial than " 'blow-jobs' and one night stands," as one correspondent wrote, was exceedingly difficult in the antigay social climate.[16] Although the word "marriage" was not used often in the letters, a repeatedly expressed desire for long-term and permanent relationships foreshadows the current struggle for legal recognition of gay marriages. Many gay people were clearly thinking about their relationships in political terms in the 1950s and 1960s. They were coming to understand that gay equality meant the right to pursue romance, love, and companionship (whether or not they called it "marriage") on an equal footing with heterosexuals. Unlike today, however, long-term gay couples in the 1950s usually went to great lengths to ensure that civic authorities did *not* recognize their relationships because they could be arrested and jailed.

Chapter 3, "Repression and Defiance," contains letters describing antigay persecution, such as getting arrested for a homosexual offense, getting kicked out of the military, or having "suspicious" mail seized by postal authorities. Homosexual behavior, described by various state laws as "sodomy" or "the crime against nature," was illegal throughout the United States during the 1950s. In 1961 Illinois became the first state to decriminalize homosexual behavior, followed by Connecticut ten years later in 1971. During the 1970s, about half of U.S. states decriminalized homosexual behavior, and in 2003 the U.S. Supreme Court decision *Lawrence v. Texas* declared all laws criminalizing homosexuality as unconstitutional.[17] A few lonely *ONE* correspondents in the 1950s and early 1960s were unable to overcome their fears of arrest and consequently avoided contact with other gay people. Most of *ONE*'s correspondents, however, accepted varying degrees of risk in order to participate in gay life. Their letters describe sporadic and inconsistent police enforcement against gay bars and other gathering places. Police raids often occurred after years of relatively peaceful free association. The possibility of getting arrested frightened everyone who walked into a gay bar.

Antigay crackdowns by the U.S. Postal Service were of particular concern to *ONE* subscribers and correspondents. Many *ONE* correspondents relied heavily on the Post Office to participate in gay life. They joined pen pal services and got to know one another, they ordered books and publications with gay themes, and some gay men acquired large collections of homoerotic male physique photos through the mail. Federal law, however, gave Post Office officials broad power to seize mail they considered obscene. For some postal officials, this could include anything pertaining to homosexuality. Getting caught with "obscene" mail (however defined) might result in fines, penalties, and unwanted publicity that could lead to professional ruin. When *ONE* first appeared on newsstands in 1953, its legal status was uncertain.[18] From the editors' standpoint, as long as they avoided erotic contents, the magazine should be constitutionally permissible. Twice, however, postal officials in Los Angeles seized all copies of individual *ONE* issues on obscenity grounds, once in 1953 and again in 1954. Postal officials reversed the first seizure after further review. *ONE* fought the second seizure to the U.S. Supreme Court, which, in 1958, ruled that the magazine was not obscene.[19] This ruling opened the way for dozens of other gay and lesbian publications in subsequent years.

The letters in chapter 3 not only express anger and frustration over police and postal harassment, but also a desire to do something about it. The cumulative impact of gay arrests, firings, and unwanted exposure fueled a civil rights impulse among gay and lesbian Americans in the 1950s and 1960s. I use the word "impulse" because most *ONE* correspondents did not know exactly *how* to improve their status, but believed *something* must be done and that they could contribute in some manner. Facing injustices and indignities, gay people increasingly came to believe that they were as deserving of equal civil rights—the right to associate with one another, the right to work for a living, the right to fair treatment from police and courts, the right to a family life, the right to pursue happiness—as any other American citizen.

While *ONE* magazine's civil rights-oriented contents probably influenced the resilient tone of many letters, we cannot assume that every correspondent's civil rights impulse came primarily from the magazine. Some of the letters in this book were from die-hard readers who dutifully absorbed every issue, but other letter writers seem to have barely looked at the magazine. Some correspondents obtained *ONE*'s address from a friend or acquaintance and never even saw the magazine. The letters give the impression that most of these people did not need a magazine to tell them how poorly society was treating them and that something needed to be done about it. They learned this from their own experiences, from people they knew, or from reading about the latest gay arrests in their local newspapers. *ONE* did, however, inspire people to express their frustrations in writing, thereby sharing these frustrations with others—a member of *ONE*'s staff, at least, and possibly *ONE*'s entire readership. *ONE*'s contents influenced the vocabulary and tone of the letters, while at the same time *ONE*'s readers influenced the vocabulary and tone of the magazine because *ONE* frequently borrowed ideas for essays, stories, and reviews from its readers. The popular "Tangents" column in each issue, which reported gay news from around the country, drew heavily from information provided by readers in letters. Thus, the influence between *ONE* and its readership went in both directions.

Chapter 4, "Incarceration," continues the persecution theme by featuring several lengthy letters from gay men who served time in prisons or mental hospitals. These represent worst-case scenarios. Even though most gay people avoided incarceration, news of such stories made their way through gay social grapevines and put a chill in gay social life.

To avoid arrest and incarceration, secrecy was very important. Gay people "came out" to one another in the 1950s and 1960s, but usually not to heterosexual family members, employers, or friends. *ONE* magazine itself challenged these secrecy patterns through its open sale on public newsstands, which accounted for a majority of the issues sold.[20] In other ways, however, *ONE* did try to conceal itself. Subscription copies were mailed in plain brown envelopes showing only *ONE*'s address. *ONE*'s staff and writers usually used pseudonyms, and the magazine did not publish its letter writers' names (these names remain confidential even today). Many of the letters in this book convey a secretive tone, as though the writer was revealing special, privileged information—"I will briefly tell you something I want kept in the strictest of confidence," wrote a man from Connecticut, for example.[21] Letters written to *Life* magazine or *Popular Mechanics* lack such secretive urgency.

The letters in chapter 5, "Representations and Stereotypes," discuss representations of gay people in popular culture and the media. Popular culture influenced how gay men and lesbians understood their sexuality in complex ways during the 1950s and 1960s. On one hand, the lack of positive, openly gay role models in the media, combined with recurrent negative images of gay-identified people as crazy, suicidal, or villainous, certainly wreaked havoc on the self-esteem of many gay men and women.[22] On the other hand, the letters show that gay people routinely rejected the disparaging stereotypes and representations of them in popular culture. In addition, despite the censorship of overt references to homosexuality in movies, television, and other mass media, *ONE* correspondents found no shortage of gay, lesbian, and queer images, insinuations, and associations in mass media. Some *ONE* correspondents railed against negative gay stereotypes and expressed worry over the social harm such stereotypes caused. At the same time, some correspondents found positive representations in surprising places. A writer from Pasadena, California, for example, described an article about homosexuality in the sleazy tabloid *Hush-Hush* as "quite good and unprejudiced."[23] Another letter writer praised talk show host Johnny Carson's handling of Liberace's effeminate flamboyance during a *Tonight Show* appearance in the early 1960s. Another writer enthusiastically offered gay interpretations of several current movies. In each of these cases, the letter writers challenged the invisibility of gay people in the media as well as the negative assumptions that so often permeated public discussions of homosexuality.

Throughout this book (with several notable exceptions, however), the letter writers were neither conflicted about their sexual desires, behavior, and identities, nor were they apologetic. One finds in these letters, if not gay pride itself, then at least an immediate precursor to the more politically formalized gay pride that would flourish later. Gay pride is usually assumed not to have existed in the gloomy "pre-Stonewall" 1950s and 1960s. The letters challenge the idea that the 1969 Stonewall riots should serve as such a stark divider between two supposedly distinct historical eras. The heavy academic reliance on phrases such as "pre-Stonewall," "before Stonewall," or "since Stonewall," tends to minimize the important continuities in gay identity and politics from the 1950s to the present.[24] Certainly gay culture experienced major breakthroughs in the 1970s, especially with the widespread legalization of homosexuality and the redefinition of "coming out" to include heterosexuals. But other developments, such as the growth of gay activism and gay pride, were around long before Stonewall. Overall, in letters to *ONE*, the similarities between gay life before and after Stonewall seem stronger than the differences.[25]

The letters also challenge the common perception that gay men and lesbians spent the 1950s "in the closet." The word "closet" neither appears in any letters in this book, nor in any *ONE* correspondence in its current usage.[26] The modern closet metaphor did not exist in the 1950s and early 1960s because there was no expectation that gay people would reveal their homosexuality to anyone except to other gay people. "Coming out" to heterosexuals was a political strategy introduced by gay activists in the late 1960s and early 1970s. "The closet" emerged as the binary opposite of this new definition of "coming out"; hence the phrase "coming out *of the closet*" replaced the older phrase "coming out to gay life." It is misleading when the closet metaphor is applied to the 1950s and 1960s because the term has so many negative connotations. "The closet" is a condescending term associated with being ashamed, frightened, or unhappy about being gay. Most of *ONE*'s correspondents were none of these things. They did not imagine themselves dwelling in some vast closet, but imagined themselves wearing masks that enabled them to pass as heterosexual when necessary in order to avoid antigay persecution.[27] A "mask" is a very different metaphor than a "closet." Closets are dark places where people hide. Masks imply subterfuge, resistance, defiance, and perhaps most importantly, human agency. Despite the hostile social forces at play in these years, these letter writers ultimately maintained control over their lives and destinies, including when to wear a heterosexual mask and when not to wear one. In these letters, the correspondents unmask themselves and tell us about their lives.

1

Biography and Self-Analysis

The *ONE* correspondents whose letters are featured in this chapter used their own life histories to explore broader questions about the nature of homosexuality. One hotly debated question among *ONE* magazine readers was whether or not homosexuality should be considered "normal." Are gay people just like anyone else except for their sexuality? Or are gay men and lesbians a distinct group of people with a distinct way of seeing the world? Does labeling gay people "normal" reduce social prejudices against them? Or does striving for normalcy merely reinforce an oppressively conformist status quo in terms of gender, sexuality, and personal freedom? Is normalcy desirable in the first place, or should gay people celebrate the fact that they are not normal? Gay activists and academics continue to debate these questions today.

In the 1950s, such questions about normalcy were sparked largely by the Kinsey Reports. Most *ONE* correspondents embraced Alfred Kinsey's controversial view that homosexuality was a normal variation of human sexual behavior. They believed his perspective was an important step in gaining social acceptance. Some correspondents disagreed with Kinsey, however, on two grounds. A minority of correspondents still considered themselves defective as human beings because they felt ashamed about their unwanted homosexual desires. Other correspondents, however, rejected the normalcy premise because they preferred to think of themselves as "abnormal" in a positive, individualistic sense, rather than in a self-loathing or clinical sense. Some of these correspondents were proud to stand out as individuals among the lonely crowd.

Coming Out

The first several letters in this chapter describe coming out experiences. Some correspondents reminisced about coming out experiences years in the past, while others wrote their letters as they were going through the process. Coming out was a major event in the lives of gay men and lesbians in the 1950s and 1960s, just as it is today. These letters describe individuals meeting other gay people for the first time as well as accepting their own homosexuality. Such acceptance might have followed years of internal conflict and loneliness, as seen in the first letter written by a 19-year-old man who admitted having suicidal feelings because of his homosexuality. In contrast, other correspondents accepted their homosexuality without internal conflict—and at young ages.

18 March 1958
Los Angeles, California

Dear Sirs,

I came out in homosexual life at the age of eighteen. Now I'm nineteen and think that it's a very happy but lonely life. A lot of times I feel like committing suicide, but I shouldn't be so cowardly as to do anything like that.

I guess the best thing for people like us is to keep busy going to college or studying. I do hope someday that I won't be lonely anymore. Your magazine is terrific and I pick up a copy each time it comes out.

Sincerely,
Richard

∼

27 November 1958
Los Angeles, California

Sir:

Not too long ago, three years ago to be exact, I saw a copy of your magazine on a newsstand in Times Square, N.Y. and scornfully laughed saying, "Now they've got a paper for Homos too," with another friend. Little did I realize at that moment that I'd become a "One" myself. I'm writing this letter, to explain what I think is one of the strangest situations. You may publish this if you so desire, without giving my address in the "One."

I'm 24 years now, and a blond, well-built, crew cut, who's usually described as the All American boy. I graduated from a College, in Massachussetts, played on the basket-ball team, belonged to the

College Swimming group, took girls out, and indulged in all the usual so called normal activities of necking, petting, etc. I had no "desire" for boys, although I was with handsome young men, and saw them in the nude.

After graduation, I came out to L.A.—two years ago, and something happened. I can't put my hands on it. Always being interested in athletics, and physical culture, I joined a leading Gym, did work outs, and really built up a physique. (I've even appeared as a model in a couple of the magazines of the male form)—under a different name. My attentions came to focus more not only on my body but on other males as well. I fought the desire, but was not able to over come it. I had an affair with another male model, an accepted Gay boy. Later I dated a girl, and to find out had an affair with her. It was a shock to realize that I craved for the male model and repulsed at the girl. I passed through many weeks of despair.

I've now accepted the situation.

How foolish we are to say that we're normal, when normality and abnormality are so close to each other?

Wish your magazine success.

      Cordially,
      John

If you do publish this letter, please leave both my name and address out. Send me no correspondence also. Thank you.

~

      5 July 1959
      Small town in eastern Kansas

Dear Sir,

Enclosed is $3.50 for a subscription to <u>One Institute Quarterly: Homophile Studies</u>. I am very pleased with <u>One Magazine</u> and devour every word therein.

Also enclosed here in is a request for some bit of information. Now, I am 25 years old—I've been out of high school since way back in '51—(seems so long) and I have known about myself since the 7th grade. I read (quite by accident) the definition of the word, homosexual, in a book on sex for young people. Since that time, I've read all I could get my hands on about the subject. Of course, here in this bleak desert [Kansas], there is not much to be found.

And what there is, is not too reliable, but some how, by the time I finished high school I had a pretty fair picture of the situation—<u>but</u>—it was not for about two or three years after high school that I ever met another gay person—at least, one who knew the score. It was a butch lesbian who introduced me to her brother who was also gay. Here my real education started. And life itself is much more real than you can find in books. Anyway by now I have been around quite a bit. To illustrate my point: I worked at the notorious Barker Hotel at 2000 Miramar in L.A. for over a year. I'm sure you've heard of the place—it's "too much"—and very educational.

But I'm wandering away from my point. I'll try to get back.

I have a cousin here, male, and will be a senior in high school next year. I also have a female cousin in Wichita, KS, who is two or three years younger then he. I am also acquainted with other high school students here and there and they all agree, and are nearly obsessed with the notion that Thursday is—All-Queens-Day—Neither will anyone who is "hep" wear green on this day as it is a sure sign that you're queer.

No one I know seems to have any idea as to what started this notion and I've been unable to find anything that might shed a bit of light on the subject. I wonder if any of you might know anything about it. It really "bugs" me that the notion seems to be so universal and so strong. There must be a basis for it somewhere—I'd like to know.

I'd better quit now. It'll probably take a 10 man crew at least a week to decipher these hen scratchin's.

Thank you kindly.

          Yours truly,
          Gregory

∼

        22 April 1962
        Midsize town in central New
         York

Dear Sirs,

This letter is addressed to all the editors, but I hope for an answer from whomever might take the trouble to answer some of the questions I have. If the style of my letter seems stilted and the prose incoherent, please blame it on my having stayed up all night writing a college paper, and it is now early morning and I am purposely writing now, as I might not have the nerve to write under saner conditions.

Perhaps I should start by identifying myself. I am a young man, 24 to be exact, now finishing my last year at college. I would have finished earlier but I left college for four years during which time I stayed three years in a religious community from which I had to eventually depart, partially because of the homosexual problem. The truth is that I have been longing for homosexual contacts since I was 11 or 12, but up until a few weeks ago never had such contact with an admitted homosexual, barring a few early adolescent experiences. This was with a young semi-prostitute in New York. I later got to know one other homosexual in New York who is a mixed up, messed up, out-of-work bum, although a very nice guy notwithstanding. Why do I go into these details which could have no interest for you? Purely because of the recency of all this for me (recent in the sense of overt experience, not desires) I am still very unsure and know little more than I did except that I want no longer to be ashamed of what I am, and feel I have the right to get together with other folks, male or female, who want to get together with me.

But there are many problems. First of all the strata of homosexual life that I have touched upon in New York seems definitely connected with criminality, prostitution, fear, extortion, etc. I have the feeling that this must be the [. . .][1] of gay life that corresponds to a similar side of heterosexual life, that is by no means representative or necessary. Please don't think I am saying this from snobbishness. Unfortunately I am personally all too much attracted by this drifting life, but I am afraid of it too. As one friend of mine put it, "These guys seem like losers all around." Perhaps my question should be phrased: must one be an all-around social loser if one wishes to live a homosexual life in our society? I would appreciate your personal opinion on this as well as any references to books on the subject.

But perhaps I have not made the problem clear. What I really want to know is whether there is no other way to meet people whom one might like to really get to know than in 8th-avenue bars and hanging around Times Square? Incidentally, if you could recommend any <u>person</u> in or around N.Y. city with whom I could speak to about this with on a mature level I would be very grateful. I realize that as a magazine you can't act as a lonely hearts club, and if it is against your policy to suggest a person I might contact just ignore this last point. (Please don't misunderstand; I am not asking for a "gay contact"; What I mean is a mature person, who could help me from his own experience think more clearly about the many problems and questions that besiege my mind.)

I should add here that I am planning to go into psychoanalysis next year, largely in order to try to find out the underlying cause of this aberration, as well as other personality problems which seem related to it. At the present time I am not one of those who try to insist that seeking homosexual relations is as "normal" as heterosexual love. I feel

I could be much happier without it and could probably make other people happier too. But as long as I have these desires it is useless to fight them, for that is certainly creating happiness for no one but only frustration and emptiness. If you would care to comment on your personal feelings about psychiatry and the (1) elimination or (2) acceptance of the homosexual desire, I would certainly be very grateful as I have no one to talk to who can be objective on these questions.

If you folks have any books such as The Sixth Man or any others that you think apply to my questions, if you send them to my college address so that they <u>definitely</u> get here before May 20th (otherwise they might get routed to my parents home and the possibility that they are opened by mistake by them, God Forbid!) please send them and I will send you the money for them right away. I would also be interested in back copies of ONE if such are available (I have only the February '62 issue.)

Finally I want to tell you how impressed I am by your magazine. What impresses me most is the combination of common-sense, sensitivity, honesty, and high level of maturity of everything in it. If nothing else, your magazine has seemed to me to be the proof that one can be well-balanced, creative, and reasonable and mature members of society, for you must surely be such people to be able to put out such a magazine. It is for this reason that I have been very frank in this letter, because I trust that you will take these questions which mean so much to me seriously and help me try to find answers, or at least begin to find out the <u>way</u> to find answers to them.

I look forward most impatiently to hearing from you, and only wish that I was on the West Coast so I could come and talk to you personally and express my personal gratitude for your magazine as well.

Your friend,
Russell

∼

2 August 1963
Omaha, Nebraska

Dear Sir:

I know you can't answer my question, but how does one find love? The one time in my life I tried to make friends with a man that attracted me—I was quite naïve then—worked for the same company that I did. I'm certain that I attracted him too, but he seemed to lead me on and then reject me. I was eventually fired, but in the meantime I went through such severe persecution that my health was destroyed both physically and mentally. I ended up under the care of a doctor and psychologist. After I was fired, I was unable to find a job in almost a years time in this city (Los Angeles) even though I have a college education. Finally my parents asked me to come home and enter a mental hospital, which I did. After I left the hospital, and as soon as the doctor said I was ready, I wrote to many companies concerning employment, and a fine company in Omaha decided to hire me. I hope I shall never give them cause to regret their decision.

One good result of all this, I am better able to accept myself as I am, and to realize that it is men rather than girls that attract me. A bad result is that the one time in my life I tried to find love I met with this complete rejection.

I know I can live without sex, since I have done so all my life, but very few men can live without love, and I am not one of these men.

Sincerely yours,
Greg

For its own legal protection, ONE, Inc., forbade persons younger than age 21 from subscribing to the magazine or participating in organizational activities. The following two letters show how this policy frustrated younger readers who felt they could benefit from being involved in the homophile movement.

26 February 1964
Small town in central
Michigan

Dear Mr. Schneider,[2]

Today I received <u>One</u> mag. and the other info. I requested . . . thank you very much. The magazine, I found, was thoroughly enjoyable "et tres 'gay' " to say the least.

One of the main reasons I'm writing is because I'm sure that what I say will be held in strict confidence . . . as a privileged communiqué. Of course, there's always a chance this'll fall into the wrong hands. But, that's a chance I must take.

You see, I'm a homophile—and I'm 16 yrs. old. Because of my age I can't, at present, support "One" or the Homophile Movement, but, as soon as I'm of age, I plan to be very active.

This's not just a figment of my imagination that I'm gay. Last year, with the help of a local D.O.[3] and the school principal, I saw a psychiatrist without my parent's knowledge. Anyway, she (the psi.) told me I was a "true homosexual."

For a long time I was unhappy with my lot (no pun intended) as part of the Lavender Set but after discovering that we were not uncommon or "queer" I've come to accept it, more or less. The book Christ and the Homosexual was a great help to adjusting myself, as also were several friends. This book should be in every teen-age homo's hands with Two by Jourdan—it would certainly make their lives happier.

The gay teen-agers will be the leaders of the movement—why are we excluded from it today when it could help so many? Some groups should be formed for the teen-age gay crowd, exclusively—there's plenty of material—both bi, gay, and hetero-gay.

We have a cause . . . too many people, I fear, look at us as "f_c_ing queers," as a peer told me. Our love can be beautiful just as it can be ugly—but so with the strait crowd. Really, I can't see why we're classed as "nuts" of some kind. Wouldn't it be wonderful if homosexuals today could walk with head high, proud of the fact— instead of hiding in the dark crevices of society like Medieval monsters. The society, which humorously we call civilization, has produced us and then regretted the fact—therefore rejecting us as freaks. A lot they've got to damn with their double standard of morality (or should I say amorality?)

At the present I haven't a photo of myself . . . but if you wish to know what I look like, there's a picture of me in the pen-pal list of March Dig mag. My address was [. . .] when I sent it in. It's still as said. The reason I'm mentioning this is probably for the sake of my vanity. I was told I look like Paul Peterson [sic]—some thought, eh?[4]

This letter is quite rambled . . . but I said a little of what I wanted to get off my chest. There's so much more to say but the space is limited.

If you wish to re-print any of this in One you may—minus name, for obvious reasons.

A reply is earnestly requested . . . as soon as possible.

Thank you for listening; I remain gaily and respectfully,

Yours—
Ray

~

15 February 1965
Midsize town in southern
Connecticut

Dear Sir:

Thank you for answering my letter. Perhaps my fears about the mails were absurd, and I want to thank you for your assurance that no one would know that I have written to you.

I was very disappointed with your rule, disregarding anyone who is under 21. Now, I am 20 years of age and do not see what the difference of a few months makes. I am a high school graduate, I work and support myself financially, and I also attend a trade school. I beg of you to ignore the few months I have apart from the age of 21, as what would be the difference? I am the only one responsible for myself. My only drawback is that I live with my parents, but I pay for my room and board. I do trust your organization and with this in mind, I will briefly tell you something I want kept in the strictest of confidence:

When I was approaching my teen years, I found I did not have the desire to be with girls as the other boys my age did. I was, however, attracted to other males, and this worried me to panic, as I often heard people speak so low of such a type of person. I then decided to never let anyone know of this nature I had, but to disguise myself to be an average boy. Oh, how often I found myself so lonely and depressed. When I reached the age of 16, I met a young man that I loved dearly, but he, unfortunately, was not inclined as I, and it broke my heart to see him dating other girls. This turned into quite an emotional problem. One day in deep despair, I went to a religious leader and told him of my problem. He was very understanding, and he counseled me up to a point, assuring me that my life was worth living and that someday, I might find someone that would be as I am. He could not help me anymore than that, but that was the first time I ever told anyone of my biggest problem. My relationship with my friend was ended much to my dismay when I found that it was a fruitless thing, only tearing me down emotionally. I went to a doctor and found that physically nothing could be done to change my nature. I went to a psychiatrist. He was the least help. He only wanted me to talk to him, and he never offered any encouragement. After I ran out of things to say and he knew my life's story backwards and forwards, he never advised or answered any questions I had. Well, I still carried on, living a quiet life, making everyone believe I was a normal American boy.

And I am still going on this way, although sometime[s] I wonder if people are not suspicious since I do not date girls. My life is very simple, I do not have anyone with whom I would ever talk to about my confusing problems of a life that so far has been disappointing and empty. Occasionally I go to New York City to see a show, but I'm always alone. I read a couple of books on homosexuality that have helped. It was from an article by R. E. L. Masters that I decided to write to you. If anyone in my family, especially my parents, ever knew about my nature, I would be dis-owned and rejected. This is the paramount reason that I would like your answer in an unmarked envelope. I have never thought that people could be so narrow minded and ignorant as to pass judgment on something they know nothing about. I would like to receive publications from you, but they would have to be unmarked, as I could not take a chance on having anyone having the slightest ideas of my orientation.

Please, reconsider your age judgment, I need assistance badly. You must have a branch in my state or at least know of one near me, if not, what about New York City? You claim there are millions such as I, but why do I fail to find any? I look like an average person and have no handicaps except age, as you pointed out, although I look older. I am so badly in search of friends my own type. You are the only one I have ever found. Please do not ignore me because of a few months of age. I would be interested in reading books on homosexuality of which I have found a shortage of in my area. Could you recommend any for me to read, fiction or non-fiction? I know I have asked a lot from you, but please give me something to go on. Please reconsider and help me. I would be most willing to pay any expense you might encounter in doing this. Desperately begging for help, I am:

Yours sincerely,
Ronald

The following letter is a detailed coming out narrative centered on an adolescent affair between the writer and an older boy. The correspondent suffered no shame or guilt over his sexuality as he became immersed in his neighborhood's surprisingly busy gay underworld. These were fond memories. As an adult, however, the correspondent experienced a series of employment difficulties because of an unfavorable military discharge for homosexuality. He offered his lengthy letter as evidence that gay people could overcome their problems and that embracing a gay identity could be fulfilling and joyful.

8 March 1960
Miami, Florida

CONFIDENTIAL
Dear Dr. Baker:[5]

I read the letter from J. K., and your answer, in the February ONE.

I enclose a resume of my life, thinking that perhaps you might desire to use a part of it or all of it to encourage him—or others.

I had a great deal more than J. K. to overcome. Tell him to stop being sorry for himself.

I regret that I must ask you NOT TO PUBLISH the attached, as there are some portions which might inevitably lead to me and possibly cause me embarrassment or trouble. The names in the beginning are not the true names of the boys involved.

Should you desire to use it, you are welcome to do so PROVIDED you delete all references to the profession of which I am a member—by changing or revising the last two paragraphs of page 9, deleting in its entirety the second paragraph of page 8, and revising the third paragraph of page 8.[6] Today, if asked "are you?," I reply "Yes—but do you really understand what you are asking? Let me lend you a couple of books which will help you to understand other people." The offer is usually accepted, and I seldom lose a friend.

Tell J. K. to live his own life, and to be proud of himself. Let him apologize to none. He must not be conspicuous, for Society frowns upon us officially yet envies us secretly. As long as he is not conspicuous, others do not give a "whit" for his sexual proclivities—just so long as they remain private.

He will be tempted—I am too, and for this reason seldom frequent the "gay" bars. And, occasionally, when I do, I am thrown with some attractive youth in his twenties who knows what he wants and is ready for the experience, and we have a "one night stand." But these are more and more seldom as the years go by.

Sincerely,
Edward

[The following narrative was attached.]

There are two statements which are frequently made by homosexuals, and which are found in many histories cited by physicians and psychiatrists. These are:
1. The homosexual's condition usually stems from a seduction in earlier years by an older man; and
2. The homosexual has absolutely no opportunity for gainful employment.

As a practicing homosexual from pre-adolescent days, whose experience has been wide and varied, I find that both of these contentions are indefensible.

Generally speaking, and personally I know of no exception, a single overt experience does not "fix" one's sexual desires upon his or her own sex. Kinsey bears this out by reporting that an extremely large number of men, and quite the majority, have enjoyed one or more such experiences during their lifetime without becoming confirmed homosexuals.

It is entirely possible and even probable that when an individual is bullied or forced into homosexual practices, as frequently occurs in prison life (but seldom elsewhere) and because of pressure or environment is unable to terminate such relations, he may become "conditioned" to being so used, and as the act becomes less and less unpleasant but more habitual or more of a "necessary evil," he may begin to find himself deriving a certain precarious pleasure therefrom—one learns to derive pleasure from conditions which are enforced or from which he cannot escape. He usually begins to develop a certain amount of affection for one or more of those who, in his mind, were originally classed as his tormentors. After a sufficient period of time, such an individual will, in all probability, remain homosexual throughout the remainder of his life.

Undoubtedly there are instances in which seduction or even rape of a youth by an older man or boy has been instrumental in bringing out a previously existent but latent predilection on the part of the victim. Similarly, and just as surely, there are many in which an initially innocent and harmless affection for one of one's own sex has, over a period of time, through affection mutually displayed, caused sex to "rear its lovely head"—just as it is bound to do in heterosexual relationships which develop from friendship to affection to petting—and more. In my opinion, this is more apt to develop in the case of an individual whose home lacks the elements of emotional display of love, or whose home is broken, and who one finds a measure of forbearance or a modicum of affection in an older boy or man. Even the barest kindness can foster love in the heart of a boy who finds little or none at home.

In such cases, the boy may soon learn to foster this attitude on the part of the other by exerting to the best of his ability such feminine attributes as exist to a limited degree in every man, even the most masculine. He seeks at any cost more affection from the one who has shown a limited amount of affection toward one who previously was "love-starved" and consequently lonely and unhappy.

If such a relationship continues for any extended period of time, innocent though it may have been in the beginning unless the other member of the liaison is extremely strong willed and [has strong] socio-moral principles, it is quite prone at some stage to excite the sexual passions of one or the other to the point that they cannot be denied. From my own experience, and from my discussions with others, it is as frequently if not more frequently the older of the two who is actually seduced rather than the younger.

As to one example of this premise, I will recite experiences of my own life after I have explored the second (to me) indefensible contention.

As to employment, if the average homosexual would only realize that most individuals are naught for his personal life so long as it affects them not, his life would be easier. Many a so-called "normal" man today is like the ostrich—just so long as it is not brought to his attention in an obvious manner, he cares little what his fellow man does, and smiles indulgently upon what he terms his fellow's "queer" proclivities—but don't let it become so obvious that he must explain his forbearance to his next-door neighbor. The average employer is no different, so long as the employee's sexual proclivities do not become so obvious as to be annoying or conversation producing, do not interfere with work, and do not result in the molestation or annoyance of fellow-employees, customers or clients. Granted that the homosexual can hold his desires under the same control that the average heterosexual must display, if he has true ability, he may compete with everyone on an equal footing.

My own life bears out that, even when homosexuality is aggravated by other matters, one may still succeed if one has ability and acts with proper decorum in connection with his employment.

I said my life has been varied. The following resume will probably persuade you, as it has me, that homosexual proclivities existed even before they were recognized by me, although circumstances and associations certainly assisted in bringing them to the surface.

When I was a child, both mother and father found that it was necessary to work to support a family of four children, of whom I was the eldest. Consequently, I found myself quite a bit "on my own." As we attended the wrong church in a somewhat prejudiced (religiously) neighborhood, I had only one real friend from the time I was about eight. My younger brother and I spent almost all our time at his home. Billy (my friend) was an orphan—his father died when he was an infant. His mother worked, and he was watched over after school by his elder brother, Ken, who was about six years older.

Ken was an athletic kid, extremely well developed for his age, with the physique of a Greek god. A perfect Adonis. He had built up for himself in one room a sort of gymnasium, and as both Billy and I were rather undeveloped, he frequently gave us "work-out" in the "gym," trying to teach us wrestling, boxing, etc., and, with sad results, to develop our bodies. He was a fine boy, full of life and laughter, and extremely kind and tender to us kids. It was not at all difficult for me to develop a hero-worship for him.

After a year of this relationship, I had grown extremely fond of Ken, and was quite attached to him. Also, I greatly admired his body which was so much better developed than my own. I used to seek every opportunity to throw my arms around him, and hug him, frequently kissing his side or chest before he would disentangle me, throw his arm over my shoulders, and press me to his side. I loved to play at wrestling with him—we usually "worked" in the "gym" with only shorts on, and sometimes nude,—and when I felt the tingle of his naked flesh against mine, I was thrilled immediately. When playing at wrestling, I always succeeded in letting him throw me, and before he could get up, I would relax and gently caress his back with my fingers as long as he would permit. That he obviously enjoyed this was evidenced by the fact that sometimes it took him quite awhile to get up! This kind of play which, I now realize, was essentially homosexual, went on for quite some time, and many is the time he would begin to have an erection and pull himself from me, jump up and run to the bathroom and lock himself in for quite a while. Many time I tried to follow him, but he would not let me in!

One afternoon, when Ken was about sixteen or seventeen, another boy came to their yard and wanted us to join him with some other boys in a game of baseball at the corner lot. Ken said he had to do some study[ing], and couldn't go. After much persuasion, he was persuaded to let Billy go, and I let my brother go also, but said I did not care to, and would go home. I never cared to take part in masculine games unless I was playing with Ken. I started home, but as soon as the others were out of sight, I went back and quietly slipped in Ken's back door and on through the house to his bedroom, where I found him sitting on a bench before his desk, studying, completely nude. I stood in the doorway for a while without Ken even dreaming I was there, just watching and admiring him, and finally skipped up behind him and threw my arms around him and started to kiss him on the neck. He was startled and asked what I was doing there, and I replied that I came back because I just wanted to be with him. He said I could stay if I would be quiet as he had to study, and got up to put some clothes on, but I begged him not to, as I told him I liked to see him and admire him as he was. He told me to sit on the bed and be quiet. I did for a while, and he seemed so engrossed in his studies he appeared to completely forget I was there. I slipped my own clothes off, and I don't think he even knew it. Finally, I got up and slipped over to the bench and sat by him. He said, "What are you doing?" and I begged him to let me sit there with him. We sat there for about a half an hour, during which I had begun to caress his spine with my fingers (which I knew he enjoyed and which frequently excited him when we were wrestling). I did not know all the mechanics then, but I knew that what I did caused him frequently to have an erection, and he derived pleasure from it. Finally, as he began to fidget and become excited, I threw my arms around him and buried my head in his lap, kissing him on the abdomen and thighs.

This kind of excitation did not take long to produce a result, and he thrust me away, saying, "Now you've done it!" I asked what, and he said it was none of my business. I asked him if that was why he ran into the bathroom when we were wrestling and things began to happen, and his reply was, "Kitten (his pet name for me), you sure are a dumb one. Don't you know by now?" I asked what, and he said if I didn't know yet, he wasn't going to be the one to teach me. Meanwhile, he was gently stroking himself. He started to the bathroom, and I ran after him, begging and pleading with him to tell me what it was. He finally told me to just sit quiet on the bench and he would get on the bed, which he did, and began to practice self-gratification. I watched awhile, and asked what he was doing, and he said, "Just finishing what you started, Kitten!" I got up and went over to the bed and lay by him and began to caress his body, and by this time he was so far gone he could not stop me. I finally succeeded in getting him to let me "officiate," meanwhile kissing his beautiful body wherever I could reach. He just lay there and writhed in ecstasy.

Afterwards, we got up, and he said, "You shouldn't have done that, Kitten, and I shouldn't have let you. Now put your clothes back on." I did, and told him I enjoyed it as it seemed to give him so much pleasure. He said, "Still, its wrong" and proceeded to give me quite a lecture on sex. He discussed procreation, heterosexual relationships, homosexual relationships, which he said were all wrong, and the pleasures derived from sexual contact. He told me that I was too young yet to enjoy it, but that one of these days I would find a woman I liked, and would get over "this foolish play." He warned me that I should not even touch a man's body again, as it might lead to a true homosexual relationship which, he said, "might ruin me for life." I asked him if he had ever had such an experience, and he said not. I then asked him if he ever would, and his answer was, "I don't know—I might, sometime, just for the thrill, to see what it feels like." I determined then and there that, if I could arrange it, his first such experience would be with me!

For a few weeks thereafter, Ken sought excuses to prevent our being alone together, and just as energetically I sought opportunities to be alone with him. He had tried to paint the "horrors" to me, but had only succeeded in arousing my curiosity and my desire to experiment with him. For about a month, I only succeeded in being with him a few occasions for a few moments at a time, which he devoted to "fatherly" talks and an effort to answer my many questions, mostly concerned with sex in all its facets. During all this time, he would not let me touch him.

Eventually, after much pleading and begging on my part and some tears, we got back to our former playful relationship, and I immediately began to take advantage of every slightest opportunity to excite him. I had learned a lot in a few weeks!

He chastised me, and often ran me home, but eventually my dogged persistency won, and the episode of the afternoon in his bedroom was repeated. And repeated. And repeated until it became a regular ritual and Ken and I were conspiring together to find ways to be alone together. Yet, all this time, Ken would stop me before there was anything more than "play." By this time, I really adored him. He was showing me the affection and love I missed at home, and I also admired his beautiful healthy young body, so much better proportioned than my own (yet, not "muscle-bound" in the present body-builder style—a true Grecian Adonis!)—a young, healthy, well-developed and handsome male.

With constant teasing and caressing, I had learned how to excite him more and more, and had taught him to lie quietly and give himself up to my caresses until he finally reached the climax of his emotions. Finally, one afternoon, I decided to risk all just as he began to quiver with emotion. Ken tried to push me away, not too hard, and as I grasped him tightly, he threw his arms around my head and pulled me closer and closer to him and gave himself completely to me! He moaned, "What you're doing to me! Stop it, Kitten, stop it!!" I raised up just enough to say, "I want to. Make me stop if you can!" He replied—and I'll never forget the agony in his voice—"I should—I must—but, dear God, I can't!"

After several minutes of intense and passionate play, Ken grasped me real tightly, squeezed me to him, and said, "Kitten, dear boy, I didn't want to, but now I've got to. Don't you ever forget you made me do it." With that, he tensed and quivered all over, and gave me his all. At once, he seemed to sag and lay back like a limp rag, and I had experienced and enjoyed thoroughly my first full and complete homosexual intimacy. I had previously been the instrument of masturbation, and I recognize fully that my efforts at caressing were definitely homosexual in nature, this experience was a fulfillment that probed the depths of hunger and desire, and fully awakened in me (and at the same time showed me how to satisfy) an ecstatic passion and pleasure I never dreamed existed.

Twice, before the end, Ken had tried to stop, but weakly, warning me of the consequences, but was in such a throe of passion that I, though much younger, had complete control of his body and mind, and he could but lie there and let me do as I would with him.

Yet the law would say I was seduced!

Afterwards, he lay for quite a while completely exhausted, while I put my arms around him and cuddled up to him. He started to talk to me, and told me that I must <u>never</u> do that again with <u>anyone</u>. I told him I did not want to do it with anyone, but only with him. He said we couldn't, because he could be sent to jail if anyone found out, and said we must not see each other anymore. I told him we couldn't do that, because then my folks as well as the other kids in the neighborhood would know something was wrong, so he said I could come over but only with my brother, and when Billy was home. I agreed, but knew I could get him to change this.

The next week, I begged him to let me see him again, and when he refused, I told him I'd tell my father if he didn't. I seemed to recognize the fact that he wanted to, but was afraid. Fear and desire overcame caution, and he consented "just once more" which became "once more" and "once more" until it was a regular and frequent affair, at least once a week, whenever we could steal an hour or so by ourselves—in the attic, in the cellar, in his bedroom, even in a deserted house down the street on occasions. He told me once, "Kitten, you don't know what you doing to yourself and what I'm helping you to do, and I shouldn't let you, but I can't stop myself." Again, and I now realize it to be so true, "If you hadn't met me, I really believe you would have eventually sought someone else who wouldn't have cared as much for you, and might have been brutal with you." He kept cautioning me not to have an affair with anyone else.

As I have grown older, I realize that Ken must have recognized the situation long before it developed as it did, and well knew (and wanted) what the final development would be, yet, while he did not have sufficient self-control to prevent the culmination of that which he really believed to be wrong, did have sufficient will-power to let me "seek and find" my own desires in my own way. He was "willing, but not eager," and I do not in the least blame him. In fact, I worship his memory—he was killed in action. He was tender, loving, and kind—which many others would not have been.

Next door to Ken was another boy about his age, who came over occasionally for Ken to go to the movies or elsewhere with him. He never knew of our private affairs, but eventually became suspicious and began to chide Ken for "always playing with a baby." Ken told him he was teaching me to be a checkers champ.

Apparently this did not allay his suspicions, as one afternoon when I was about fourteen, I was supposed to have locked Ken's back door (to which I had a key by then), but either forgot to lock it or the other boy, Joe, had somehow gotten a key. I toyed with the thought Ken might have told him or given him a key, but really don't believe it. Anyway, Ken was then about 19 or 20, and Joe was about the same. Suddenly, while Ken and I were "playing" together, we suddenly realized that Joe and a cousin of his were standing in the bedroom doorway watching us and leering. Ken jumped up, and Joe said, "You're too late, now. Go ahead and have your fun, and if you don't I'll have you both in trouble." Ken went over as if to fight, and Joe said, "You can beat me alright, but if you touch me, I'll have you and your little friend in jail before night." I ran over to Ken and threw my arms around him, and Joe said, "Go ahead and have your fun, because Jim and I are next!" I started to cry, and he said, "Quit crying, you little fool. You've been hiding away with Ken long enough and it doesn't seem to have hurt you yet, and we're not going to hurt you any more. You just be nice to us, too, and no one will ever know the difference." Ken lunged at Joe, and both boys grabbed him and threw him back on the bed, and told him, "Now, you either be a good boy and do what we say, or we'll take you instead of your little friend, and still turn you in."

I had visions of Ken and I going to jail, and begged him to agree, but he said no, whatever happened. Finally he gave in, especially after they said that if we didn't agree willingly, they would force me anyway. I didn't realize then that we were all in the same boat. Joe then insisted that Ken and I finish what we had started, as they wanted to see it all, so we did. Then the other two came to me one at a time and had their pleasure with me.

Neither were at all rough, and I soon found that while, with Ken, it was pure adoration, with Joe and Jim I found myself enjoying sex for its own sake and for the pleasure it obviously gave the other party. And, once they had found this outlet, they did not intend to let it go. So, while Jim soon left for his hometown, it continued to be Ken, Joe, and I. Eventually, over Ken's objections, though by this time I had little reluctance, Joe began to introduce other youths, some in their late teens, and others in their early twenties. By this time, I had been introduced to other practices, and so would let them use me in any manner they desired.

The boys organized a Glee Club, and I knew that I was to be there at their practice sessions, which soon were held at various boys' homes—depending upon whose parents would not be there. I went ostensibly to "hear them practice." By this time, the group consisted of some thirty boys, ranging from seventeen to twenty-two.

Gradually, as the "novelty" wore off, the group began to fade. Ken moved away, but continued to write me occasionally until he was killed in WWII.

Meanwhile, as an excuse for having me with them, Ken and the others had made me sufficiently proficient in checkers that I became local champion, and held the title nine years. The newspapers actually praised Ken and a few of the others for devoting their time training me so well! What people don't know about relationships!

Life moved on. Some moved away, others got married. I was in High School, and began to have clandestine affairs with one or two of my "chums." Also, through the Glee Club, I met people I never would have met otherwise, and though these meetings were usually under the guise that they wanted to meet the Checkers Champ, I soon found their real reasons.

I learned that even those who used me for their sexual satisfaction only, must jealously guard my reputation lest their own be spoiled. In our teens, no—then Ken played his part, and I do know he had my best interests at heart. He could lick anyone who got out of line, but could not prevent two, four, or more from participating. His threat to kill the one who hurt me was always respected. And, as I and my contacts became older, they sought to have a legitimate justification for our friendship.

My contacts became less and less, and my reputation grew. Eventually, I entered into teaching, and, with the exception of one or two friends at home, had no contacts in my hometown, but occasionally went to a city about 200 miles away to seek forbidden pleasure. Yet I was always careful.

Eventually I was inducted into the Army with the National Guard. Two kids, and really kids to me, knew my past history from their older brothers, and, having been cut off from all relations with my former group, I soon took up with them. I would go to a hotel for the weekend, and they would visit me. And soon, a few of their friends were introduced.

Eventually, I was transferred as a result of having contracted malaria, and so sought new friends. I learned that one's passions must be satisfied in some way, and became somewhat careless.

During a "homosexual purge," I served as reporter at a trial of some thirty officers and enlisted men, quite a few of whom I had known, but, fortunately, my name was not mentioned.

Eventually, one man suspected, with whom I had had no contact, plead that I had seduced and practically raped him. He knew I had had contact with others, and gave the names of several already convicted, who, when questioned, admitted relations with me. At my trial, I proved by the sworn testimony of a full colonel that at the time I was alleged to have been having an illicit affair, I was actually working in the Colonel's office with him and several other officers, and that we did not leave our office until 2:30 A.M. I was still convicted, dishonorably discharged, and sentenced to five years' hard labor. And the trial took place in my home town! Many friends, some who knew, and some who didn't, came to my rescue without avail. Two U.S. Senators plead unsuccessfully for a review. I went to Fort Leavenworth, and tried to die.

The prison Chaplain, God bless his soul, gave me back a will to live, and with his help, I was able to help others. The prison psychiatrist was "gay," and had had affairs with several inmates. As I rejected his subtle advances, he was persuaded my conviction was in error.

Meanwhile, the charge upon which I had been convicted became public knowledge among the prison "population" due to inmates working in the offices, and—a common procedure in prison life—I had to permit myself to be "adopted" by a couple who could use me as they would, but prevented me being "fair prey" for any and all who desired sexual satisfaction. That is one of the horrors of prison life. One youngster, about 18, convicted of being homesick and leaving his mother's skirt tails for the first time in his life—the army calls it desertion—was raped 14 times by men at knife point, and he entered the hospital with a ruptured anus!

I was eventually offered restoration, accepted, and after a period of several months in which I was given much more freedom (and had many more affairs—I found the homosexual practices rife among those with a little more freedom than the main population), was restored to duty and my dishonorable discharge erased.

I then served at various posts, including one at which I served as Chaplain's Assistant for quite a while, and enjoyed serving. Meanwhile, I continued to have "affairs," but very circumspectly.

Eventually I was discharged and granted an honorable discharge showing a certain number of days "lost under A.W. I04["]—the provisions under which I had been offered and accepted restoration. I could have been (and was offered) parolee status over a full year prior to my release for restoration.

I found the date of my original National Guard enlistment wrong, and very foolishly sent my discharge back to the War Department, at their request (after I had written of the error) for "correction of the typographical error in the date." What was returned to me was an executed dishonorable discharge plus a "limited" (not recommended for reenlistment) discharge covering my tour of duty subsequent to restoration.

My home state Congressman fought for three years to have this perfidious action withdrawn, but the noble War Department blandly stated that a dishonorable discharge is not subject to review.

For over a year, I then worked for Navy Department in Washington on a very important project, and at the time I left, was scheduled for immediate advancement several grades. This despite the fact that my immediate superiors were aware of my army history. I left Washington due to my health, and for the next several months underwent medical treatment.

Meanwhile, pressure was still being brought to bear upon the war Department to review my case, and as the pressure became heavier, my records conveniently "disappeared." I still have the dishonorable discharge. I've quit fighting this.

By this time, I was pretty thoroughly disgusted, and, while undergoing medical treatment at a large seaport town, I threw caution to the winds and became quite well known among the sailors.

However, I soon got hold of myself, and after a few months came to the city in which I presently reside, it having been recommended by the doctors that I come here for reasons of my health.

I sought work, and, a gentile, found it with a jewish businessman who sought only ability. Persuading him to try me out, he found me satisfactory.

Through his contact, I began to work for his accountant, also jewish. I was urged to take the CPA examination, and told my employer the whole story. I also told him that I still, but quietly and circumspectly, engaged in homosexual activities.

I took the examination at his urging, and am today a well-respected Certified Public Accountant, with many friends in business and professional circles, some of whom know of my inclinations, some merely suspect, and others are ignorant.

I make no secret of the fact that I am unmarried, am never seen with girls, and do not hide the fact that I am buying a home with another man my age with whom I have been living for some five years. We have friends in at home, but no wild orgies. I have occasional circumspect affairs with other friends, but quite quietly at home.

A few years ago, an important local Government official investigated me as a result of an application for a position in General

Accounting Office which I had filed before leaving Washington. He had my record with him, and apologized that he would have to rule I could not hold a Government position for another five years. By this time, I would not have accepted had it been offered. However, this same official considers me a friend, and we have quite a bit of professional and official contact.

Today, despite my homosexuality, I am one of the highest paid employees of an accounting firm in my area. I realize that, were I to enter into practice for myself, scandal concerning my past history or my present homosexual activities might easily cause me to lose everything. Yet, I am almost ready to believe that this, too, can be overcome, and I have sufficient respect from business and professional men that even this could not completely ruin me.

I will undoubtedly remain homosexual to my death. I do not deny it if asked. I do not flout it. To me, it has become as "natural" and right as any other method of expressing one's individuality—so long as I do not injure or annoy anyone else and do not make myself an object of disgust by careless practice in public.

This brief history of my life is in itself a very strong argument for the two premises I set forth in the beginning.

Therapy

The letters in this section describe experiences with psychological and psychiatric therapy. In some cases, correspondents sought psychoanalysis or aversion therapy to change their sexual orientation. The letters show that such efforts were doomed to fail. Other correspondents, however, reported benefits from therapy as long as it did not try to change their sexual orientation. Therapy helped many correspondents cope with the stresses and anxieties of being gay in a hostile society. Many mental health professionals understood that changing an individual's sexual orientation was neither possible nor desirable.

> Published in *ONE* magazine,
> February 1953, 15-17
> Los Angeles, California

Dear Sirs:

I am a physician on the staff of the U.C.L.A. School of Medicine, and while my prime interest is in the field of cancer research and treatment, many of the technical procedures developed for the study of hormone disturbances in cancer are now being applied to the problems of the sex psychopath as represented by the two or three hundred cases under observation at Norwalk State Hospital. Your quotation from Dr. Bowman's report to the State Legislature appearing in "One," Jan., 1953, pages 8-9 is unintentionally misleading in that it implies that basic research on homosexuality is now being conducted by the State of California Dept. of Mental Hygiene at U.C.L.A. Although this was undoubtedly a part of Dr. Bowman's original plan, the study now in progress concerns primarily "antisocial sex behavior" involving acts of violence and attacks on minors. Homosexuality per se is not an essential part of this problem and therefore, does not form a specific part of the investigation.

I have discussed your organization with those directly concerned with the above program, and you will I am sure, be interested to learn, as I was, that the law-abiding, socially useful homosexual is rapidly becoming of little legal interest, and prosecution of this large group is being discouraged throughout the state. For the first time, a distinction is being made, and attention is being directed only to those who, by force, violate the freedoms of others for sexual reasons, and the well-adjusted homosexual is considered as separate from this group as the usual heterosexual. If nothing more comes of the current state research program, I am sure that you will agree that this is real progress. Those to whom I talked regarding your society felt that before long, the Committee to Outlaw Entrapment would find itself fighting a straw man, since the legal emphasis is decidedly shifting in the above mentioned direction.[7]

However, even if the possibility of entanglements with the law should in this way be forever removed from the life of the homosexual, there remains, as you point out, the tremendous prejudice of the surrounding heterosexual world against something they cannot understand. This prejudice is based on lack of facts regarding homosexuality, and the unfortunate part of it is that the science of medicine does not have any substantial body of information to offer in explanation of this constantly recurring natural phenomenon. One of the reasons has been the failure on the part of homosexuals themselves to recognize this lack and to do something positive about it in an organized way. If they do not produce the necessary data, it is unlikely that anyone else will.

It seems to me that your society is in a unique position to make worthwhile basic contributions to human knowledge concerning homosexuality. With such a large cooperating group, research projects could be undertaken, and the data so obtained be reported in the scientific literature to become a permanent addition to medical and then to general information. It does not seem to me that the homosexual can successfully demand that the world accept him, even by the subtle maneuver of demonstrating his conformity in all other phases of life as long as the present ignorance exists, and as long as the homosexual himself doesn't actually know whether he is "normal" or "abnormal."

I believe that the Mattachine Foundation could best achieve their goals and conclusively demonstrate their sincerity of purpose not by the defensive approach of saying, "see how many brilliant people are in our group" or "see how harmless we are," etc., but by being the first to explain scientifically WHAT THEY ARE. Such a positive approach could be the beginning of a great movement in the right direction. In any field, facts speak for themselves, but without them there remain only theories, emotions and intuition, which impress no one except a few who might find it temporarily convenient to agree.

I have taken the liberty of presenting a physician's view of your work[.] I would be very glad to hear the reaction of your readers to these ideas. You may print all or part of this letter with signature, if you wish.

Sincerely,
Philip M. West, M.D.

~

24 April 1955
Suburb of San Francisco,
California

Dear Sir:

Ever since discovering that ONE could be purchased locally, I have been reading it regularly beginning with the October issue of last year. At that time I was in favor of subscribing immediately, but held back after discussing the matter with a European-born friend of mine, an ex-Nazi refugee. He advised against it fearing that THEY might get a copy of the list. Fear, being the contagious thing that it is, I refrained, knowing that I could purchase it locally. However since I apparently missed the March and April issues, I shall send in a subscription in a few days. Currently, I'm unemployed, and it won't be until late this week, before I will know if the budget can stand it at this time. The magazine is beginning to mean so much to me, that I shall probably strain a notch or so. Every issue I have read from cover to cover, including some of the past issues which I found at the City of Lights.[8]

The more I read, the more firmly convinced I have become that the time is ripe for an attempt to campaign for acceptance in a society, which while so preoccupied with sex, acts most of the time as though it does not exist. Ever since the Grand Inquisitor from Wisconsin got under way I have strongly resented the implication that because of what I am, I am also a traitor to my country, if not an avowed communist.[9] The distance between non-conformity and treason is infinite, and frankly I can't see any homosexual with a degree of intelligence embracing communism. Feeling the way I do, I have come to the conclusion that it is far better to make an earnest attempt to alter the situation, rather than going in for passive resignation, and saying that it cannot be done. Benjamin Franklin, I believe, once made the statement that if we don't hang together we shall surely hang separately. And the climate of this country is such that this could well apply to our own minority group.

Your magazine makes a splendid forum for the airing of ideas, because judging from some of the comments, some confusion and even hatred exists amongst our own group. There are those who hate the more flamboyant types, which is based on the fear of being classified with them, but on the other hand, we are in no position to sit in judgment upon them. We should realize the pressures, the frustrations, that cause them to act as they do. When you get beyond the surface of some of them, as I have bothered to do, you will discover that they, too, are not as blithely happy, as you would be led to believe. Then there are the male homosexuals who despise the female of the species, and vice versa. That, too, is another form of stupidity.

One aspect that interests me, is the various types, one might say, those who were born, those who acquired the pattern, those who claim to have entered the homosexual world as their preference, the bi-sexual, and a type I haven't seen mentioned in ONE, the amoral type, to whom sex is a matter of whatever is available at any given time. Kinsey's insistence that a person's sexual pattern is set at a very early age, as early, I think it was, as the fifth year, and possibly earlier, caused me to do a self-analysis last year, by taking copious notes, to see which of the first two types which I just mentioned, I belonged to. The result, based on what I have managed to read during the past twenty years, leads me to believe that I fit in the first category, and that the pattern showed signs of evolving as early as my fifth, or sixth year. At that time I wasn't truly aware of the situation until I had reached my late teens, which is another story. This leads me to wonder if the theory that the tendency isn't latent in all of us, isn't the most logical one. If so, that would rule out those who claim to have decided upon it as a matter of preference. I have met one person making that claim, and have wondered if it wasn't sophistry on his part.

There is a lot of confusion on the subject, even in the medical and the psychiatric professions. This I know from reading, and limited contacts with those professions. Years ago I read a book by some German author who went right into some length to explain homosexuality as influenced by some conjunction of the moon and the planet Uranus, of all things.[10] Sounds fantastic, but it was actually a reference text to a law course in a New Jersey college. Then there was the ranking psychiatrist at an Army hospital, who told me that he knew positively that mutual masturbation was the preferred form of homosexual intercourse. When I laughed uproariously, he was quite insulted. Sounds absurd, but I can even top that one. A woman doctor in Oklahoma City, once purchased a copy of a book called "Sexual Frigidity in the Male," and was seen, by a thoroughly reliable friend of mine, painting out the illustrations of abnormal males on the grounds that they did not EXIST. All this convinces me of the necessity for more discussion on the subject, so that all of us are better informed, eventually, on the whole subject.

I think that ONE is contributing considerably in this field, by publishing reviews on books, and articles, so that the uninformed can learn of sources that are more reliable than can be found in the average public, or school, library. The February issue, I noticed, mentioned a book, which discussed the fact that repressed homosexuality can lead to alcoholism and stammering. It can also lead to people showing symptoms of diseases, which they don't have. I know of one case where a young man showed many of the symptoms of epilepsy. His doctor, in delving into his background, etc., finally discovered that it was a case of repressed homosexuality and that his feelings of guilt, following any sexual indulgence, produced the external expressions of epilepsy.

Well it is high time that I brought this to a close. When I start to write a letter, I lose sight of the fact that brevity is considered highly admirable. I am submitting the enclosed book-review, which may be of some value, unless I have been beaten to the draw in the issues I have missed, March, and April. Let's keep on with the struggle, because any progress is far better than none at all.

Very Sincerely,
George

Published in *ONE* magazine,
July 1955, 18–19
Pasadena, California

Gentlemen:

Herewith a layman's rebuttal to Dr. Ellis' article "Are Homosexuals Necessarily Neurotic?"[11]

One wonders just what is the norm on Dr. Ellis' scale which appears to slide from neurotic to neurotic. He states that an individual is neurotic if "his sex desires are exclusively oriented toward members of his own sex." My dictionary tells me "to orient" means to adjust or correct by referring to first principles. If we go along with Dr. Ellis, there are no first principles since he calls the exclusive heterosexual neurotic also. Therefore, away from what first principle is the homosexual oriented? How do we recognize or diagnose the neurotic if we have no constant by which to evaluate them?

Dr. Ellis envisions a neurosis-free adjusted being as one capable of all feeling and experience, with no exclusive interests or desires. In short, an individual completely obscured by experience and environment.

Phooey!

I think he presumes much in calling homosexuality a neurosis. There is a homosexual neurosis to be sure, just as there could be a compulsive neurosis to close doors but door closing itself is not a neurosis. Furthermore, I doubt if many "exclusive" homosexuals feel it necessary to "adjust" to their homosexuality and thereby lose their "guilt" about it. In fact, the homosexual has to "adjust" to his homosexuality no more than he has to "adjust" to the color of his eyes.

I conclude from Dr. Ellis that to be a well integrated, adjusted and normal individual, one's personal life must be cluttered with all psycho-sexual experience from A to Z and in equal portions. There is nothing quite like compounding a neurosis to send an individual "running to his analyst" to be adjusted out of his adjustment.

It seems to this writer that therapists who advocate individual adjustment as the panacea for all psychic ills in one breath and speak of "this neuroticizing society" in the next are a little less than certain as what exactly is at fault.

Since the fact of being alive includes a continuing inter-action between the individual and his environment, and since neither is static, it seems a shame that we view man's variety so negatively. Should all the mountains become hills and all rivers ponds because it is arbitrarily decided that these are the better or even the desired forms of environment?

The problem (if one exists) which the homosexual has is no different from the need every human has for identity. But, to achieve a personal and social identity does not require life-long subservience to society-conceived, unproven theories of what constitutes a normal, well-adjusted human being; all this being based on the probability that there is or should be such a thing.

It is a waste of effort to pursue the study of human vagaries and behaviors without considering the social, intellectual and probable sexual evolution of the whole human species. All else is indeed "wishful thinking."

          Miss D.

          26 June 1960
          Sacramento, California

Dear Dr. Baker:

As a subscriber to "One" for the past several years, I have enjoyed your very rational discussions, and am thankful that someone can give sane advise on homosexuality.

I am enclosing an article from the "Sacramento Bee" newspaper, which was published a couple of weeks ago. It is a syndicated article so perhaps you have seen it. The advice given by "The Council" is fine down to the last two sentences where we run into the old, old advice, "See a psychiatrist."

Dr. Baker, is there *any* proven case of a homosexual who has been permanently converted by psychotherapy? I have never heard of one, despite the words of various so called "authorities."

I personally know of three men who had psychotherapy treatments. Let's call them Joe, Hal, and Ralph.

Joe was arrested for abnormal sex practices, but put on probation on the condition that he would consult a psychiatrist, which he did. Following the "treatments" he abstained from any sexual practices for nearly a year and then drifted back into homosexuality. Hal, who was disturbed at being a homosexual, was sent for treatment by his minister. Following this treatment, he married a very lovely girl. They have been married for eight years and have a six year old son. Hal however, has again taken up sex relations with other men to the extent that he keeps a lover in an apartment in another city. He is a salesman and spends much of his time with his lover by telling his wife that his work keeps him out of town. Ralph was given a dishonorable discharge from the Armed Services when he was "caught" with a buddy. He was consequently kick[ed] out of his parent's home, and came close to having a complete breakdown. His older brother however, in an honest effort to help him, talked him into consultation. This happened three years ago, and Ralph is now referred to as a "tramp." In other words, he has sex relations with any man who is available and willing.

I have heard of other similar cases, but have never heard of any homosexual who permanently became heterosexual due to psychiatric treatment. Have you?

Sincerely,
A. V.

∼

22 March 1961
Brooklyn, New York

DEAR SIR:

MORE ABOUT THE NUDIE-WUDIES AND ABOUT THE ADJUSTMENT. WELL NOW ADJUSTMENT AND BEING WELL-ADJUSTED SOUNDS TERRIBLY INTELLIGENT IN THE TALK, BUT I FIND IT VERY DIFFICULT TO FIND WHAT IT <u>MEANS</u>. AFTER LISTENING AND ADDING UP ALL THE TALK, IT SOUNDS TO ME THAT THEY MEAN "WELL <u>YOU</u> KNOW, LIKE ME" (BEING SUAVE AND NURSING A SECRET ULCER,) AND THAT'S ALL I COULD GET OUTTA POPPA FREUD. BUT <u>HIM</u> YOU REMEMBER WAS REALLY ALL OUT FOR THAT HETERO JAZZ. FOR <u>HIM</u> THAT WAS <u>IT</u>. WELL THAT'S FOR HIM, NOT <u>ME</u>.

I HAVE LOTS OF NUDIE FOTOS (AND THEY AIN'T EASY TO GET). FOR ME THEY ARE ALL, EVERYONE, SPRINGTIME ALL YEAR ROUND JOY HAPPINESS AND LOVE LOVE LOVE. I GUESS YOU MIGHT CALL IT AWE-INSPIRING BEAUTY IF YOU WANNA. AND I DON'T CARE TO HAVE MY BEAUTY EDITED BY SOME EDITOR WITH SOME SICK JUNK IN MIND BECAUSE <u>ALL</u> HE CAN THINK OF IS THE TOILET. I WISH HE WOULD KEEP HIS WELL ADJUSTMENT TO HIMSELF. THE NOSE LEAKS? THE EYE LEAKS, THE EAR LEAKS, ETC ETC. HOW CAN ANYTHING BE BEAUTIFUL TO ONE LIKE <u>THAT</u>. I AM NOT ADJUSTED, I HOPE THE HELL I NEVER AM. YOU ADD UP THE MOMENTS OF HAPPINESS IN YOUR LIFE, <u>I'LL</u> ADD UP MINE AND I DON'T CARE WHO'S THE WINNER. STEUART ISN'T SO MAD MAD MAD, I CAN THINK OF LOTS OF EXTINCT DINOSAURS WHO TRAMPLED THE EARTH WITH INVINCIBLE TRIUMPH. THEY WERE AWFUL BIG YOU KNOW, LIKE THE HETEROS, BUT CULTIVATED STUPIDITY. HOMOS <u>HAVE</u> TO LEARN AN ALIEN INDEPENDENCE OF

MIND (HOW CAN THEY AVOID IT IF THEY MERELY STAY ALIVE?) AND THIS IS THE SECRET OF ALL NEW HUMAN KNOWLEDGE. THEIR INSIGHTS FORCED BY CULTURAL FRICTION COULD MAKE THEM TOPS IF THEY CAN SHUCK OFF THE HETERO QUALITY OF SELF COMMISERATION.

ABOUT DOB, MAYBE YOU CAN GET YOUR FOOT IN THE DOOR OF A 'RIGHT' BY NOT EVEN ASKING FOR IT (I DON'T KNOW EVEN IF HISTORY SAYS NO, BUT IT WAS WRITTEN BY JERKS ANYWAY) BUT MAYBE YOU HAVE TO AT LEAST OPEN YOUR MOUTH AND ASK FOR IT.[12] AND MAYBE PUNCH FOR IT WHEN YOU CAN. THAT'S WHAT THEY USED TO DO.

THE STORY 'THE SCAVENGERS' WAS AT FIRST DEPRESSING, BECAUSE IT IS SUCH OLD HAT, BUT IT DOES HIGHLIGHT THE FACT THAT HOMOS ARE USED TO GETTING SMASHED AND CAN GET UP AND BRUSH THEMSELVES OFF. BUT DON'T BE A HEROS, DEARIES, THEY GET BURIED FAST. INSTEAD TAKE UP, SAY, BIOCHEMISTRY.

         Philip

24 November 1961
Small town in northwestern
Ohio

Dear one;

I've recognized myself as a homosexual for five years. I was introduced to Gay life at the age of 10, not by others, but by older neighborhood boys, at the time I was terrified, but later on I enjoyed it. This period went for two years. During the remainder of Grade school and High School I was dormant, and inactive, I never dated girls. Never attended the co-ed parties. In my yearbook during Senior year I was considered quiet, friendly, and independent. My Senior quotation was "Women disturb me not." This wasn't my idea. There must have been another in my class that I didn't recognize. At this time I began to wonder whether I was homosexual or not. After evaluating myself I admitted to myself I was. I thought I was the, "<u>only one</u>." Not until I reached 20, did I visit a Gay bar, I was glad to have friends that understood my innermost feelings. At this time I experienced my first love affair. My worst problem came into view when my three sisters began heckling me about getting married and raising a family. I shrugged them off for as long as possible. I finally broke down and told them everything. My one brother-in-law was very understanding, to a certain extent, but insisted on Psychiatric treatment. It proved useless. Eventually I was bluntly kicked out. I've been on my own since. I had to reconcile with my loved ones. To this day I have to live two lives. And I'm still not trusted with my teenage nephews, even tho I would never have anything to do with them sexually.

So, I'm gay; no matter what I do to get away from it, the innermost attraction for men is there. There is nothing more I can do to restrain from it.

What would you do in my case?

Troubled,
Daryl

P.S. How can I get in touch with Dr. Blanch [Baker]. I am a Psychiatric nurse in an Ohio hospital. It would be interesting discussing viewpoints with her. This is my first subscription to One.

∼

7 August 1961
Midsize town in eastern Texas

Dear Mr. Lambert:[13]

I have secured a copy of One from Central Sales and I must say that I found it very interesting and only wish that I was able to send you some money to help you with such a good cause. I did not realize that there was someone in this world who really care[s] about the homosexual and all the torments and troubles that they go through each year.

But I am writing to you because I must get some things off my chest and I will feel much better since you are a stranger and one with an understanding heart, I feel that my problem is off to its self [in] that I am the only one who has such a problem and therefore I have a longing in my heart for some comfort. You see Mr. Lambert I have been a homosexual all my life and yet I haven't had any experiences, you see I am 25 years of age and I am living with my parents who by the way is very possessive with me. My Mother still treats me as thro I was a child, if I go anyplace then she must go also and whenever I get any mail she must read it first if she knows anything about it and this is one reason that I am a homosexual as the female to [me] means someone who is rought and giving orders all the time. I do not have a friend to my name and I do not have any hobbies that I know of, the only thing that I do is look for work and to watch television all day and night and it is getting on my nerves and I do know that I am emotional [and] upset most of the time.

I know when I go apply for work they must look at my nails which is terrible and it is getting so bad that I cannot write for making mistakes as you can see, you see I bite my nails and suck my thumb all the time and this seems to get rid of a lot of the tensions that I hold inside. Of course if I had the money I would go to the Doctor but if I should mention it to Mother then she would have a fit of somekind and I would never hear the last of it.

I would very much [like] to leave home, to get an apartment or room and to find a job and to live my own life, I know if I got away from home I would not be under so much tensions. The problem is how to leave home when you donot have them expenses that you can't face for the lack of money, and no job prospects and how in the world could I ever tell my Mother the reason for leaving.

Mr. Lambert I do pray that you will be able to give me the advise as Iam unable to find a solution to my problem and it has been going on 7 years now and Iam getting worse each day. I would like to settle in California if given the chance to live my own life because of the Educational opportunity but I understand that in California you must live there for one year before you can get a job so this problem I will not have to worry about at all as I would never have the money to live on for a year.

May God Bless you and everyone on your staff for the fine work that you are doing and I pray that before it is to late you will be able to give me the advise that Iam so bad in need of.

Sincerely;
Larry

PLEASE HELP ME BEFORE MY LIFE IS TORE TO PIECES AND I HAVE TO FACE THE MENTAL WARD

∼

16 January 1962
Knoxville, Tennessee

Dear Mr. Glover,[14]

I appreciate your information and openness to discuss a situation such as many of us face today. I am thirty-three and a Navy Hospital Corpsman veteran of state side Korean duty during Truman's war. I can tell you that this charge was placed against me similar to the Col. Sutton case. I was allowed no council and heresay evidence was used against me. I was discharged Undesirable and three months later in 1953 I had a complete schizophrenic reaction which kept me in a state hospital for 10 months. I found two other cases who were trying the mental "illness" gimmick to get discharges changed, one whose name I remember, [. . .] had changed his name by being adopted by [a family in Oklahoma]. He was trained as a telegrapher-yeoman. He admitted it to get out. I had 15 electric shock treatments and 45 days of insulin shock therapy. I am still suffering the after effects of the weight gain. I went from 175 to 256. During the period after my discharge from the hospital, my mother died of cancer very suddenly and six months [later], I had another flare up. In this case I was turned in by a Nav-Cad Navy pilot who told the hospital doctor (we both were patients of an act with him), I suffered another relapse about a week later when my grandfather on my father's side died. I was released three months later. These records got into my Veteran's Administration records. The stigma will follow me the rest of my life. My name is also in the Boy Scout "blackmail" list when I was 17. I have found a woman doctor who understands me who is a psychiatrist. I consult with her. I am still under the V.A.'s care. It cost my family nearly 5,000 in payoffs to the American Legion and politicians to change the discharge. I finally received an Honorable conditions one April 1956 under the same clause which releases pregnant WAVES from the service. I wonder if they consider me a case of promiscuity of adulterous or incestuous relations with other servicemen??!! Such are my trials.

Now for my academic background, I have 275 quarter hours and at 45 quarter hours an academic year, I have 6 years of credit with six hours to spare. I have a bachelor's degree in anthropology from [a large university in the midwestern United States], and have worked on a Masters degree in history at [a different university]. I'm 33 and like most of us, unattached, not in the double ring male ceremonies.

There are some points which interest me in the field of WHO are inverts. I notice so many of the muscle magazines on the stands. There are brief references in the literature to these types who must be narcissistic in the Freudian oral stage. (He means infantile here). I refer to Stearn to PP. 65-75, and pp. 117-124.[15] Jack Owen mentions some of it in the Beach Bums. I wondered how many of Milo's 601 S. Vermont Ave. Los Angeles 5 are of our kind? I have noticed the rising star of Larry Scott, Evrett Lee Jackson and Chuck Young. I know some from the Indian side of the issue that it is true that among the Pueblos, and Plains that the berdashe was a transvestite who took squaw's clothes and did women's work. He was lived with by a brave at times. None of these Cherokee (Jackson) or Young (Apache) would take the female role but they are definitely the males who would live with the berdashe in the ancient days. Today we call these types TRADE??!! It makes one wonder when one has . . . been through such places where psychiatry is effective and having had as much anthropology and abnormal psychology as I have! As for looking for causes for our dilemma, read the accompanying article from the Oct. Cornet. It might be of interest to you all. Also read the part in Phillip Wylie, Generation of Vipers about on the influence of this mess.

My bibliography deals only with books I have heard of authors who wrote on the subject or mentioned it in their works. I went as far back as 1920 and found the listed entries. I know the Christine Jorgensen case is found in the Journal of the American Medical Association between May 20–June 1, 1953 in time streak. I think the article is by Hamburger who castrated "it." I will keep out for the look for interesting things.

About our local situations here. There are a few descreet ones on campus here in town and some of the professors we think are BI's or "ladies in retirement." I am not in school and what books we have on Homo's are in the Special Collections room under lock and key. The public library has none. I compiled the bibliography for another gay friend and another Librarian-old maid who I trust closely. She is head of the reference dept of the library about 100 miles from here. I have not even begun to extract the ARTICLES on the subject yet. Let me know if I can do any local research for you all. I am in contact with a group who I can trust. Thank you for your prompt mail. I can not come to the conference but will give best wishes from here. If you ever hear of any "interested" individuals in this, Louisville; Nashville, Chattanooga, Ashville, Atlanta area let me know! We might form a chapter of the Mattachine here in the Southern Appalachians. By the way, police are strict in Memphis but not so strict here locally. No homo news in the paper for months. Most of the swish kind and wall scrawlers go through the YMCA—many draftees stay there. Police bait I say. I appreciate any information you can furnish. P.S. my avocation's historical research, library science, genealogy, archaeology, hiking, and Indian lore.

Sincerely,
James

Sexuality and Gender

The following letters offer lesbian and gay perspectives on the complex relationship between gender and sexuality. Some of the ideas expressed in these letters seem strikingly progressive (particularly those written by ministers, interestingly), while several reflect outdated thinking (such as the claim that women are responsible for all sexual repression in society). Lesbians especially had much to say about these issues.

> Published in *ONE* magazine,
> October 1955, 27
> Santa Barbara, California

To all you MEN:

I just read your magazine for the first time—and I want to tell you how horrible you all are. You know very well all homosexuals are men, and there are not any women homosexuals. How dare you have a "Feminine Viewpoint" section when the only feminine viewpoint comes from the feminine men? I see lots of homo men but never in my life have seen a homo woman. I'll bet that Ann Carll Reid is a man and you're just trying to fool the public. Why don't you leave women alone and out of your lousy magazine. You don't have any respect.

Mrs. B.

> Published in *ONE* magazine,
> June-July, 1956, 45
> Atlanta, Georgia

Dear Editors:

As a heterosexual I find your magazine of great interest . . . when I first read it I was somewhat annoyed at the idea that the homosexual considered himself as having the same rights as the heterosexual . . . my understanding had been so very limited. . . . I kept on reading each issue however, and finally realized it wasn't just for curiosity; I began to understand the reason and justification for such a publication as yours. . . . The knowledge obtained has been of value in my association with my heterosexual friends, surprising as this may seem. There seems to be much of the hetero-homo in all of us and understanding of their actions and feelings has greatly improved since I've learned more about our "other side." . . . I wish I were more of a writer and could explain these things more clearly. . . . I hope you can reach more heterosexual readers. They have as much a need for your magazine as the homosexual.

Mrs. G.

Published in *ONE* magazine,
December 1957, 30
San Francisco, California

Dear Sir:

An opinion expressed by Mr. A. C. of Galveston, Texas did, and I quote, "make me so damn mad" that I would like to answer him. Women for the most part who are lesbians try to be as inconspicuous as possible, not because we are ashamed but merely because it is easier to get along in this world when considered "normal." When a man is pointed out as being gay he receives one glance, a woman receives a second, and a third. Is it any wonder then that we prefer to keep quiet? Be that as it may, I'm sure that our women will come forward and present to the public their ideals, dreams and problems.

Another opinion expressed by Mr. L. of Baltimore, Md., gave me real food for thought. Agreed, homosexual love can [be] and often is beautiful, and our society does provide the world with a great number of its better artists, authors, musicians. But I think it's a darn crime for any active homosexual to seek out and force attentions on any innocent youngster. If a person is destined to become homosexual they will on their own without any help from us oldsters.

Miss L.

∼

31 July 1960
New York, New York

Dear Mr. Slater:[16]

When I said, in a previous letter, that I am never sure you receive the clippings I send, I meant that I don't trust the Post Office. If you were to acknowledge receipt of every letter and clipping sent to you, you would need two full time secretaries plus [a] large quantity of paper, envelopes and stamps. Unfortunately, ONE cannot afford that. Therefore I thank you very much for your short nice letter of July 14.

Back to our Post Office. I don't trust it because we New Yorkers are going now through a "decency wave." Therefore, the Post Office may open anything, examine it and throw it in the waste basket if they feel like it.

As regards New Yorkers, let me say that they are narrow-minded, stubborn and appallingly misinformed. Their lack of understanding and inability to change their mind is most shocking. They may ignore a lot of things and yet utter sharp opinions on such things. Arrogantly, they make awkward statements about things they do not know at all.

They assume that they are always right. They never admit that they are wrong.

New York should be the most cosmopolitan city in the world—but it is not. New York should be the most tolerant city in the world—but it is not. New York is a conglomeration of "small towns" with all their gossiping, witch hunting, bigotry and so on. People here waste a lot of time poking their nose into their neighbor's business.

New York enjoys a constant stream of visitors from all over the world; yet, New Yorkers look scoffingly at a woman gracefully wrapped in a sari and openly laugh at a handsome hindu man with a turban. They may even make insulting remarks. Nor even the United Nations Headquarters have been able to make New Yorkers more worldly. Xenophobia in New York is a fact.

New Yorkers want desperately to be "distinguished"—through ostentation. Status seekers to the back bone, they are up to anything with the sole purpose of overshadowing the Joneses.

We all like money. The more the better. But money alone do[es] not make a person distinguished. Nobody can be distinguished without money but something else is required in order to be that way; among other things, talent and education. Ignorance and stupidity cannot go together with distinction.

Everybody knows that the city of New York is facing a most difficult problem: the Puertorican [sic] problem. Books have been written about it but New Yorkers do not understand it yet. To New Yorkers, Puerto Rico, Latin America and Spain are the same thing. I myself have tried unsuccessfully over and over again to show them how wrong they are. They keep repeating: "I don't understand . . . I don't understand. . . .

They do not want to understand.

Even "West Side Story," the highly successful musical comedy, shows the same mistakes. "West Side Story" is supposed to show one side of the puertorican problem in New York and, scattered here and there, one can spot touches of flamenco dancing and a brief pantomime taken from the second act of "Carmen"!

A few months ago I was listening to the radio. I had tuned the WQXR. It is the radio station of The New York Times. A program of Spanish works was about to start, when Mr. Abram Chasin, musical director of WQXR, said, as a matter of course, that the best Spanish music has been written not by Spaniards but by foreign composers. Therefore works by Ravel, Lalo and Rimsky-Korsakoff were broadcasted.

Mr. Abram Chasin had thus ignored completely Joaquín Turina, Enrique Granados, Manuel de Falla and many others!

How could a musical director of the radio station of The New York Times be so ignorant? When a person that holds such a job acts that way, what can you expect from plain, ordinary people?

I started to write a letter to him in protest, but after a few paragraphs I changed my mind and tore up the letter. After all, I figured, he will read it and throw it out. But others protested, I guess, because a few weeks after, WQXR broadcasted a program of Spanish music with works by the composers I mentioned above. Before the music, the same Mr. Abram Chasin tried, very poorly, to explain his ridiculous statement of weeks back.

Let me quote now a few lines from "The Past Within the Present," an article by Faubion Bowers published in Dance Magazine of June 1960. (I enclose this number herewith.)

> "I remember, not so long ago, that a distinguished radio commentator expressed surprise when I mentioned "Japanese theatre," and asked me what language it was in. More recently, a prominent playwright with a success on Broadway explained away the fact that the Japanese had never asked to perform his play on the ground that, "after all, there are no theatres there."

When a distinguished radio commentator and a prominent playwright talk that way, what can you expect from plain, ordinary people?

Female impersonation in the Kabuki Theatre is the most interesting and important side of it and, as such, should have been widely and openly advertised. All the publicity should have been done around that fact, which should have been stressed up. But those connected with the show thought otherwise. They were of the opinion that such a publicity would have been a bad publicity. . . .

The Kabuki audience was integrated mostly by lovers of theatre and dance. To them, the Kabuki traditions, foreign and remote, were things they had to put up with—in order to enjoy the show. Therefore, they all knew about female impersonation in the Kabuki Theatre and being slightly more open minded than the ordinary citizen, accepted it. But plain Mr. and Mrs. New York kept repeating: "No girls in the company. Men dressed as women. Why? I don't understand. . . . I don't understand. . . ."

New York is controlled by women. They are very powerful here. Men are afraid of them. Women have instilled into men's head the notion that intelligence is a feminine quality. Therefore, knowledge is for the exclusive use of women.

Everybody here is fully aware of homosexuality. Therefore, every man tries to show off his ignorance and stupidity—in order to be masculine. Since intelligence and knowledge means femininity, every man pretends desperately to be ignorant and stupid—to please everybody.

New York is the intellectual and artistic center of the nation. Mountains of books, magazines, newspapers and all kind of literature is seen everywhere. One may think that New York is a city of learned people. But it is not. New Yorkers read and read (those who read) and then keep repeating: "I don't understand. . . . I don't understand. . . .["]

Conversation here is expected to be shallow and nonsensical, kept alive by a succession of empty sentences without connection with each other. Any attempt of starting an intelligent conversation is considered of a very bad taste. To have a personal opinion is considered antisocial. To think is a crime. The people keep away from a man who thinks and acts intelligently as he is considered a dangerous character. <u>Only women can think</u>.

Men have no personality here. Women have smothered it. At home, the wife takes all initiatives and makes all decisions. Men have lost their authority. His wife and his children have no respect for him. He is only a seminal necessity and a provider.

Men here are completely dominated by women and most of them actually believe that women are more intelligent than men; than [sic] women are superhumans; that women should be the leaders.

On the other hand, everybody watches everybody. In our place of work we have to control our emotions all the time. We have to watch our moves, our attitude. We have to keep our face rigid; no smiles. We have to control our eyes. They have to look expressionless, indifferent, inconcerned—particularly when we talk. Defamation, calumniation and slandering is rampant.

If we act warmly; if we are slightly demonstrative; if we are, by nature, friendly, we become a "suspect." And if the boss thinks that one employee is "interested" in another employee, either one is fired—or both.

In every place of work there is somebody who claims to have "X Rays" in his (or her) eyes. He, or she, claims to be infallible. And once a "suspect" is caught in a most innocent, but in the opinion of the "expert," revealing gesture or situation, that "suspect" is doomed. Needless to say that the "expert" is always either a repressed homosexual or one that, for obvious reasons, cannot attract anybody. The latter is the most dangerous type.

Men live here in constant terror of being "branded" and do the most ridiculous things in order to show others how straight and he-men they are.

Enclosed please find two numbers of Dance Magazine. In them you will find something about Kabuki. Also the Kabuki booklet, a beautiful thing for your library.

Please send me the January 1956 ONE magazine. I enclose herewith [a] money order for one dollar for that purpose. If it is not available any more you can keep the money as a small contribution to ONE.

Good wishes to ONE.

Yours respectfully,
Fernando

P.S. (1) I love New York.
     (2) I don't hate women.

∽

2 July 1962
New York, New York

Dear ONE:

Ignorance on sexual matters is appalling. Sexual education should be widespread. It should be a subject in high school.

How people could be tolerant and understanding toward homosexuality as long as they know so little about heterosexuality—sex in general?

Most heterosexuals are sexually frustrated, unsatisfied, repressed. In sex matters most of them are abnormal individuals, although they are considered normal just because they are heterosexuals.

Very few heterosexuals have normal sexual relations with a woman. Most of them, when in bed, demand from the woman the most unmentionable things. The gamut of aberrations, in them, is infinite. And they call themselves normal! Yet, when they face homosexuality, they get shock with indignation.

Who is to blame for so much ignorance? Women.

Men are for thorough sex education.

Women insist on keeping their children in the dark. They assume that their daughters and sons are absolutely virgins when they get married.

They know they are fooling themselves. But they prefer to perpetuate this make-believe.

Mothers want their daughters and sons to be popular. Therefore, girls and boys are strongly encouraged to go out with their boys and girls friends—with the inevitable petting and other stimulants.

They know that. But they pretend to ignore it.

Sex, sex, sex everywhere and by all means. But no sex outlet except marriage.

Sexual education? No, for heaven's sake!
What do mothers want then? Marriage.
They know that once boys are grown up, it is difficult to dominate them.
Therefore, mothers need an allied [sic]; the future wife. Once sons are married, the mother comes to terms with her daughter-in-law and both of them together dominate the young husband.
Ignorance is the thing women appreciate most in men. And as far as sex is concerned, women (mothers) try to keep their sons in complete ignorance.
Venereal disease is one aspect of sexual education—perhaps the most important one.
Women are so selfish that they prefer to expose their sons to venereal disease rather than accept sexual education. And they consider themselves more intelligent than men!
You, ONE, are doing a noble job on educating the heterosexual public. However, the public make your job too hard because of their own ignorance on sexual matters. They['ve] got to know themselves first. Once they look at themselves as they really are, your task will be easier, because to know is to understand.
Heterosexuals are at the present time awfully unhappy. They have to do away with all their own prejudice, stupidity, hypocrisy, prudery and cowardice.
We need a new philosophy of life—a new american way of living. The sooner the better.
Heterosexuals are so cruel toward homosexuals because they, the heterosexuals, are so unhappy themselves. And dominated by women!
Once they set themselves free—from prejudice, from women and from churches—they will be then sexually happy and tolerant toward homosexuality.
As for venereal disease by homosexual contact, it happens quite often. However, when a man gets infected by homosexual contact, he never tells the truth to his doctor.

           Fernando

           16 November 1964
           Baltimore, Maryland

Dear Sir,
I don't know if you get letters from people with a real big problem, or if you can help them, but I do know I need help and you

are my last hope. If, after reading this, you can help me at all, I'd be most grateful.

Its going to be hard to put my problem into writing, but I'll try to get all the facts across. You see, outwardly I'm a woman, but inside I have a male's emotions. In fact, at times, I become 2 different people. For awhile I'm a woman, and even act like one then all of a sudden I'm a man. This change doesn't . . . show on the outside only on the inside. I never know when this change is going to happen, it just does. Only one fact remains permanent, that is, I have no love or emotions for men. I only fall in love with other girls, but not all the time because I don't seek feminine company. What I mean is—here in Balto. city there is a place called "Cicero's" where Lesbians hang out. Since I don't consider myself a Lesbian I don't hang out there and try to pick up some girl. I <u>want</u> another girl's company, but I won't look for it. She has got to come to me because she wants to or else its no go. I don't think someone should be forced to live or associate with someone who isn't normal.

Right about now I'm so darn lonely I could scream. I've tried to take my life twice in the past 3 years. Sometimes I get so lonely and depressed I can't bear to go on any longer.

I work in an office because I prefer filing to factory work although I know others like me prefer working where they can wear pants, etc. My work is O.K. because they accept me, and don't know what my problem is. If they found out I could be fired as I have been before. However, it tears me apart inside when the fellows in the outer office come into the filing dept., and goof off with the other girls I work with. By goof off, I mean, hugging them or patting them in some way, you know. It tears me apart because I realize that I have no one, no one at all, never will. In other words, I'll never marry, and experience married life. Men and I get along as long as they just talk to me, but if they try to get fresh then my other side (the masculine side) shows thru, and then there's trouble. There is only <u>one</u> fellow in my whole office that talks to me, and he is like a brother to me. That is the only feeling I get for them. I'm satisfied living with this abnormality, but by the same token I can't go on living without love and affection. As I've said before this can only be accomplished by another girl. Therefore, the reason for this letter, and my plea for help. I want to know:

    a) If you get letters from other girls with the same sort of problem?

    b) If you know of any who might live pretty close to me?

    c) If you know of someone who doesn't have my problem, but would like to be friends with me?

I guess this is like a "Lonely Hearts" letter to you, but you're my last hope. I'll enclose my address and phone number so that if there is someone you know of they can get in touch with me. Also do you have clubs here in Balto. city? Where? Can I obtain some of your magazines? If I can't subscribe to it, where can I buy them? Because there is more to my problem, and would take too long to write, I'll be glad to explain it further to someone who wants to know a little more about me.

I appreciate you reading this, and because I'm hoping so strongly that you can help me, I'm thanking you in advance. My address is:
....

My phone number is:
....

I'll be waiting anxiously to hear from you or someone who might be able to bring a little happiness into my life. Oh, also I am white, and 25 years of age.

Sincerely yours,
Lori

~

3 November 1962
Brooklyn, New York

Dear One:

I have just emerged from a "Computer User's Symposium." You will notice of course, that everything I have to say is polarized in the sense that I <u>see</u> things in a certain way and am selective, because much is going on, but a small part is captured, except by generalizers.

Firstly, I observe that men are deliriously happy to get-together. Of course, they have a common base, as in all cases, say baseball, but in this case computers, which is merely the pretext. They love the power of their own bodies and minds, and of their so charming but incremental and ornamental differences. (Cocktail Hour) In this sense they were 99% (a guess) a set of homosexual people. (There were four women (brava), and about 300 men.)

Of the 99% there was 50% who were permanently camouflaged (a guess) from cradle-to-grave with wedding ring prominently displayed, and a careful mask and cautious departure when too much ebullience or joie-de-vivre raised its merry head.

There was of course, the most subtle of communicative interplay, . . . somebody watching someone else who was watching someone else, . . . some boisterousness, and some penetrating half-smiles.

There was a shattering intensity of abstraction-ability (not surprising among mathematicians and organizers-of-thought people.) No pride.

Above all, there was a striving to belong, and be with someone, perhaps a reaction to their lonely and individual efforts to make something out of nothing, which is the usual task of an abstractionist.

As an example, it is very difficult, usually, to get across that there <u>is</u> a set (of something) (anything), but the most you can call it is a set. Numbers, oranges, balls, penises, breasts, bodies or stars or particles. Most minds get lost in the concept because they have preconceived ideas of what belongs in a set (of anything). In this sense what you do <u>not</u> say in mathematics is as important as what you <u>do</u> say.

In addition there was a large element of combativeness (as your own experience would lead you to expect).

Some assertive and destructive, but mostly an emotional expression of uncertainty.

Computer usage and the conception of what such a tool is, or ought to be, is in its first sparkling jump into existence, of awareness, of possibilities.

(The same as I <u>see</u> One to be).

Not yet burdened with the heavy tradition or customary usage (the gravitational, stubborn pull that kills us all.)

The large content of emotional drive, or of neutral wait-and-see attitudes displayed in the congregation is of course due to the qualitative, and therefore inconclusive nature of the papers presented. There was not a sufficient statistical background to utilize extant methods of assessing the <u>value</u> of experience.

Computerization and space technology is presumably a glamorous occupation. However it is not that at all, it is just plain tough.

Beating off stupidity is the only occasion for one to scream. You can't be two things at the same time, both patient and impatient, can you??? (Well, we'll do our best!)

The accommodations were considerate of one, and luxurious (if you looked at it in that way.) We stayed at the Marriott Motor-Hotel in Phila.

I sense that the décor was a combination of homo and hetero persuasions. I mean that that is what the artists were.

Your cover for October was adroit, being suggestive rather than immediately instructive regarding a mode of existence, which really exists, but which is invisible (and unnecessary, to the Bull and Cow citizen), but a great strain on the remnant of thinkers who have the intolerable burden, (almost) of locating themselves between the urgency of their body needs and of intelligent self awareness and of otherness awareness.

So keep trying, and if you have to do without (mostly of approval) why then so-be-it, but stay, for you have something that nobody else has (although they may assume that they have everything, and have it made.) They don't and neither do I (have it made) as we say.

It may be that I have been boring in some degree and not a [Dancer?], but then we are all confined by our Reach. And so I shall be explicit via physical experience, for what profiteth it a Man to gain his Soul, and lose his Body? (This is a wrong question, at best, profit and lose, gain and cost, but it is the familiar song that everyone sings.)

I pointed out to the boys in the Anofice [sic] (20 to 30 yrs, me 50) that they took a great joy in touching each other, by handshake, by touch of thigh or butt, or whatever. Unconsciously, but not any (careful) more!! Our operators are advanced from the Mail-room by the selection of a puritan who can face everyone because he has restrained himself from fucking them!

Al is the leading intelligence, who touches my knee in conversation, but constrained by Religion (Roman Catholicism, whether he will get out of his shell I don't yet know, . . . how Glorious do I have to get?)

Tho I am Simplicity Personified!

Paul is burdened with the Bull-Cow-Safety factor.

Al is a prize! (Not to be overlooked.)

Paul is a got-it-made but pitiable human.

Paul (23) has a signed and sealed Sex Contract (married.)

However Paul (and not Al) observes that there is a Customer Engineer who has (presumably) only a High-school education and no background in electrical theory. And therefore that Paul can tread in the same path and become a gadget fixer. And between comfortable fewkings [sic] gain money by Circuit Tracing so that he may do more of the same.

. . . .

I had a souvenir from the Symposium in the way of a keychain with bottle-opener, etc.

I said to Eric; "would you like a copy of my Key," remarked upon as being so enormous. (The key to the Kasle you know.) YMCA

He rejoined with, "What would I want with a thing like THAT!!!!!

I said, "Men get together for more reasons than you have in mind, scornful as you are. I might talk Baseball or the theory of Electricity that you desire to know about."

"But since you know everything about me and yourself in advance, I propose that you get a textbook on "theory of electricity" and study by yourself."

———Later, when Eric was talking about the problem of Money, Wife, and Child, I said, "Well, you can't have Everything." And he said, "That's for Sure!" He knew that I could do without him much more easily than he could do without me.

Love,
Philip

(Much to his credit) from now on I am a Scandinavian Iceberg!

In the following two letters, clergymen rail against sexual hypocrisy in society and make passionate arguments for social acceptance of gay people. Their letters are powerful reminders that religious figures and institutions have long held diverse opinions about homosexuality.

3 March 1963
Suburb of Detroit, Michigan

Dear Editor

After having read many of your interesting and informative magazines, I finally decided to write and attempt a thank you note, for what I believe is a wonderful dedication to this present day society.

To be able to help the world to understand that the "Homosexual" is as human as any next door neighbor, is a tremendous task, however I think that you are going great.

I have read down thru the history of many of our own very important writers, historians, generals, and the like have been "Homosexual" and in some places in the bible there are hints that Jesus himself was soft and feminine, how true this [is] I cannot attest to even tho I have read the bible thru and thru, you see I am an ordained Minister and have had to read and study bibliology.

The society that we live in today have too many things that lead to depravity and sex offences, other than the "Homosexual," I refer to such things as the filth that can be found on any newsstand in these United States and elsewhere, also in our movie theaters on the screen, to me there is more suggestive sex in the aforesaid mentioned than in the actual heart and soul of the "Homosexual." I find in drive in theaters that teenagers see maybe 5% of the movie and 95% sexual pleasure, and statistics prove that the up trend in illegitimate children is appalling, rape and murder are also on the upward climb, and those offenses when examined by our finest doctors are usually men and women from very well bred families and are also married, with children, and are of rather good intelligence, and then too there are those of lower intelligence and poor families that have been deprived of proper education, these self same people are almost always so called normal as far as "Homosexual" tendencies are concerned.

The Rapist, Murderer, Extortionist, and etc, when examined most usually never have any "Homosexual" tendencies, and seem to abhor the thought that they could be or ever have been associated with anything as low as a "Homo," or fairy or queer as they are so often referred to. I have asked many people throughout the country in law agencies and the like how many "Homosexuals" are guilty of such aforesaid mentioned crimes, the answer is always the same, "Almost no percentage."

I have given council to many of the Gay set and find that in letting them decide for themselves is always the best answer to their problems. I feel that if they are gay so what as long as they can make useful citizens of themselves and do not become a hindrance to the so called normal set. I almost believe that I hate the word Normal as it implies too much, and besides what is normal?????? and what is abnormal???????. The things that some of our teenagers do for kicks can be classified as abnormal, but somehow it is not. Tasting forbidden fruit, for instance, such as dope, sex, muggings and all of the rest of the things that we read about in the newspapers this is supposed to be close to normal for the modern day way of life. To be different, in ones way of thinking about sex is supposed to be the unforgivable sin, I say that it is not who are we to play God and to know what the individual feelings are of those that live around us, Love in its true sense of the word has no boundaries, some of us Love animals, some flowers, some cars, boats, trains and the many many luxuries that money can afford, but those of us that find true love in any form are indeed fortunate. I feel that to have found true love and friendship in male to female or male to male or female to female is the only one thing that God intended us to do, all things to me are to be or they would not happen as they do. I also feel that no one person in this or any other world can say that we do not have the right to love as we please whether or not we do it in private or out in the open. I have had many men come to me with the problem of being in love with one of their own kind and have also indulged in this practice myself, I have found that the true honest "Homosexual" is kind, considerate, temperate, tolerant, extremely intelligent and on the whole more than a true citizen in any community, and in a great many cases he has been known to be a hero in time of disaster and war. Somehow the so called society that we live in find the "Homosexuals" to be loathsome things preying on the innocent youngsters of the world, yes I suppose that this is true in some respects but these are so few in number that they do not even need to be mentioned. I have also noted that if a child, a teenager, or an adult does not wish to partake of "Homosexual" practices the "Homosexual" does not pursue the issue for fear of being caught or even worse beaten into a pulp, or preyed upon for money or blackmail or both. The homosexual in my opinion is the most persecuted human in this country, the land of the free. I therefore say that you are on the right track and I believe that you have made great strides in the one thing that we need in this country, the right to free thinking, free loving, and the true freedom of doing and performing that which is best suited to our individual feelings in the privacy of our own homes.

I have read your articles on Miami Beach, and have also reread them about umpteen times, I hope that it has had some effect on the understanding population of that fine city. I have read your various other articles and must admit as with all things some were good and some were not so good, I most enjoyed the article about "Illinois" and its new laws regarding "Homosexuality," I say good show. I will also ask if you have read an article in a New York scandal sheet about the new process of brain washing willing "Homos" to cure them of their plight, this is being done in England and that is something else to talk about another time. I have some friends in England and have been told by them that there is a greater amount of freedom in "Homosexuality" there than here, what has happened to our so called democratic way of life where a man can pursue the right of freedom and free thinking, don't you believe it, I have had too many young people just out of service tell me too much of what is going on there, and also of the things going on out here in this civilian world.

Thanks for listening to my rattling on and on and may God bless you. I will write again if I have any more to say, and you can decipher it, my typing is absolutely atrocious as you can see but somehow I think I have gotten my point over to you, by the way do you people ever send photos of your staff????? I would like to know what you look like.

God Grant Me The
Serenity to accept the things
I cannot Change
and The Courage To Change The Things
I Can
and The Wisdom To Know The Difference
In Gods Name, Bless You

            Very Truly
            Rev. Gene

> Published in *ONE* magazine,
> October-November 1956,
> 39
> Oklahoma City, Oklahoma

Editors:

Although, with Derrick Bailey, I think the Church has never intended to reject the homosexual, I suspect that whatever enlightenment may have come to us as a result of Biblical scholarship and tended to break down the "Sodom-prejudice" has also been to some degree counteracted by the Protestant "Reformation," which brought with it a tendency to misunderstand the nature of Love and Sin. If one fails to understand that Sin is a matter of will and not of nature or of act, then of course, he may reject the homosexual in spite of the fact that no act of the will caused that psycho-sexual orientation.

It is a fact, and a regrettable one, that homosexuals by the hundreds have sought aid in the churches and been turned away. It is also a fact, unfortunately less well known, that many homosexuals have been and are being helped to the opportunity to love, to know love, and to find peace in the context of the Christian Community.

I appreciate your magazine. . . . Most of all I appreciate what you are trying to do.

Reverend R.

~

> Published in *ONE* magazine,
> October 1953, 10–11
> Tulsa, Oklahoma

Sirs:

The following you might call my "Credo":

I believe in Homosexuality as a Way of Life. I feel no sense of guilt or shame. I know that I, as a homosexual, can be an asset to the community in which I live and a good citizen of the land which gave me birth. Realizing that others may not understand my way of life and that they may seek to deprive me of my social and civil rights, I can still say with all sincerity, "Father forgive them, for they know not what they do"! I affirm my undying conviction in the Fatherhood of God, the Brotherhood of Man, and the Immortality of the Soul. I pledge my utmost to the task of securing equal rights for those of my people who merit and desire it. I abhor any form of totalitarianism which seeks to enslave the spirit of man. I pray that the injustices and misunderstandings of our people will soon be a thing of the past. I believe that no nobler bond of affection exists than that love which unites the hearts of two men. With these ideals I know that I can be a happy, satisfied, well-integrated individual whose life will merit the respect of mankind.

[no name published]

∾

Published in ONE magazine,
June 1955, 19
Toronto, Canada

Dear ONE:

Anent the many moral implications involved with homosexuality, I submit that the chief fallacy in traditional thinking lies in the assumption that all deviates are heterosexual who, via immoral thought, become homosexual, and who, via moral thought can become heterosexual again. By developing this assumption it is easy to claim that all deviates are self-made, and unnatural.

Fortunately, many persons look twice at this notion, and sense its untruth. We are gradually coming to understand that nature produces homosexuality, as well as heterosexuality, by making the components for the former predominate in some mortals. Against the background of this idea, it is recognized that homosexuality is natural for some persons, and that, as with heterosexual attachments, homosexuality needs to be refined rather than frustrated.

[no name published]

∾

Published in ONE magazine,
September 1955, 28
Los Angeles, California

Gentlemen:

I am not one of your subscribers, nor am I a homosexual. I am an elderly married woman. But I am a friend of a number of homosexuals, and so am fairly acquainted with their unique and special interests.

Your magazine came to my attention, and I cannot fail to be impressed with its aims and objectives. From the standpoint of both a minority group, as well as the majority, they are certainly good.

From what I have gathered from your magazine, it appears that practically all angles and phases of homosexuality are being dealt with as progressively as possible. However, there is one factor which, so far as I have ascertained, has been omitted. This omission, I surmise, is due to almost complete lack of knowledge in this department. I refer generally, to the spiritual factor—but specifically, to the esoteric and occult aspects of homosexuality. Here is a field, vast, vital and utterly important to every homosexual, as well as to every member of the normal society which he or she contacts.

My personal experience in this field, over a period of many years, has been intensive and extensive. In America, unfortunately, there is still almost complete unawareness of these matters. So far as I know, no psychologist, psychiatrist, or member of the clergy of any denomination, has admitted availing himself of the available information. Abroad, the case is different. There, the knowledge of which I speak, is made excellent use of, by people qualified by education, labor and sincerest interest, to employ it.

May I offer the names of five authoritative textbooks, containing this information? They are:

Sane Occultism, by Dion Fortune
The Problem of Purity, by Violet M. Firth
The Esoteric Side of Love and Marriage, by Dion Fortune
Psychic Self-defence, by Dion Fortune
The Perennial Philosophy, by Aldous Huxley

The first four are published by RIDER and Co., Publishers, Hutchinson House, Stratford Place, London W. 1, England. The last named by Harper and Brothers, 49 East 33rd Street, New York 16, New York. Incidentally, for the happiest results, they should be read in the order named. Any reputable and enterprising book dealer in this country can furnish copies of all these books, if they do not already have them in stock.

In your most worthy effort to be of greatest possible assistance and encouragement to your readers, you cannot, in all faith, fail to offer this opportunity for this extended and specific understanding to these same readers.

I trust that you will, at some time, publish this letter, letting those who avail themselves of the information given, make their own choices and decisions.

Mrs. E.

Published in *ONE* magazine,
March 1956, 28
Calcutta, India

Greetings from India:

I am anxious for the Indians here in Calcutta to become acquainted with ONE—the copy which gave a list of mannerisms to avoid. Due to India's attitude regarding homosexuals I suggest you mail it 1st class.

In the National Library here I found an interesting translation from the ancient Sanscrit of Vatsyayarias Kama Sutra which deals with the love precepts of the Brahmans. I copied most of it. It was written about 500 A.D. There is much homosexuality in Bali and I was fortunate in getting some interesting information, also about the Gurkahs here in India.

Mr. S.

2

Love, Sex, and Relationships

A major goal of the homophile movement was to attain free association rights so that gay people could legally meet one another and form relationships, whether those were short-lived sexual relationships or long-term relationships with deep emotional bonds. Most correspondents (the male ones, at least) experienced little difficulty finding willing sexual partners. In a social climate that demonized and criminalized homosexuality, however, the letters describe frustrations and difficulties in trying to establish long-term relationships.

Falling in Love

The first four letters in this chapter capture the excitement of falling in love. Love grasped *ONE* correspondents when they least expected it—while traveling in a foreign country, for example, or during an evening volunteer session assembling the latest issue of *ONE* magazine. These gay love affairs were rebellious acts in a society that characterized such relationships as immoral, unnatural, and illegal.

>   3 March 1963
>   Columbus, Ohio

Dear <u>One</u>:

    I have always meant to write, but never had the necessary impetus before.

    I lived in Los Angeles almost all my life. My parents were there and I had many gay friends. I have a good profession and achieved success in my field at a very young age. But my parents, friends, and career could not make up for a great lack that I had always felt.

I met a young man, a sailor, who came into L.A. on leave. The first time I met him, I knew I was "hooked." I saw him on all his subsequent leaves and fell deeply in love with him. He was an unusually fine boy and I couldn't deny what I felt for him.

There came a time when his duty in the Navy was finished and he was to return home. I had to make one of the biggest decisions of my life, and I did.

I gave up my possessions, my job, my family, my friends, and the sunny climate of California and returned with him to the snow and ice of Ohio.

I stayed with he and his family until I was able to find an apartment. I had an excellent job waiting for me here, so there was no problem.

I love him very much and we have grown ever closer. I see his family often and they have become an important part of my life. My young man is adjusting nicely to civilian life and is working hard in a good position. We have a wonderful group of friends here, many of whom are "partners" and have been together for several years. We are young (I am 24, he is 23), but have no fear of the future. There is nothing that cannot be discussed between us. I'm glad I have waited until I could write you a happy letter. Enclosed is a check for a year's subscription and also a small contribution. You have given me courage and strength over the years far more than you can ever know.

Sincerely,
Trent

~

18 September 1958
United Kingdom

Dear Bill,[1]

I arrived back on Tuesday a day late after a good holiday. Bill is still in Spain and returns here early October and of course we hope to hold him! Apart from other pleasant things that happened, when in Vienna, a very handsome American chatted to me for about an hour at the Prater nude sun-bathing roof which is 100% gay and at the end of it mentioned that (being so very rich) he thought that the next day he would go for a few day trips to the north of Vienna which is the oldest part of Austria. I said how nice and we parted. Next day I bumped into him near the dressing cubicles (where people take their friends—so convenient) dressed immaculately and looking more good looking than before. As I could think of little else the night before, I was surprised and pleased to see him and said so and added that I thought that he had gone away. He said Would you come with me and I said Yes and reflected—I have almost no money and he said never to worry. At six he picked me up and we sped into the hills and down into the valleys and knowing Americans and their silences, I chatted about the fabulous art collections of Vienna the impossible beauty of the Robes of the Order of the Golden Fleece (a mere 12th cent. effort of petit point pastel shaded and gold threaded magnificence which would make any seamstress weep with joy offset by the Royal and Heralds robes in almost plain rich red and blue velvets with collars of treble rowed enameled crests painted in reds and blue of powdered gems on etched light gold) and the Royal jewels the vast collections of painting including Breughels, Goya, Rembrandt, van Dyke in the palace art galleries and carved rock crystal set off with gold and gems and ancient volumes bound in cloth and the paintings highlighted with seed pearls. The sky was too beautiful and I looked up at it and recited snatches of poetry that matched the mood. He drove on with his perpetual mona-lisa smile and then I sang—Spring is here, why doesn't the breeze invite me, the stars are near, why doesn't the night invite me, maybe it's because nobody loves me—(this, by Ella Fitzgerald, is my favorite number) He said—maybe it's because of the singing and we both laughed and the state had been obtained. The universe lay in the cup of one's hand and there was nothing one could not do. I thought—he gives me a pleasant holiday, I shall give him what gifts I can and together we painted and seared each other with love so that for a week after I could feel him burnt into my body. Next day we sat overlooking the Danube at Durnstein (the castle and town where Richard Coeur de lion was imprisoned) and the Austrians around us in the courtyard were laughing and drinking. He smiled on at me and those lovely grey eyes were far better than wine. I said, unnecessarily breaking the silence Do you know why we get on so perfectly? He answered, because we are so cosmopolitan. It seemed that physically, emotionally & intellectually we could use these states as we pleased but what was a particular joy to me was that although he said he was no mystic, the breadth of life he'd lived had taken him well into the tremendous energies of the spiritual planes which was why he was so healthy and sane. I met two others like him—our dear Rudolph and Rolf.[2] When I sat in Rudolph's presence for a few hours I thought, what is enfolding me with bliss and happiness—it wasn't his physical appearance, but gosh, he was radiating, not healing, nor will,

nor love, but Goodness. And with Rolf it was the same. I went to the
Club and among other guests was introduced and England received
a special cheer. I whispered to Rudolph, they look bored with Rolf's
speech: he said, no, Rolf is telling them the same story he always tells
them about an older man and a minor. They hang their heads and look
uncomfortable because they ALL have a guilty conscience!! ARCADIE
too were kindness itself and their only criticism of Americans was that
they never have the decency to write or answer or take note of what
magnificent strides had been made in France (I was thrilled to listen
to descriptions of 1984 conditions) I said I'd try to explain this to you
but also I firmly pointed out the difficulties with different languages
and the slight isolationism of the U.K. and U.S. I have some interesting
cuttings, ordered the n/papers and you'll be getting them in two weeks.
Specially a letter of how Canadian diplomats are (only and always,
presumably) chased down the Dilly by hordes of queers with satanic
faces. This man is we believe, a journalist. The H.L.R.S. crowd I visited
last night.[3] H.- Smith will soon be installed as Sec. full time as they
have the money necessary. They will first ask people and let me know
who would like to receive the Review. I am of course anxious to have
a reply to my very last letters now that I'm back in harness. A friend of
mine has subscribed to ONE but he is in a monastery he says—there
are those outside our Holy Mother who are ever ready to condemn—so
would you send me an extra copy now? John [. . .] sent a wire with a
phone no. while I was away but they have not heard of him so if you
can contact him, kindly let him know I'm home now. Do check my last
letters as I haven't space here to recap on suggestions and questions.
In one of the paper cuttings you will see a reference to THE BRITISH
JOURNAL OF DELINQUENCY. I have seen this and it is a must for
you. You write as above to c/o INTERNATIONAL UNIVERSITY PRESS
INC.; 227, WEST, 13th ST., N. YORK II. It will cost you about $1.50 and
ask for the Special Edition on Homosexuality. I don't think there's any
more news. Hope to hear from you soon.

Yours,
Brian

P.S. This just came through: £4 paid by [. . .]. This is good for 2 years.

26 February 1962
Brooklyn, New York

Dearest Miss Jackson:[4]

I have just read your article (As for me). True we have no
pattern to grow up by, and we sure are a hell of a lot different, not

only sexually but mentally. I whole heartly agree on a Homosexual
Anonymous pattern, as I'm sure the majardy of us do. A place where
one homosexual helps another, as for understanding the cure for that
would be a suitable mate, that is the dam root to all our problems.
I am a well-adjusted homosexual, and try to make a happy life for
myself, but it sure is no fun doing it alone. As for guidance uniquely
geared to his or hers own needs, and that Homosexual Anonymous
can give it to her or him, just what did you have in mind. I must
confess that when I came out into Gay Life, which really isn't so
gay, I was 14 Yrs old, and in New York at the time you couldn't wear
enough paint, or dress feminine enough, or swish to much, as I came
out with a loud crowd, I know now that being loud was only a release
although I certainly do not regret a bit of it, as those to me were the
only years when gay life was gay. I all so did it to attract the male eye,
and I sure did, I was the Honey and they were the bee. Oh I had lots
of fun and dates, but somehow I just didn't find the suitable male, as
I prefer someone older and more mature than myself, that was quite
a problem, as the bees were my age or slightly younger, and just as
wild and reckless as I have been. I was married a couple of times, but
we really didn't have much in common, as I wanted to settle down
have my own place and live happily ever after. How often I dreamed
of meeting the right person, settling down and making him happy
and giving my all to him. As he would to me. I met a fellow when I
was 18, he was very different, than the fellows that I've been dating.
He had four degrees, a very culture and most brilliant person. He has
contributed an awful lot to me, he showed me a different side of life, a
more finer side, which I eagerly excepted. He took me to plays, Elegant
restaurants to dine, and his friends I thought at the time way above my
level, they consist of Doctors, Lawyers, Writers, ETC, he had opened a
new world to me. Of course I conducted myself properly, as I did not
want to embarrass him in front of his friends, I didn't mind no makeup
or any form of glamour, I even got use to a white shirt and tye. Most
of his friends sense I was what they called a GUTTER QUEEN, and
they said crule things to and about me, I realize now that I should
have felt sorry for them, in spite of all their money and culture, I had
something there money or culture could [not] buy, and that is YOUTH.
I did try to like them, but they just wouldn't get off there horse, god
created everyone equal, I wonder. I had to get back at them, and I sure
did, he took me to Fire Island one weekend, he made me [wear] tight
pink shorts and shirt, when I stepped off the boat, they sure flipped, I
still wasn't satisfied, that evening a bunch of the Sayville boys strolled
into a bar, I ran upstairs and put the pink outfit on, my hair was long
and naturally curly, well those boys sure flipped, I put the jutebox on,

and sat with the Sayville boys, and to top it off I walked out with all of them, leaving the other queens with there tongues hanging out. I'm 22 Yrs old now, and learned an awful lot. If I had loved, as I did only a different kind of love, the fellow took me to plays, etc. we would have had a happy life together, as he was deeply in love with me, we went together for three years, and believe it or not, we never had sex, and that sure is unusually for all they think about now is sex, which to me is, and always will be secondary. How sad it is when someone has so much love to offer, and no one to give it to. I sure this is the story of most gay people. That's the problem, solve or do something about that. And only than would we really have a so called Gay Life. But the letter column which states, and I quote (UNDER NO CIRCUMSTANCES DO THE EDITORS FORWARD LETTERS FROM READERS TO OTHER PERSONS NOR DO THEY ANSWER CORRESPONDECE MAKING SUCH REQUEST) the battle is LOST. I've had a rough time with my family of six sisters, but now they are sort of adjusted. The sister that I am living with now, she sure is like the weather, one day I can tell her my escapades, the next day she would give me a rough time, but deep down she has a warm heart, and a deep feeling for the lonely ones, my sisters and I don't have much, but we do have a strong bond of love between us, that is worth more than anything else in this world. She happen to notice a copy of one magazine lying on the couch, she told me about it the next morning. It's true the storys and poems are delightful but as she said, for a homosexual magazine, as now changed to Viewpoint. How on earth are we helping each other, we have no pen pal to write to, or clubs to meet one another. If we don't have togetherness, we will continue to have plenty of loneliness. And that will turn the adjusted homosexual into a nut ready for belvue. As far back as the magazine has been published, your short article is the most sensible that has ever been written, now all we need is results. From our so called friends. I know an awful lot of elderly homosexuals, that want and need someone badly, as we all do. It's a shame, after work they get together and drink themselves into a stupor, until they fall unconscious, only to wake up the next morning with a beautiful hangover. It disturbs me that I and MANY MANY ETC. others will end up the same way. Its tragic to see some of my friends buy love, as there is no price on real love, and how many of us find it, for without love we really have nothing. So lets wake up and face the facts cold as they are, what can and will be done, if nothing is done, than as my sister who is so called normal, as I know that no one is absolutely normal, quotes "ONE MAGAZINE IS A TOTAL WASTE." As the poems and stories sure don't ease the pain of a lonely heart, I rather waste the money on a movie. And I'm sure so would many others. After reading this shall we say letter, you must think I'm a bitter person, well I [am] far from bitter, I'm just plain discusted. I would deeply appreciate if you would have the time, at ans this letter, or better still, published this letter in HOMOSEXUALS VIEWPOINT. AS THIS IS MY VIEWPOINT, AND IT IS OUR MAGAZINE ISN'T IT. OR WILL THE LAW BE ON YOUR NECKS OR THE POST OFFICE. IF THE EDITORS ARE DARING ENOUGH TO PUBLISHED THIS LETTER, I'M SURE YOU WILL GET PLENTY OF RESPONSE AND THE BALL WOULD START TO ROLL, IT'S ABOUT TIME WE DID SOMETHING ABOUT THIS RIDICULOUS SITUATION. I['m] sure I spelled some words wrong, but I am typing this at 11.00 P.M. and am very tired, do forgive me.

       I remain
       John

      21 March 1965
      Los Angeles, CA

Dear . . . ,[5]

In a day or two I shall be winging my way home to my address [. . .].

I have many problems (and who hasn't) which I hope, somehow, to work out. The way is not too clear at the moment but I am determined that I shall be able to return to Los Angeles to again meet the friends I've met here. When I return [home] I'll write Don Slater a line about how much ONE has done for me.

As I left ONE the other night I appreciated so much the simple gesture of your coming over to the stair-case to bid me goodbye. Your action gave me a warm feeling—that I was going to be missed. I can picture you yet—your smiling countenance atop that beautiful yellow sweater!

Permit me a few observations and a frank exposure of some secret thoughts.

First, I like you. You have a cheerful disposition. The underlying thought in your writings has struck a responsive chord in me. <u>Sham</u>! How <u>I</u> know what <u>that</u> means—you'll never realize what I've endured for <u>years</u>. <u>Love</u>—one man for another! In only a few instances have I known this and you pictured my sentiments so beautifully in one of your stories.

It may sound maudlin but it's on the level. There is something in you that attracted you to me. I saw something in your eyes, as well as your written words, that told me you have much love and compassion for your fellow <u>man</u>. You draw me to you, secretly, as a magnet, but being the backward old goat that I am I refrained from making any advances.

But, "honest confession is good for the soul" and so I'll tell you this: how I yearned to hold you in my arms, to run my fingers through your hair (god! What beautiful hair) and to press your lips to mine! I have been starved for affection, [. . .], and not all gays are particularly interested in this. But those who crave it as I do have made some sublime moments for me here. If I read people correctly, I feel sure you are a <u>sincere</u> lover.

This is not to embarrass you, nor is it a bid to ask for your indulgences if and when I return. I just want you to know I respect your intelligence, your sincerity, and I appreciate your kindness towards me. Something in your eyes told me that you sensed the difficulties and heartache this old gay goat has experienced. I am most grateful to you and all the other fellows—where I have really felt comfortable, the first time in years, at ONE!

The best o' luck to you!

Sincerely,
Peter

Cruising and Casual Sex

During the 1950s and early 1960s, there was no need to travel to a "gay mecca" like Fire Island or Hollywood for a casual sexual encounter, although people did (and still do) take advantage of these gay enclaves. In these letters, willing partners were easy to find in cities not known for having gay reputations such as Pittsburgh or Knoxville, in small towns and suburbs, and even in isolated lumber towns in the Pacific Northwest.

Sex represented many different things to these male correspondents. For a Philadelphia correspondent, gay sex was a religion. The human phallus was his God. For another man, gay sex was painful and confusing, but nonetheless emotionally necessary to him. The writers' candor about sex in these letters is a striking contrast to the sexually neutered contents of *ONE* magazine.

∼

7 April 1958
Vancouver, Canada

Dear Sir,

I promised another fellow to write to One Inc. about an experience of his. I told him I was almost certain there was nothing your organization could do about it, at the same time advising him to forward 50 bucks per annum to One Inc. in his own best interest. Here is the why and wherefore of what happened to him.

He is a well established very competent high school teacher usually taking schools at isolated industrial sites, i.e. pulp and paper mill towns, mining and logging locations. He is a reasonably well built man, 5'10", 170 lbs, intellectual looking, well turned out. [Fred]—his first name—has always struck me as very honest, frank, straightforward, uncomplicated, a little lonely perhaps but not noticeably neurotic as us gay people go. We maybe see each other twice a year just for a couple of hours at a time and he tells me how he is making out, I might or might not trick with him, more to oblige him that out of any yen for his type—oh it's not that he's so old, under 45, but I hunger more for those elegant types under the Y.M. showers with those svelte curves swelling pectorals and firmed biceps or else those casual working stiffs in their high boots white safety helmets turned up trousers and opened neck shirts. Well yesterday when I see Fred again the first time to talk to since last August he tells me the following which I'm sure is nothing but the truth.

Seems he came to town from his teaching job for a weekend first week of Feb. He goes to the Hastings Steam Bath looking for sex, one out of the three where such a commodity can be found. Just by the by him and I and many other joes of our acquaintance trick indiscriminately at all 3 and we ain't never so far contacted any V.D. that we know of, but then could be yours truly is just plain lucky as I screwed the scruffiest whores in Calgary London and Brussels with no safe during my six years in the Can. Infantry whilst on a protracted normal kick. Well as I was saying our teacher friend went to the steam bath and while there he gets well enough acquainted with another gent to take him to his room. This pickup seems nice and average 5'9", 165 lbs, light reddish brown brush cut hair, nice looking butch until one knew him well and then his nellyness became obvious. Said his name was [Bill Barry], lived in these parts with his mother, was out of work, getting by on unemployment insurance, was an A1 trick, 50-50 no holds barred. Fred and Bill hit it off fine, Fred paying his way for Bill to visit him in the auto court 60 miles from Van. near the school where he was teaching for 3 week-ends. A week ago Wed., March 26, Bill turns up late at night from a taxi at Freds. He is under the weather from liquor, demands $100. and some of his clothes and if he does not get same threatens to tell the school principal that Fred is a homosexual. Fred laughs at him, tells him he'd better leave or he'll throw him out. Bill manages to get into an ivy league shirt coat and pants of Fred's after which they really start to mix it. Now Fred's main concern is to be rid of him and not to get hurt too badly in the process as he has to be in respectable shape for his classes comes 9 a.m., so he rushes to the cabin next door where 2 normal loggers who he is friendly with, knocks them up out of sleep and asks their help. They are only too glad to be of assistance once they are dressed. They slap Bill around a lot and he starts to scream like a real gone prima donna. They threaten to tear him limb from limb if he don't cease and persist pronto. He does for awhile, protests his innocence at the same time trying to put Fred in a bad light. When Fred tells him he is foolish he gets quarrelsome again and antagonizes the loggers again so that they lay into him so vigorously that Fred begs them to lay off for their own good so as not to run the risk of an ensuing lawsuit for assault and battery. When they heed him, Fred call the cops—the mounties—to make Bill leave. When they arrive they insist he get in their car so as to end the disturbance which has become considerable, with the entire occupancy on the scene some of them being Fred's fellow teachers. 2 A.M. by now.

Next morning a phone call comes for Fred in the principals office 10 mins. before school is to commence for the day with the principal and six other staff near the phone. Fred answers it and it is Bill saying he has given the cops the low down on Fred and they are coming to give the principal the low down dope on Fred. Fred say go ahead, bring your friends along and although he is inwardly quaking at the dread prospect of a scene he has a hunch Bill is bluffing. Well that is the last he has seen of the cops or Bill but the latter did threaten him with the retaliation of his friends as a reprisal for Fred's reliance on the loggers. So outside of a few bruises and the loss of some clothes he seems to be okay, while he has no physical fear of Bill there may still be a mess waiting for him when he returns from the Easter recess.

This is not the first case of attempted victimization of men whose only fault that I know of was their good heart and trusting nature. The main reason that I go to bat for Fred is that I consider him a good asset to the gay people. He is a good sport, friendly, civilized, tricks with all and sundry regardless of color or creed, never disowns the acquaintance of gay men in a normal social environment. He is not too hep at what One or the Mattachine Review is getting at but mainly because of his own narrow interests rather than hostility or indifference. What his political, religious, or philosophical outlook is I would not attempt to state as I haven't a clue; that of the daily press and the popular magazines I imagine, with the homosexuality wedged in any old place in his psychological make-up.

    I realize there is not a hell of a lot One could do about it, the immediate problem of hoisting potential blackmailers with their own petard. But seeing as how another staunch fighter in this business of gaining sexual freedom lost his two-bit federal civil service job because he asked a 12 year old if he wanted a blow job and I did not report the injustice of his firing to you at the time. I felt I simply must pass the word along in Fred's instance. If the supervisor of my gay civil service friend had told him no more of that I'm confident he would not have verbally offended any teenagers while on the job again. But instead they just up and dismiss him, and the guy himself wouldn't hurt a flea, I just wish to beat sixty there have been someone around willing to put their lips around my nob when I was but 12. I'd be a better man now and especially the fellow in question, who of what a revelation it was when he first blew me, better even than the technique of this mean right low down Normajean that shares my board but not my bed and hasn't and won't give me the benefit of her lips where it would do most good this past 18 excruciatingly frustrating months. And it ain't as though your correspondent is just some bedazzling trade, more than game am I to kiss her all over for 90 mins. at a stretch. But her goddamer is lost in an endless reverie of elusive chickens. Things are fast approaching the pretty pass of me nurturing my income to the extent where I'll have the recourses to waft a bill in front of the nose of any right desirable undraped shape that catches my eye with a "Hey Mac do you want to make yourself a fast few bucks." Please don't feel obligated to reply to this but should you want to show it around best change Fred's name, physical characteristics and the auto court part. This Bill Barry I can't place offhand but most likely could if I inquired around. Fred tried to trap him with a cheque but he insisted on cash or the alternative of causing a big squawk. Please don't take offense at anything I say, as I said before the world as I know it is a hard old double dealing place.

                                           Sincerely yours,
                                           Gary

8 March 1962
Knoxville, Tennessee

Dear Mr. Legg;

I have received my first copy of the magazine. I find you treat our problems with delicacy and thoughtfulness. I am inclosing a movie review which was given me by a cousin who is a bachelor. In the February issue, I noticed an article on the theme of gay bars and how we should have friends outside of our gay set among the "straights." I have had this same experience but most of my bar going has been in straight bars. There are rumored to be only one gay-like bar in our town for men only. We have a population of 350,000 over 500 square miles and this town is a drawing center according to some of our psychiatrists who I have talked with from the surrounding little towns. The "Y" has been clamping down on the more obvious wall scrawlers, but I was told in a three month period, 12 were evicted quietly. The reason for this is because of the "Y" having a contract with the Armed Forces induction center for housing the draftees and service volunteers. Even these little 18—23 age group have made overtures to me when I lived there. It seems to be the only place where it is obviously so. The Navy "Y" in Norfolk was full of overtures. I was in the area in 1951-52 and it was quite common. I was at hospital corpsman school at the time. Returning to the article of Gene Guillardo, I feel we have to merge in the background and make friends with the Bisexuals, gays and the "straights." We must live in a HETRO or a play on words HURT-O-SEXUAL world. I think you are all doing a good job and I am glad to hear about the Illinois decisions.[6] I am inclosing a movie review which appeared in Feb 5, 1962 Newsweek. Best regards, and I will keep in touch with you.

Sincerely Yours;
James

P.S. negotiate my check as soon as you can, my balance gets low towards the end of the month. Thank you!

∼

29 July 1962
Pittsburgh, Pennsylvania

Dear Fellows,

Long before this I intended writing an account of the goings on in and around town but there has been no time to do so. It seems to me there should be little to report as one would expect things to be much the same here as elsewhere. On the other hand, a fellow from Youngstown assured me early in the summer that there the heat is really on. My sources of information here vary from one who assures me that all the places downtown (including the swank <u>Cork and Bottle</u>) are infiltrated by plainclothesman to another who declares Schenley Park completely safe <u>even after dark</u>. My own feeling is that the truth lies somewhere between. Usually at noon I cruise some combination of the University, the Museum, and the park. Not only do I make out well, but meet numbers of others who have done the same for years. Always around midsummer the young crowd (and I don't mean the debutantes) begins to appear and play for an occasional fast buck, but this type is easy to spot and easier to ignore. The police do check the park regularly, but more, it seems to me, to remove the undesirables than to reduce the activity there.

The Concord Café (best known in town) has a uniformed guard on duty at all times. This, I understand, grew out of an incident last winter when several young ones jumped across the bar one night and wreaked general havoc. This is a relatively quiet place, though, as are also the <u>Cork and Bottle</u> and <u>University Grill</u>—the only three gay bars in town, incidentally. The rest room at the Concord, however, is amazingly unsupervised.

The fifth floor T-rooms in Jenkin's Arcade (a general office building) downtown were especially active in past years, but because of a gang of young delinquents they are now locked at all times with only those working in the building having keys.[7] After the hair raising experience I had there last summer (and I was <u>not</u> cruising) I feel this was unfortunately necessary for the sake of general public safety.

The Y (except for a downstairs T-room in the daytime) is dead. This is not only my own experience, but the report of others. On several occasions, in fact, I have been escorted from Mellon Square to a room at the Y.

The bath (Schune's), on the other hand, is quite active, and despite the squalor and dinginess of the place attracts a very fine crowd. People come from Ohio, West Virginia, and in general from an area of a radius of at least 100 miles. The nearest similar establishment is in Cleveland—a fabulous spot according to Pittsburghers. Some Clevelanders, however, recently informed me that their best was no longer in existence. They come to Pittsburgh!!

There is a club downtown where dancing, etc. occurs. Quite a place from all reports. The "Daughters" belong too. Theoretically it is restricted to members or guests of members, but I have heard that out of towners can get in on their own. On several occasions I have been tempted to try to crash the place, but usually I was engaged in some more worthwhile activity. I may still try before the summer is over.

Several weeks ago I learned that the late June prison protest (the water tower climbers) was not without interest to us. One radio news reporter actually announced, they say, that 11 of the 13 involved were "perverts." This was not in the papers. I did read, however, that two are getting more lenient treatment than the others because of their "cooperative attitude." The Press also reported that they were all watched continuously, while on the tower, through strong binoculars and records were kept of what they did there. Rumor has it that the leader has been transferred so often (he has been in almost every prison in the state) because wherever he goes he makes his desires known and proceeds to do any and all who are willing.

One of the fellows here at the house is Catholic and I read with interest one of the Church's attacks on the recent Supreme Court rulings. I especially enjoyed the headline: <u>Court Outlaws Prayer, Promotes Homosexuality</u>. (This was in a local campus publication for Catholic students.)

My face is more than a little red to enclose this single portrait of George, especially after reading the recent <u>Confi</u>. I have been extraordinarily short this summer. I do hope my extra job this fall (I am teaching two nights a week at [a community college]) will make a difference. I hope, too, that you survive the present emergency for I am determined to treat you better financially this coming year than I did in the one just past.

As I shall be leaving here in a little more than a week, please mail all future materials to my [Southern California] address. I will not be returning directly home, but the intermediate points are still uncertain.

Perhaps you have already heard that when I return this fall I shall leave my heart back here. No Greek God, I assure you—BUT—

Best wishes and Good Luck!

          Sincerely,
          Ed

P.S. My typewriter, unfortunately, is in California.

          15 June 1963
          Midsize town in central
          Illinois

Gentlemen:

Thank you very much for sending me your April issues of ONE. It is my first experience with this or any similar magazine on this subject. I particularly enjoyed "My Coleus Romance" and "On the Corner."

I wish you would keep my name in your mailing list to receive any special offers you may have from time to time.

As I know you have as one of your basic goals that of fighting for the rights of the individual to know what he wants to do with his life—what he wants to read and to see and to feel and to experience, I am requesting your assistance.

I get a great sexual satisfaction from looking at photos of the male organs. This gives me a greater erotic satisfaction than <u>almost</u> anything else. It is a pleasure I can resort to conveniently when those few friends who really mean everything to my life are not near to me. This is a pleasure I enjoy in my own bedroom in the privacy of my own home without having to "prowl" public places and arouse suspicion. I live in a small town and all eyes are on the suspect and unbearable gossip spreads fast.

In my opinion being able to satisfy my need to observe this beautiful part of maleness in this way should be more socially acceptable than frequenting shower rooms in pools, gyms, etc. where my attention to men's privacies is obvious and usually proves only embarrassment for both of us. Society, unfortunately, has the view that this one area of only a few square inches is "dirty" and "vulgar" and that in no case should this extremely important and absolutely vital organ of the male body ever be glorified or even photographed. The truth is, <u>every</u> act of the male from birth to death is controlled by the awareness of his possession of this maleness and every behavior pattern is fixed for him for life just because he has this piece of masculine flesh between his legs. Since it is so wonderful to him and can do such wonderful things for him and since every man is more proud of his penis than any other muscle or pound of flesh on his entire body, I can't understand why society will not let him be open and obvious about this beautiful tool which means so much to <u>every</u> man's life.

This right to appreciate God's holy creation in its entirety is being denied me and every other man who admires the beauty and perfection of the human body. I have a sizeable collection of physique photos and I enjoy seeing the perfect masculine form with all its grace, musculature, and potency, but as you know, none of these ever shows the exposed scrotal area although it is quite permissible to expose almost every other square inch of body surface in every conceivable pose and stimulating, suggestive position. I want the right to appreciate 100% of the masculine physique. All I want is to look!—I don't need to touch, I don't need to seduce, I don't need to degrade anyone. All I want to do is look—in complete uninhibited privacy.

I'm sure enlightened, progressive leaders such as yourself will want to help me obtain such frontal nude photos. Certainly as forthright and vitally interested as you are in the problems of the homosexual and in promoting his rights, you must have a collection of such photos yourself, privately, and have the source of this material at your disposal. I know there could be fines and serious trouble for selling and buying such so that physique photographers are not willing to admit that they have them and do not want to risk sending a few dollars worth through the mails. I am a responsible single man, age 30, and a college graduate. This would be handled in the strictest confidence by me.

Will you please give me the name or names of sources of nude photos which could be purchased by me through the mail. I want a large number of different models in various positions and physical states for purposes of comparison. They should be completely exposed, close-up and clean shots. I will pay well to get them from any source whatever by mail. If you have any in your private collection that you could send me, please advise.

Please tell me what you know about such sources and it will be worth money for the help if delivery is guaranteed. I have written to almost every photographer in the USA. Please help me!

Sincerely,
Michael

31 October 1962
Philadelphia, Pennsylvania

Dear Mr. Slater,

I am very gay and want to join a gay club but how does one go about joining? I found the addresses of the two societies in this area and wrote to them directly. Their addresses appeared in the Mattachine Review and their names are the Janus Society and Homosexual League of New York.

The first time I wrote to each of them I enclosed a self-addressed, stamped envelope. I enjoy reading ONE and found, in the September issue (Tangents), some advice from Sal McIntire who says—in so many words—that readers suspecting the local post office of causing uncalled-for poor mail service should write to ONE.

My complaint is this: When I wrote to the Janus Society the first time, I received no answer. I wrote again after a week and a half passed. The second letter came marked "Unclaimed," "Box Closed." If the Janus Society no longer holds that Post Office box, why didn't my first letter come back?!!

I worship the male organ of generation much like it was worshipped thousands of years ago. To me, there is no form of communion sweeter than taking the actual Phallic God into my throat and swallowing the "come." I have been without this love act and companionship for a very long time lately and, needless to say, want it very badly. This is the reason for wanting the fellowship of a gay society.

There is no need to be afraid of me, I have no police record and am NOT connected with the police in ANY manner whatever.

I practice my religion quietly and detest the loud-mouthed, swishy queens; of course I am not one. The last Buddy I had (lived with) was a big, handsome Dane. Boy! What a lover he was! Big, deep, powerful strokes (15") and, once he got started hunching, there was no stopping him until he shot his last drop. I love a man with a big cock and isn't afraid to put his heart and soul into fucking me like a wild animal. But I draw a line: I have my communion with white men only.

If the primary aim of homophile clubs is to convert or rehabilitate the homosexual then please count me out because I will not quit my religion. Let the gay person turn away from the Christian religion and he can live his gay life fully without the slightest feeling of guilt. Look at the Bible and you can see how the Jews first set themselves up as the Master Race, crammed their religion down the throats of peoples all over the world then look again at how the golden calf (a phallic symbol worshipped by the children of Israel while their self-chosen leader, Moses, tarried so long on Mt. Sinai) demolished the Ten Commandments. This proves that the God of Abraham, Isaac, and Jacob—the same God that Jews and Christians worship today—is FALSE; the phallic deity is true and endures forever.

I am not just "laying this on thick" as a big joke, I seriously mean every word written here. Hoping you have read it all and are willing to lead me to a gay society like the ones I mention earlier, telling me how to join it (or them), I am

         Sincerely yours,
         Leroy

         22 October 1964
         Suburb of Oakland, California

Dear Sir!

My name is Neil. Not too long ago I called up Don Slater on the telephone. The telephone bill for that call (telephone call) came to exactly $7.00. I now think that it would have been better to invest my money in some other way or form.

When I spoke to Don Slater on the phone he/you promised me that if I would write a letter that you/Don Slater would send me a personal reply.

At the present time I have sixteen issues of ONE mag. (eleven are back issues). On the phone you (Don Slater) said that I should also subscribe to "One Confidential." At the present time I am not prepared or able to do so.

I have all the "Quarterlies" #5 to #18.

If you are not available, I would very much appreciate if perhaps one of your staff would answer the following questions for me.

What exactly is a HUSTLER.

What   "   " " QUEEN.

What does the word "FRIGGIN" mean?

In SEPT. 1964 issue—Miss Destiny says, "I slept with a lot of fish." What is a "fish"?

(Don Slater told me that he interviewed her personally).

To my way of understanding Oral Copulation is the easiest and most common expression of love. I am curious about Anal Copulation. I personally know of two different cases of Anal Copulation. The first man (a Mexican) said that it hurt a lot (the penis in the rectum). A twenty-four year old boy told me that he tried it (anal copulation) with a negroe. Anal copulation to him was painful. (Actually there was almost no penetration). The Negroe said that the 24 year old boy was not cooperating and that rather than being relaxed he was tense. Anyway, this 24 year old took an old broom handle and sawed it off so that it was about ten inches long. He put a greased prophylactic (condom) over it and shoved it up the rectum. This is supposed to be practice for the real thing. A broom handle does not feel too bad. My question is: What can you tell me about Anal Copulation? Also:—Is Anal Copulation something that someone has to get used to, or is it something that always hurts.

In the June 1964 issue there are two men on the cover. Is <u>William Edward Glover</u> the gentleman wearing the glasses? He also has a checkered shirt.) Who is the man next to him in the short sleeves.

Concerning Sadist-Masochism. I do not think that I go for this kind of stuff at all.

I am not sure that I understand SM at all. (Don Slater told me on the phone what SM means). But the explanation was not clear.

When I was in my early teens and before, I used to take off my clothes and try to hit myself with a leather belt. Is this something like masochism?

SM is all right with me if it keeps itself within the proper bounds of propriety. If SM is carried out to its Nth degree it can become quite hideous. Maybe you think differently—if so—I would love to hear from you.

With very few exceptions—all homosexuals with whom I have come into contact with were circumcised. Also an extremely high percentage of homosexuals with whom I have come in contact with were also Roman Catholics. It is my understanding that in general Roman Catholics are not circumcised. I would appreciate your comments on the above statements (Roman Catholicism and circumcision.)

Don Slater promised me over the telephone that he would faithfully answer any letter that I wrote to him. If he is not available I suppose it is permissible for other workers who are in the <u>Truth</u> to answer my questions.

Sincerely yours,
Neil

Seeking Serious Relationships

The letter writers in this section wanted more than casual sexual encounters, they wanted serious, lasting relationships, relationships in which sexual behavior might play only a minor role. Several of these letters complain about the fact that gay bars served as central sites of gay and lesbian social life. Some correspondents did not drink alcohol or they found their local gay bars seedy, unappealing, or attracting a disreputable clientele. But avoiding gay bars made it more difficult to meet and get to know other gay people who might be interested in a serious relationship. Individuals who avoided gay bars and other sites of gay social life risked isolation and loneliness.

∼

10 February 1957
Small town in northern
Montana

Dear friends,

Have occasionally read your magazine and must congratulate you on the fact that your contents are more wholesome than the majority of heterosexual periodicals on the market. Seems to be permissible to corrupt society, and even the young, in movies, on TV, and in the current magazine, so long as it is between the sexes. I have been considering a subscription if I may be assured it will come to me sealed and without any obviousness appertaining to the nature of its contents, for I am in one of James Barr's disreputable positions in my community. You may recall I purchased from you copy 394 of his play.[8] He challenged, "Generally I dislike Politicians, Men of God, and Intellectuals. I like psychiatrists, university professors, writers and people who work with their hands." My dearest friends are university professors and writers and people creative with their hands. When I was a student in high school, I read Quatrefoil, and later I read Derricks, consequently I was delighted several years ago to obtain his play, which outdistances considerably the current Tea and Sympathy, though not necessarily Gide's plays.

I would very much like to present him with a critique on his book, play, and short stories if you think it cricket to give me his address. You realize that homosexuality in ye olden times, in Greece, i.e., was not the effeminately disgusting spectacle it makes of itself in public nowdays. Men were still masculine, not always virile in the rugged sense of manliness, as many of us are born with extremely sensitive natures; lovers in those days went side by side to battle. The most important aspect of love in those days was not solely the consummation of a physical act. They did not drift from bar to bar rubbing legs and from body to body. They concentrated on the idea of falling in love, just as any boy and girl does nowdays, and they made an effort to make their love last, like a marriage, something moral and stable and redeeming accomplished with their lives. All this la-di-da, limp-wristed exhibitionism is disgusting; it is even revolting in current best-sellers; the homosexual who acts this way is suffering from infantilism; maturity of mind and body is both necessary. You don't always win your enemy by joining his ranks, rather, as in Christianity, you win the opponent by the example of your life. Perhaps some chaps are effeminate by nature; if so, then live with dignity, if you like to cook, bake, sew in the privacy of your own home, and if you are so fortunate as to find a directly opposite chap, masculinely rugged, whom you cherish for his virility and he cherished you for your feminine attributes, then live together with dignity and you will not be creating such disapproval in the community. Many homosexuals are asking for the kick in the pants that they get by society, in turn, they, like nominal Christians, do as much harm for the ideals of your fine organization, as the nominal do for the idealism of Christ's cause. Barr's writing is not always top-rate, his ideas often far in advance of present day realization, but I like the way he supports the dignified homosexual, not the chaps who live nervously their nights and days in anticipating of "blow-jobs" and one night stands.

It amuses me to enclose a little satire my buddy and I at college composed ad libitum one afternoon when we had been doing collateral reading on Jung, Adler, Freud, [and] James for psychology class. I was reminded of it recently while working on a section of my book, actually a number of short stories like Derricks, or John Horne Burns' The Gallery, interesting people whom I have known, fictionalized to a certain extent, but who have made profound impressions on my life, like Dante in the Divine Comedy, whose eye is on the mountain of God but whose ascent is barred by three beasts, a lion, a leopard, and a wolf. The book comprises the three kinds of people who barred my way to the mountain, the last was a man who set out to prove there was no God. So it goes. What fun!

Self-enclosed addressed envelope if you wish to give me Mr. Barr's address as well let me know what back copies of your magazine are at present available if I were to purchase a number of them. If you feel that I should address my critique to James Barr in care of your ONE, Inc. I shall, of course, do that. Thanks for listenin' fellas.
Sincerely
Alex

14 February 1957
San Diego, California

Dear Ann,[9]

I have hesitated so very long to write this letter. I realize that probably you will find its contents somewhat unusual, but after much consideration, I can figure no other way to attempt a solution to my problem.

I am unfortunately a Navy man. It isn't that I begrudge the time I am having to spend in the service, its only that the military life at this moment is offering nothing but disadvantages. One of these disadvantages is; I am here in California, knowing no one and have not the vaguest idea where to go to meet anyone.

I have been reading your magazine, (I'm forced to buy it at the newsstand rather than a subscription, for obvious reasons). I am sure that you don't deal in this sort of "directory service," but I would like to have your advice on just how to meet some gay people of the above average intellectual level.

I am a graduate from Texas Christian University, with a degree in speech and drama. I enjoy good music, good books, good plays, ballet, and many of the other so-called "finer things of life." And lets face it . . . . . . its very seldom you meet people who really appreciate these things in gay bars. At least in Texas gay bars.

Having been in gay life only a little over a year, I am still not exactly sure how to go about meeting someone who would be interested in more than just a casual one night friendship. I was introduced to gay life by the young man with whom I was in business. Now that I am in the Navy, he is living with someone else, even though we are still in business together. Although I have met many gay people, I have found very few with whom I felt I'd like to form a lasting relationship.

Tell me, Ann. Aren't there any gay people in the world besides me who like to live a quite [sic] sort of life. Not in the bar every night . . . perhaps a cozy little apartment . . . a hi-fi . . . TV . . . the theatre occasionally, a movie now and then, to the mountains or the beach on Sundays and just occasionally a wild party with friends, just to let off steam.

Perhaps after the ideal relationship I had with [Tim], I have set my sights too high. God only knows, if there is anyone like the people I've described, they aren't looking for anyone to keep them company.

Well, there is my problem. Where and how do I go about finding gay friends like these? Just in case you should find time to answer my letter, I am enclosing a stamped, self-addressed envelope to make it more convenient for you.

I certainly think that you and your staff are doing a terrific job with the publication. I don't know if there is any way in which I can help (financially), other than just buy the magazine. If you do accept contributions to help defray the cost of publication, I'd like very much to send you a check. It's really wonderful to read all the different ideas set forth in ONE. Its been quite a comfort to me since I've been here.

Thanks for taking the time to read this, even if you don't find time to answer.

Sincerely
Dave

∼

26 December 1957
Brooklyn, New York

Dear Ones:

My homosexual life has started at the tender age of 15, I am now 19, I have had quite a few affairs (ONE NITERS) I have read a few love stories where two homo's can actually find true love. I am 5FT 4INCH,

Black curley hair, i'm not concede, but i have been told by admires none of my liking (TO YOUNG, DON'T WORK, PREFER MATURE MANLY TYPE) that i am pretty.

I like to believe that a homo's life can be happy as any other life, You are probably wondering what's mine and a lot of other's problem, being pretty can also be a handycap. Every time i go into a bar and a fellow buy's me a drink (DON'T DRINK) there's always strings attached three strings SEX. I and i'm sure that other homo's want more than sex out of life. The other day my friend was telling me that Walter Winchell mention something, about us homo's having a MATRIMONY BUREAU on the East Side in Manhattan. Why don't we have a Lonely Hearts Club, sometimes i feel like a sexpot, i and also other want someone to LOVE, DO THINGS WITH, MAKE A LIFE FOR OURSELVES. We're tired of going in bars waiting for a pickup whether you go in a suit or not. We still all want the same thing. Mine and also other live's will just be wasted going into bars, hoping and praying that some day we will find our mate. That doesn't sound like much of a life, well it isn't. I hope something can be done about it before we just fade away, Lose faith or take our lives, it is a desperate situation, i have know quite a few young fellows who have taken their lives, due to lack of lonelyness. I am very glad about One mag and i buy it every month in spite one still isn't helping us. All tho i must admit it has given me a little courage. but we are still in the same predicament, How can we fight for our freedom, we really have nothing to live for, I wish you would pay special attention to this letter, not only for myself but also for others. and i am sure that there are others. If we can somehow form a group and get together and perhaps pair ourselves out, we won't be so lonely anymore, and we will also feel stronger and fight for our rights. If you feel that you are not ready for this step, Please drop me a line so that i know that i have tried.

Sincerely yours,
Toby

P.S. [. . .] IS MY REAL NAME IF YOU INTEND TO ENTER MY LETTER IN YOUR NEXT EDITION PLEASE USE THE NAME OF (TOBY)

Published in ONE magazine,
March 1955, 42–43
New York, New York

Dear ONE:

There are many of us who have little use for the gay bars, for the thrill-seeking crowd whose entire orientation is on the physical . . .

I prefer to believe that the gay bar crowd is the mere lunatic fringe element, warped and at least partially useless in any battle for social acceptance. I know that this attitude would anger many of my acquaintances, but I cannot retract it . . . Most of the gay crowd whom I have met thus far are superficially intellectual, with a veneer based on the false assumption that it creates an aura of sophistication. But how hollow it is under any sort of close inspection, and how pathetic. How much more enjoyable is the company of the thinking homosexual whose mind is not constantly racing erratically along the groove of an evening's pleasure. I do not mean to be irrevocably condemnatory of the gay bar element. But I prefer others for my friends or companions.

[no name published]

Published in *ONE* magazine,
June 1955, 20
Seattle, Washington

Dear ONE:
"I REMEMBER," in your excellent February issue, moved me greatly calling forth some almost-forgotten recollections from my own earlier years. The principal in this brief story (and I have seen many like him) is indeed to be pitied. As for myself, I revolt so drastically against tradition as to believe that in this modern age not even women need to be "kept" by men, even when the men happen to be their husbands. So you can judge my reactions to the spectacle of a man being kept by a man, or a woman by a woman. With Twentieth Century educational advantages, and with all professional and most non-professional occupations open to either sex, it seems incredible that any person could be so wanting in pride and a sense of personal freedom as to be unwilling to stand on his own two feet, in economic matters. Evidently something is seriously lacking in our social leadership.

[no name published]

Lonely and Isolated

Although gay social life (such as bars, cruising areas, or lesbian softball teams) existed in most cities and many towns, not every gay person would necessarily find it. Gay social life was usually camouflaged and intended to be unnoticeable to straight people. Some *ONE* correspondents did not know where to look for gay life in their local areas. Other *ONE* correspondents had family issues or careers that influenced their decision to avoid gay social life. Several lonely correspondents lived in small towns, but the letters show that a person living in New York City might be just as isolated from other gay people as someone living in a small Midwestern town. This is one of the characteristics that demonstrates the universality of homosexuality; one could find it, or not, just about anywhere, but some gay men and lesbians were too afraid or uninformed to look for it.

∼

8 August 1955
Small town in western Illinois

Dear Sir,
I have enjoyed the April 1955 edition of ONE and am anxious to get other editions to send to my girl friend in Germany who has requested that I send them.

I am wondering if you have received the money order for two dollars and fifty cents . . . mailed July 26th via air mail from [a small town], Ill. If you have not received this please let me know so I can report the loss to the Money order department . . . I have not heard from you concerning the subscription nor have I received any copies of your good publication.

In traveling, it would be good for some of us to be able to have a small pin, as an emblem or club button (or card)—however, I suppose it wouldn't be kept a secret as to what it stood for but some sort of identification would sure be helpful—as well as to where to go for eating and drinking. While visiting Los Angeles last month, I didn't know where "MY KIND" would be found and was directed to places by one of the Los Angeles ministers—in fact he took me, for he was "One Of Them."

Hoping to receive copies of ONE soon.
Evelyn

∼

13 December 1957
Midsize town in southern Wisconsin

Gentlemen,
I am wondering if there is a "drug" that will control or dull my homosexual desires. I have taken "Miltown" (a tranquilizer) sometime ago, and it seemed while I was under this drug that my homosexual

desires and drives were <u>decreased</u>. Now that I have stopped taking it, my drives are building up again <u>as bad as ever</u>. Will drinking lessen my desires? I'm so lonesome and blue, and am ever looking for a partner to strike a romance with. I even cry over it. Would you advise me to find myself a partner whom I can show my love and affections to, or go on suffering the rest of my life, or find some drug that may help me. I had seen a psychiatrist sometime ago, and of all people I had to fall in love with him (but him not with me). Now he has moved to another town, and I miss him so. I dream of him continually, and I wake up to find its <u>only a dream</u>. Boy, what a heart broken story. What shall I do? Can you give me any advise as what to do? Do you think finding a partner would help me some? Is there something I can take to kill these drives? I am 32, never married, the reason is obvious. Just <u>where</u> could I find company? I'm <u>so</u> <u>lonesome</u>, God knows just how lonesome I am. Please let me hear from you regarding the question I have raised. Thank you.

As ever,
Harold

P.S. When I am alone with some fellow I "take to," I get a real strange feeling, a feeling which haunts me and seems unexplainable, a certain quietness comes over me or both of us, I'm not sure. What is this??"

∼

14 April 1958
New York, New York

Dear Editor:

I wonder if you could please help me with my problem as follows, for which enclosed please find a self addressed stamped envelope. I'd very much appreciate whatever aid you can give me.

I am 26 years of age and though never having the opportunity to gratify my sexual feelings, I am homosexual (active role) I am going mad with need, which is causing me nervousness and great unhappiness. It's on my mind day and night, you can readily understand this is torture. The sight of a mans buttocks or organs although merely through his cloths sets me aflame. When traveling in the trains I try to get close enough so that I can at least fondle there buttocks etc. but am usually never successful leaving me frustrated and distressed. At one time I was threatened with blows, the urge is so unbearable I've been considering suicide.

I've tried to satisfy my sexual hunger with illustrations I drew but they were found by my folks and I was reprimanded and made miserable afterwards.

I know my nerves will calm and depression will disappear if only I can satisfy my sexual desires at least one time with a good looking understanding man.

I appeal to you, please, please, help me with at least some advice as to how I'm to go about this. Only you can understand my situation. Please do not fail me.

I'd be grateful for a prompt reply. Thank you very much for your attention and courtesy.

Very truly yours,
Carlton

~

Published in ONE magazine,
July 1958, 30-31
North Island, New Zealand

Dear Mr. Gregory:[10]

I'm an old man now. I've craved affection for 74 years. I crave affection more than sex, but believe me, both desire and performance are possible and extremely delightful at 74. I've never run round looking for sex, but I've often looked into a man's eyes and desired to love him, but dared never speak. I've been in love with a man many years and never even spoken to him. Such is the torture of the law in this country, and yours. They talk of British justice. There is no justice if a man's a homosexual.

Our doctors don't understand us at all, and don't want to, nor do our lawyers. They call us <u>perverts</u>. What rot! What God made us, so we remain till death. I married, thinking love for a woman might grow. What a fool I was! How could it? For a homosexual man to marry a woman as I did is wrong and against God. He made me that I should love men and want a man's affection, and I sinned when I married.

You may think that at 74 one has no strong desire. Be both disillusioned and encouraged. Desire, I believe, lives till a man's last breath is out, anyway, in me, desire still lives strongly.

Believe me I do understand all the different types. Some I think could behave a bit better, but it's hard and perhaps stupid to put up the fight I do to remain outwardly respectable and within the law.

Mr. C.

~

7 June 1963
Buenos Aires, Argentina

Dear Sir,

I read you information about "our" life in U.S.A. with great interest. As I am the only member of "Arcadie" living in this city, and perhaps continent. My No. is [. . .]. I am also member of Der Kreis of Zurich, Switzerland, No. 3481. And I receive also some times our Dutch magazine, our life in USA seems wonderful.

I wish to know about our One magazine, and specially I shall be very interested if you can send me penfriend's addresses or if you can give me address to any USA's friend.

I am an Argentine young men, 28, working in the building business and professional. During my free hours I love to make art and I made Paintings Exhibitions here with success.

I am very fond of good music, literature, theatre, films and opera and ballet. And my preferred sports are swimming, rowing, yachting, walking, tennis, fishing, etc. and to make beach's and sea's live every time I can.

Physically I have 6 fs tall; 178 lbs.w.; blue eyes; brown hair. I love very much to travel and know every exciting place in this continent and Occidental Europe, I was in Europe until some weeks ago.

My purpose writing you is to find Northamerican penfriends. As I am here very lonely. All my friends are in Europe. Mr Baudry the director of Arcadie of Paris, knows me. And you can ask information about me to him. I consider myself some kind of extra official delegate of "Arcadie" in Buenos Aires, Argetine!

I have not friends "like us" here, except those foreigners coming from Europe and that I know through friendship's message in Der Kreis, Vriendshap, Eos, etc. Here "we" have not reunion places, no bars, no magazines, nothing serious, and the people, "our people" very persecuted, is perhaps because of that very weak, have not the sense of friendship and is not very good in general. So I have "conventional friends," some girls. But I have not a real friend.

There are so many Americans here now that after to read your report Mr. Legg, I though that perhaps some One's friends are here and I don't know them.

If you can't to send penfriend addresses, perhaps you shall know some Club for "us" who does? Or even if some friend is coming here you can send my address to him, I understand that by law you can't send penfriend's addresses, but perhaps you could use me like your One's delegate in this city and country. Can you?

My address now and in the future is: [...]
Pablo

~

24 January 1964
Suburb of Los Angeles,
California

Dear Sirs,

I just read your Dec. issue of <u>One</u> my first encounter with your magazine. On page 20 you spoke of homosexual meetings. Do you know where these meetings are held in [the San Fernando Valley]. [...] I am 17 and very interested in receiving help. At the present I live off of Physique magazines consisting of only nude photos of men, and showers after P.E. class where I have several favorite lovers. I have never told anyone I was homosexual but I feel that through your organization I may find satisfaction for my sexual hunger.

I am a Christian and so are my parents and family. They must never find out because they would worry about my life after death.

I don't know if you arrange for lovers but I will tell you my statistics and what I want in a man.

I am 17, 5'11", 130 lbs, thin but well proportioned, attractive, not feminine but not real masculine, I am a virgin. I want a man 17-35, 5'6"-6'2", 150 lbs-215 (not a 5'6" man of 215 lbs.) large chest and arms, muscular, large thighs and a fat rump (not too fat but fat enough so it looks tempting in tight pants). I don't care about what kind of cock. A manly masculine face. It doesn't have to be at all handsome just masculine. I guess I'm asking for a lot but that's it.

I need your help. Please refer me to someone or someplace locally where I can meet someone else who is gay.

Questions

Is it against the law to make love to another homo in private?

Where is there a homo meeting near me?

Are all homos swishes and real feminine or are there athletic muscular homos? If so do they ever fall in love with more feminine homos or do they prefer masculine ones?

Is blowing dangerous? Why?

Do sexual relations help the hunger or increase it?

Do the meetings mentioned on page 20 provide you with a mate or what?

Enclosed is a stamped self-addressed envelope. Please sent your reply in it.

Thank you for your time and consideration, I am so thankful for your magazine which has given me a new hope.

Yours,
Bill

---

27 October 1964
New York, New York

Dear Sirs,

I am troubled by a recent experience I had. I have always felt "different" from most of the boys and since 15 or so when I met my first homosexual I always knew this was the type of life I enjoyed. I participated and enjoyed all types of sex activities with other men and boys except that I never let anyone fuck me.

Recently I began to get this feeling that I would like to be fucked. One night while I was taking a shower I noticed another man with a hard on. I decided that if he would I would and so I proceeded to bend over, drop my soap etc. to arouse him even more. He came closer and began to pat my ass and buttocks. He played with me and then suddenly he struck. Bells went off and I guess I jumped to the ceiling. It really surprised me that it hurt so. Yet I love this sensation it produces and I want this type of company again. My problem is what can I do about the pain? Is there any exercises I can do. It hurts so much that I am afraid to try it again yet emotionally I have to have it. Over here in Italy I have tried but don't like to go out with the Italian gay set. The language problem bothers me for one thing. Yet being in the Army the tension and strain on me is enormous. Certainly my family doesn't even suspect. Yet I flirt with constant danger every time I take a shower. I want male companionship in the worst way the lack of which drives me to the very brink of disaster. What can I do? I have tried going to female prostitutes and they leave me cold. Many times I cannot even get an erection. I work in the Telephone Communications field and if I receive a dishonorable discharge I doubt that I could find another job. They are so fussy. I have 5 ½ years left to go in the Army and I certainly can't forget about sex. I just go simply wild standing in the shower watching all those men. Can you help? Please!

John

4 March 1965
Small town in northeastern
Florida

To whom it may concern:
I am not really sure how to go about this. Though you may not believe me; this is the first letter of this nature I have ever written so I am a little leery, but of what I am not sure. Please bear with me then as I may ramble and make this too long.

I am 25 years old and even though I am not married I have had sex relations with girls and women at least as often as the average man and perhaps even just a little more once in a while. Also, when younger I masturbated a great deal and still do sometime—I guess because I enjoyed it but also I think, because in playing high school and college football, later community living in the service, thus showering etc. with an awful lot of boys and young men I received a lot of kidding because my sex organ is smaller than most people of my age. This hurt at first but later as time wore on I got used to it, and it doesn't bother me any more, except maybe once in a while.

So at first I was deathly scared that I would never be able to satisfy any girl. And so I masturbated an awful lot, but I have a good friend who is a doctor and one day I went to him. On one visit when I got to his office—he had a prostitute waiting, and she really taught me how to live. I truly loved it and have gotten all I could of it and at every possible opportunity since then. Just being honest, I love to make love and I guess I love all the different means to use enjoying sex.

My trouble now and it is A REAL PROBLEM is that I am engaged to be married this October. My girl is sweet, lovely, all-American kind of cute wholesomeness and has a body so perfect it defies description. On top of all that—she loves me very much and I do her with her wholesomeness and intelligence and treating me like a king without qualification when I'm with her <u>BUT***</u> -- <u>HERE IS MY ***</u> <u>PROBLEM</u>! ! !

Lately just once in awhile I have gotten a sort of feeling as if maybe I would at least like to try, maybe just once and maybe from now on, homosexual experiences. However, I don't want to go to jail trying to find a way to find out, that is for sure. I do, very much, want to try at least once, some kind of experience because I don't want to get married without really knowing how I feel—what kind of sex I really enjoy and want most for the rest of my life. I sure don't want to get married—then too late, find out that I'm more homosexual than heterosexual. My girl is too wonderful to have that happen to her—she just doesn't deserve it.

So here is my request to you: will you send me some literature to read, pictures, brochures, newsletters, places to go, perhaps in the vicinity of Daytona; since I am and will be in that vicinity for 5 or 6 more weeks getting over an operation.

If you send me anything, please send it in a plain wrapper, marked personal and confidential because once in a while some member of my family is inclined to open my mail, and I don't want anyone to ever be hurt by anything that I do—even though they shouldn't open the mail in the first place.

Also, right now, please don't send me any requests to join some group or organization. Once I know about it, etc., then I might join, but first I want to know what I am doing, if it represents what I want etc.

Thank you. I would appreciate hearing at your convenience, remaining

Respectfully,
Robert

Pen Pals

Over the years, many *ONE* correspondents requested (and sometimes demanded) that the magazine provide a pen pal service. *ONE*'s editors refused on the grounds that the magazine might be shut down for "aiding and abetting criminal activity." In 1959, *ONE* published two opposing editorials debating the merits and demerits of gay and lesbian pen pals, and many readers shared their experiences—some favorable, some not—on the topic.[11]

17 September 1959
Midsize town in northeastern Texas

To Pedersen and Lambert,

I quite enjoyed your complimentary pieces written on the subject of Pen Pal Clubs—Lambert has been hiding his talent for caricature from the readers of "One." No, of course "One" can't risk running a Pen Pal Service.

But I suspect Pedersen is right in believing that such correspondence does sometimes produce good results of some kind, that is, more good than bad. Someday "One" may be in a position to run such a service. Now your first duty would seem to be to keep mag free of ruinous legal entanglement.

About 16 years ago, when I was very young, very neurotic, and very isolated, I entered an ad for correspondence in "The Saturday Review." The response was gratifying—I was constantly writing letters to people scattered all over the country. How I found material for so many letters I don't know. Gradually—or in some cases quickly—we wrote ourselves out; and not one romance came of it, directly or indirectly. (I still regret having broken off correspondence with a Calif. artist who was quite ___ from all angles.) But like Pedersen, I can say that the correspondence had some positive value, for myself at least. For one thing I got a lucid view of what went on in the minds of other gay people. At that time I knew I was gay but my experience had not included acquaintance with other gay people. And so by the time I went to New York and met gay people, I was somewhat prepared for the novel experience—and trying, at first.

A few of my correspondents lived in New York City and those I met of course. I had in fact already decided, on the basis of photos, that none of them were material for a romance. (Two or three in NYC thought, if not romance—at least—and that was a bit awkward.) One of them became a substantial, although never a close, friend. Another, who had his writing about Henry James published now and then, was a person I visited for intellectual conversations—a few times every season over a period of 5 years. But two NYC correspondents, who were a "couple," helped me indirectly by introducing me to Ron H. No, I'm not about to tell you that was romance at last. Here was something else I needed very much my first year in NYC—a place to go in the evening. I can't imagine what I would have done if I hadn't had Ron's place to go to—later on I found other things to do—but that first winter I needed a refuge from the impersonal world of the great city. I'm sure all those evenings of aimless conversation with the small crowd at Ron's could have been spent more constructively, for all concerned. Anyway, it was a place—and Ron, a warm, kind person—where we "refugees" kept body and soul together. . . . An ad for correspondence in "The Saturday Review."

A last remark: I agree with Lambert it's no use complaining about conditions that can't be helped—but it's a pity that too many gay people lack the force, the urge, the intellectual grasp, to want to change conditions which are to them anti-life—I include myself among the "too many."

Albert

19 September 1959
Brooklyn, New York

Dear Don:

I read the September issue with great interest. I am glad that this "pen-pal" business has finally come to a head; so we all want a pen-pal. You've finally uncovered our most secret longing. (Most of us are tired of sending away for free samples . . . Now, we want a pen-pal.)

Seriously, I think that we should have our pen-pals, and that you should provide them for us. I read both articles carefully, "WHY NOT A PEN-PAL CLUB," by Lyn Pedersen, and "SICK, SICK, SICK," by William Lambert. I really wanted to know what was what, so I read every word carefully, and I must say, that I am in favor of Lyn's approach much more that that of William. Why NOT a pen-pal Club . . . ? William says that dire results will come out of having pen-pals; well listen, Billie. . . . Dire results come of any situation that is not handled properly; and the little examples you give, are not conclusive, by any means. If we gay folk want to go out and have things "happen" to us, we can do so very easily, not only with pen-pals, but with many other associations. If what William writes is so, then we should close down all gay bars, and all means of one homo meeting another. We should live in a little sealed, isolated world, simply because one guy might possibly, (if you know him well), beat up another, or steal his precious treasures. Let me tell you something, Billie . . . that has been going on for many, many, many years; with, or without pen-pals! It is, on the whole, the results of immature thinking, or just plain stupidity; and besides, why should you worry. The results of stupid reasoning are going on right this minute, close at hand, and far across the vast regions of the world. Relax, Billie. They wouldn't listen, even if you told them. And as far as the lonely ones are concerned, the shy ones, the ones who live in small communities, and whose only pleasure is the mail-box, I say for them, and for all of us, we should have a pen-pal Club.

You ask us, William, "Why am I lonely?" Then you proceed to answer this question by supplying answers from your own experience. I could give you a few more answers to add to your little list; but I think, instead, you should read Lyn's article; he gives them, also . . . and better than I could. Sure, maybe Joe did beat up Oswald, but I still think that the main issue here is the alleviation of loneliness, not the guidance for those who cannot think straight. And sometimes, whether you believe this or not, a great good can come out of people communicating with each other. Let me give you an example, Billie-boy . . . Last year, a certain writer, who had an article published in "ONE" Magazine, received, from the editor of "ONE," a letter of enthusiasm from a reader. This writer answered her letter, and established a fine friendship. The letter came from a fellow in London England, and then, other things followed, books, and papers. I was the author of the article, and my new-found friendship was with [Brian Huxford], in London; though him, I have met Harry Otis, the author of "The Keval." These friendships are two of my most prized possessions. And it wouldn't have happened to me at all, if Brian hadn't written a letter, and if Don Slater hadn't sent it on to me; and if I hadn't replied to that letter, I never would have met Harry. Pen-pals? Sure, pen-pals! Maybe a few bad ones do get through, Billie, but the good out-weighs the bad, certainly.

Hey, Don . . . What happened to my story: "Some of My Best Friends Are Jews" . . . ? If your lawyer is still reading it, give him a little help, will you? I'd like to know whether you want it or not. I finally found a great agent here, Sidney Porcelain. He has brought some of our Homosexual literature to the fore. Wish me luck, and let me know about the story.

Love to you all,
Jason

~

7 October 1960
Wilmington, Delaware

Gentlemen:

Your Pathetick Appeal arrived today. I hope the enclosed will be of some help, and I'm only sorry I can't give you more.

The Pen-Pal question continues to pop up with the persistence of the proverbial bad penny. A couple of years ago I spent some fifteen months in England. Because of the nature of my work, I was thrown [in] with upper-middle class and upper class society. Like many of our ilk I am very reserved on the surface and a boiling tornado underneath (the metaphor—or simile—is mixed, but it's late). I subscribed to a correspondence "club." I met some eight or ten people and they were as dreary as the most violent opponents of the idea could wish, --but I met one . . . and that one made up and compensated for all the boredom of the others whom the most charitable could only describe as jerks. That it came to nothing lasting was no one's fault; he had to return to Australia, I had to return to the States. But even if I never see him again, nor find another, the subscription rather paid off. While I can agree with every cautious, sensible objection to the idea of a correspondence bureau, my agreement must be tempered by my own experience. Despite the witch-hunts in London and elsewhere, I feel that the English have far greater respect for individual freedom than we, and what would—and does—work in England, could be dangerous and disastrous here.

I am very grateful for the work you are doing and I wish I might do more than send paltry cheques. I have had editorial experience, and if you wished, I would be willing to do proof-reading. Forgive me, but the magazine needs it badly. The story "Fata Morgana" had some serious typos and my own story had a couple of blunders. I suppose that sending galleys across the continent would be too complicated, but if I could help, I should be very willing to.

Please—could I have a couple of copies of the July issue with "The Forgetfulness of Mr. Meunier" in it?

All the best.
Sanford

~

25 September 1963
London, United Kingdom

Dear Mr. A.

I just read your letter in the august issue of ONE.

I did not read the article about Homosexual maridges but I believe myself in maridges. I think Homosexuals should have a "NORMAL" life as Hetero sexuals (!). Should be no different between the two.

I can see, your problem is just like my. Your letter seems to me if I had written it. In London the situation is so similar.

I had belonged to a pen club. I received frustrating letters when we met I discovered my pertner is not suitable for me. On other ocation I received an obscene letter, the other one did not want to share my spiritual need only the phisical ones.

I am 33 years old. I admit the worries and frustration made me over weight. I am 13 ston. [182 pounds] 5' 8" tall. Darkblond and have blue or greenish blue eyes. I [am a] semi old fashioned, romantic typ. I am not feminin looking but my mental in many way. In love making I am [the] passive one. I am not handsome not rude. Just ordinary looking. I have elementary schools and a college education. I was a nurse in Hungary but here I work what ever comes. I am writing sort stories in Hungarian magazines. I like music classical or modern. I like art, both. Cinemas theatres, swimming, fancing, sailing.

Now[a]days I am not going anywhere because with out a partner I cant see the joy of life so I am staing home.

I would like to have a "NORMAL" life with some one to love and belong. To have a normal social life. I have relatives in various towns of Europe, friends in London whom I would visit more often if I would have a partner to go with. Just like other people. It is not written in some ones forehead some one is a Homosexual.

Since I have not partner I am not going nowhere. You see yourself what happened in the bar. The same happens here.

I feel very very <u>alone</u>.

I would like to know you better and welcome your letter please wrote to me.

Yours sincerely:
Elroy

P.S. I am very sorry my typing is not so good in English, but my hand writing more awful.

Married Couples

The final two letters were written by married homosexuals. It is unclear in the first letter whether the correspondent was male or female.

∽

Published in ONE magazine,
August 1955, 21
New York, New York

Dear Sirs:

You're doing, basically, a good job—though I'd like a little more fiction and a little less esoteric hogwash.

My wife and I enjoy reading ONE, and we're only sorry we can't leave the magazineform in plain sight in the apartment.

[no name published]

∽

11 July 1956
Midsize town near Montreal,
Canada

Dear ONE:

I read the other night at my girlfriend's home, your strong article in favor of us whereby we should have the same rights as the homos have; I am 29 now and have been a lesbian for many years having had my first experience in a Nudist camp while in Europe with my husband back in 1947. We still live together and he does not mind a bit my way of thinking about love for lovely feminine friends, on the contrary. However, here in this part of North-America, especially in this province, it is very difficult to get together and live together as our Laws are very strict.

It is impossible for us to receive ONE and I am writing you this note to find out if you have a way whereby by sending you my subscription, I can receive without this publication being refused, your interesting magazine. Possibly by sending same 1st class Mail will it reach me here [. . .]?

I do not know if this is possible, but possibly you could pass along my name and address to someone or a Club you would know that would be interested in exchanging correspondence with the writer as I would like very much corresponding with American Lesbians about my age.

Trusting to hear from you.

Yours very sincerely,
Megan

3

Repression and Defiance

The letters in this chapter provide firsthand accounts of antigay persecution during the 1950s and early 1960s. *ONE* correspondents described aggressive police officers, invasive postal officials, and antigay politicians. Some correspondents lost their jobs because they were homosexual or suspected of being homosexual. An emerging gay civil rights impulse is evident in many of these letters. By sharing their outrage with the magazine, these correspondents contributed to a growing chorus of gay protest.

Politics

The first several letters provide a range of gay perspectives on national politics. One correspondent praised a speech by George F. Kennan, former U.S. Ambassador to the Soviet Union, in which Kennan criticized antigay policies in the federal government. Another correspondent asserted (incorrectly) that the Soviet Union treated gay people better than the United States. The first letter is from a man who was trying to convince newsstand operators in Washington, D.C., to sell *ONE* magazine. After describing these efforts, he turned his thoughts to the broader antigay hysteria pervading the nation's capital during the early 1950s.

30 October 1954
Washington, D.C.

Dear Mr. Lambert:

Enclosed is my check #347, in the amount of $3.25, which is for the sale by Bill's [. . .] Smoke Shop, 9th St. near F, N.W., Washington,

D.C., of the 25 copies of the October 1954 issue of One. Six cents per copy were retained by both Bill and myself as our Commission.

Bill talked as though the 25 copies sold out rather fast. I asked him if he would like to have 50 of the November issue and he indicated that he would, but said it was up to me. I inquired if he had had any complaints as to its legality on the newsstand and he said if I really wanted to know whether it was legal, I would have to see Roy Blick. Blick is and has been on the "vice squad" of the Washington Metropolitan Police Department for many years and confiscates through the police power certain magazines, books, etc. I saw the nudist magazine "Sunshine and Health" on the Main Street newsstands in Los Angeles, for example, when I was there in June, but this magazine, according to Bill, is "illegal" on the newsstands in Washington. However, he does have one or two other nudist organs.

So in view of Bill's equivocal manner, I will "leave it up" to you, since he wanted to "leave it up" to me. Actually, I suppose he would be glad to have them in view of the fact that they sell so well, or at least he said they did.

I certainly have no intention of contacting Blick on the matter and would not recommend that anybody contact him, as he is a very ferocious type of person and is the one who trains the plainclothesmen here to solicit homosexuals in parks and theaters. I saw Blick once and regard him as a very ignorant and misinformed person. Since Senator Hunt committed suicide, Blick and Leo Rover, United States Attorney here, have seemingly quietened down on the homosexual issue and very little appears in the papers any more about the homosexual "morals cases." One of Blick's detectives, as you may know, entrapped the Senator's son in Lafayette Park about a year ago and Lester, Jr. was convicted. The Senator was deeply hurt over the matter. Then Senator McCarthy, I understand, threatened to damage Hunt's chances of getting reelected to the Senate by exposing the story to Hunt's constituents. In addition, Leo Rover had Lester, Jr. indicted, the story goes, when the latter was later subject to Army induction. Of course, this act and McCarthy's, too, were essentially political, since Hunt was a Democrat and McCarthy and Rover were Republicans. Marquis Childs wrote a very interesting article on the Hunt suicide which you may have read.[1] I have been told that the Washington Board of Trade and the Evening Star newspaper were also instrumental in putting a stop to publication of the homosexual entrapment stories.

I am telling you these things so that you can form a more intelligent decision on whether to send me the 50 copies of the

November issue. If One wishes to send them, I will deliver them to Bill's just as I did the October issue.

Sincerely yours,
Brad

∽

Published in ONE magazine,
April 1954, 28-29
Baltimore, Maryland

Dear Sir:

George Kennan, former Chairman of the State Department's policy planning staff, has recently sounded off in a way that I think merits acclamation from ONE and all its readers.[2]

Speaking at Princeton last December, Mr. Kennan at first requested that his remarks be kept off the record. He repeated the address very recently, however, at the annual Christian Conference of the Relevance of Religious Belief to Problems of Everyday Living, and changed his mind about no publicity, permitting the Princeton Alumni Weekly to print his speech in its issue of February 12th.

The pertinent part of Mr. Kennan's address follows: "Let us, for the love of God, keep out of the ranks of the finger-pointing holier than thous—the people who sublimate their own sex urge in the peculiarly nasty and sadistic practice of snooping on others and exploiting the failures and embarrassments of others in this most excruciating of problems.

"In particular, let us not fall into the sort of immature Philistinism that seems to have taken possession of our government in its latter-day preoccupation with the morals of the public servant. What has gone on in Washington in these recent months in this regard has brought the greatest dismay and disgust to many of us older civil servants, not only because it seems to us to rest on a very faulty understanding of human nature, but because it implies the existence in our midst of angels, disguised as security officers, equipped to pass judgments on the sinful remainder of mankind. Surely nothing could be more un-Christian than this."

And later:

"It seems to me that the greatest sin to which Christians are susceptible in questions of sex is really the sin of intolerance and lack of charity. Whoever makes other people's personal problems more bitter, and by holding these people up to ignominy, is the man whose conscience should really burn him. . . . He is the man who has most to fear for the safety of his soul. . . . He is guilty of the deadly sin of pride, and I suggest there is none deadlier in the eyes of our Maker."

Whatever our religious beliefs—or lack of them—and whatever our cavils at such phrases as "failures and stumblings"—we who are homosexual should commend Mr. Kennan. Such words from a man until recently very high in public life are of tremendous significance, it seems to me a tremendous step in the right direction.

[no name published]

∽

31 October 1960
Suburb of Los Angeles,
California

Dear Mr. Slater:

I wish to take you to task for the editorial appearing in the October issue of ONE.

You state that homosexuality and communism are inimical. I disagree most heartily and think I take my stand because of perhaps a deeper comprehension of what the degree of "freedom" will be under such circumstances.

Due to the intense propaganda for the past fourty years against the newly born economic system of socialism (communism does not exist anywhere in the world except for being the name of various political parties) the mass of people have been brain-washed to the extent that they will not try to understand of what has happened and is happening all about us. Consequently we have become accustomed to using the word "freedom" carelessly, realizing that it is all relative whether in the USA or the USSR and furthermore depending upon the individual's concept of such.

I think that only when we have a greater degree of socialism in our life with its consequently greater liberty of trying to understand the various sociological problems, will homosexuality have a chance to be understood properly. The problem in the USSR, as I understand it, is handled much more sensibly than in the USA and in time I think they will make great strides in solving the problem in all its ramifications.[3]

Historically we know of many revolutionary heroes who struggled and gave their lives for the emancipation of mankind who themselves were apparently leading homosexual lives. With the proper understanding of the Soviet Union and its evolutionary drive there is nothing incompatible with homosexuality. Certainly one can not say that our own government offers such liberty that the homosexual feels free to go about his business and not covering up a bit. Try getting a civil service job, corporation job, or anything else of that nature and freely admitting that you lead a homosexual life.

I think that Martin and Mitchell were completely aware of what they were doing, and when they stated that they considered a "woman was a woman" it showed much deeper thought that we attribute to them.[4]

But anyway my point is—I for one do not agree that a homosexual can find no solace of thought or ideal drive from Marxism. I find my greatest stimulation for my fellow brother through constantly preaching the merits of homosexuality and Marxism.

Enclosed find an extra piece of green paper for what it is needed.

Sincerely,
Henry

~

Published in *ONE* magazine,
April 1958, 28
"A New England State"

Dear ONE:

I want to tell you how much I enjoyed "It Is Natural After All," by Wicks. I have believed this after a great deal of research, and from some sort of intuition within my own personality. Keep up the good work. It is a long hard pull to enlighten people, but we do have a few scientists on our side. There is a solid wall of Puritan superstition under ages of make-believe that society seems to think is the truth. But by gradual and persistent enlightenment it will give way to the light of knowledge.

Mr. J., House of
Representatives

~

6 January 1961
Austin, Texas

Dearest ONE:

Well, here it is. We both had an uneasy feeling about the Kennedy brothers, and those of us who were idiotic enough to vote Democrat this time (and the miserable thing is that we could have swung the election), are going to pay the price for letting a do-goodie promise of the Never-Never Land of Liberalism, or the winsome smile of a pretty candidate swing our vote. There were warning and signs, and perhaps all of us failed just a little. It has long been our view, that ONE should take a more active interest in politics for the sake of homosexuals.

Once, we wrote, but did not mail a proposal to ONE for a column to be written here and forwarded to you, on a non-partisan basis. We did not mail it: the writer half of this marriage was busy preparing for the publication of his first novel, and the scientist half is less interested in politics, though he shares the interests of his partner, naturally.

We, as homosexuals, must wake up to the fact that if we do not exercise our vote with even more discretion than the ordinary American citizen, we are waltzing toward oblivion. The homosexual vote of censure should and must be exercised, until we can demand consideration for our vote. Nothing on earth staggers a politician, quite like an organized minority. They can be swift and sudden death, and for witness, please note that Mr. Kennedy was elected because of his appeal to two minorities.

Prejudice elected John Fitzgerald Kennedy! Catholic voters united for him; Protestants did not unite, though they were smeared in practically every edition of New York's papers before the election. Even the dear old decadent South has less prejudice, than the pro-Kennedy partisans.

Shame on us!

Affectionately to you, your
staff, and all our friends.
Timothy and Geoff

∼

Police and the Law

The federal government's classification of gay people as national security threats fueled a wave of antigay police crackdowns across the country during the 1950s and 1960s. Whether swept up in a gay bar raid or entrapped by a plainclothes police officer in a public park, the possibility of being arrested was a major concern for the correspondents below.

∼

1 August 1960
Brooklyn, New York

Dear Friends—

I seem to have missed my July payment, so here 'tis for July and August. Sorry, but guess it was overlooked because of my vacation end of June to July 10th.

Went to Provincetown and the Eastern Seaboard "touchiness" has reached there too. Weathering Heights, one of the most popular places for straight and gay didn't get their license this year. A technicality—applied a week late—but I understand the Town Meetings have been rather disheartening at several appeals. Voice vote, and the preordained decision is "No." Responsible town fathers objected "because a parking lot is near my home and I hear high-pitched voices screaming 'Let's go to Weathering Heights' and it annoys me so I vote 'no.'" Wish I could have gotten a copy of the town's weekly newspaper which quoted it verbatim.

The Atlantic House and Town House—two other well-known places—supposedly lost licenses for 10-day suspensions because State Cops were both propositioned and appalled at the carryings on there. Number of arrests in both places. And all the other places, straight, gay, and mixed are worried. Rumors are rampant that there will be Midnite inspections of rooming houses (but not what they'll inspect "for") as well as pictures (of what?) having been, or to be taken at other places and rooming houses. St. Peter's R.C. Church has the town mothers leading the drive. One of their Sunday bulletins had the announcement that it is the parishioners religious and civic duty to attend the Town Meetings to vote against "homosexuals who are trying to make Provincetown their haven of lewdness."

A general feeling of caution, concern, worry, and fright seems to pervade the town. As one townsman said, "State Cops wearing Bermuda shorts are playing a constant game of hide and suck."

But I had an enjoyable time. We're still there in large numbers, but have no voting rights, of course, and those property owners who do are intimidated, but still manage to vote for us in about equal number to the anti group, even tho' the decision is always against.

Best wishes,
Gregory

P.S.—So they say—
"Allegro" in Philadelphia raided twice. Carted the boys to jail for a nite for "frequenting a disorderly place."

Atlantic City bars closed down for 10 days because of a murder. No details, tho.'
NYC still quiet and closed down fairly tight, so streets are busy.

~

26 August 1962
Midsize town in northeastern Texas

Dear Bill Lambert,

Yes, I suppose you're right, the bar directory idea isn't feasible. N.Y.C. bars that flourished in the late 40s were not in existence when I returned for a visit in '56. But the two mainstays in Dallas (Villa Fontana and Gene's Music Bar) have lasted through the past seven years, each having changed names once. And last week I found the same sort of crowd in the Cork Room in San Antonio that I found 4 years ago. S.A.'s Marine Room's sign was glowing—but I didn't go in to see what was going on.

The Fort Worth friend you mentioned is probably [. . .], who went to L.A. for a vacation.

I think you received a missile from a native of Fort Worth—from young literary Mark. He used to ignore "One"; now he waits for each new issue to appear at Newsland in Dallas. So you see, your critics will read you, if only to seize an opportunity to tear you apart. When I saw Mark last week he had not had time to read all of the Aug. issue. Mr. B.'s letter evoked a wry smile from him. I merely commented that I wondered why you put the eye-poking lines in the Letters' section—not that I doubt that some policemen need a poke—but obviously gay people can't use physical violence to cope with that problem. . . . Speaking of the police, I have some reason to suspect that the Dallas police, or some of them, are particularly zealous in using their authority to give tickets for violations of traffic laws or to hold persons for investigation, if they think the victims are homosexual. It might be called petty harassment. The evidence is insufficient for a generalization—maybe I can get some inside info. from a patrolman I'm acquainted with.

Yes, I realize that "One" is probably better informed about the bars and other conditions than any other group in the country—aside from the grapevine yours is almost the only news. Give us as much info. in "Tangents" and "Letters" as you can—that is worth publishing.

Albert

~

25 May 1957
Wichita, Kansas

Dear Alison,[5]

Glad to know you're patiently carrying on—I'm afraid I'd not be so patient. When they "woof" at me or my friends, I have always "woofed" back so vigorously they backed off. Those who are most prone to persecute homosexuals, I have found, have a guilt-complex of their own and a little plain talk clears the whole thing up. Back in Missouri several times I challenged the district attorney when people were being persecuted, even pushing him out of the way to explain a few facts to the grand jury. It got so when I got interested in a case, they soft-peddled it for they knew I wasn't to be intimidated. It's our country, too few politicians would welcome the public into their bedrooms. Why should they get to pry into ours?

By the way, the reason I didn't renew my subscription is that I just stopped getting "One" and no one said "boo." When my first copy came, two back issues were enclosed. This is probably why my subscription ran out before the year was out. This is OK by me. Enclosed is my check for the legal fund and renewal. Hope it helps.

How they could find anything objectionable, I can't understand with One's *tame* editorial policy. Keep it legal but stand up to them— they'll back down. They expect homos to run and hide as so many do.

By the way, I've been invited to be a member of an archaeological party flying into the Andes in Peru. Can't spare the nine months altho' trip sponsored. There's always so many constructive things to do, it's a shame some people just get into trouble. These men wouldn't have asked any but a Lesbian to go on such a trip. There's definitely a big place in the world for us if we aren't afraid. We are what we are just as others are what they are and all have their places.

Enjoy hearing from you. Good luck.

Sincerely,
Helen

~

5 July 1957
[No return address]

Dear Sir:

You wrote to me not long ago, and recently the Supreme Court of USA—enacted a law whereby no one can be arrested unless the police will upon demand—furnish the names and total secret files to the defendant.

Hence—I wonder if this new law will have any effect upon the many entrapments, wherein a plain clothesman, will approach a person and pose as a fellow sufferer, and, try to win this person's confidence—then—upon doing so, have the person break a law.

Then arrest the person upon the charge of this violation, what ever law is broken.

I hear of other types, where we have a decoy hired or forced by the police—to entrap another fellow sufferer, and, when they both go home together—then—the police follow them.

It would seem to me, that such things cannot be so easily done with every file and record and name of all participating officers and their stool pigeons being exposed to the public record.

Then—the fact the second new law states, "no one shall be forced to testify against himself, as the security of the individual, and his freedom, supersedes the society as a whole."

I am writing to ask you what you have observed legally, since these two new laws have passed the Supreme Court, is the situation better—or is it not altered.

Evidently you did not notice, I do NOT write for myself, but for a friend—who in these days of persecutions, wishes to remain anonymous.

He realizes there is a great deal of hate for this, hate so great it [is] a little frightening, and, like Nazi Germany and its hatred of Catholics and Jews—but—we hope it will not end up like Germany ended, in Gotterdammerung.

A friend wrote to him—from the east—and said, Manhattan, is the most tolerant—and, whilst it is against the law, it is rarely intolerant—and, there are very few persecutions and entrapments.

He talked to a lawyer who said, "Manhattan has always been lenient—and Los Angeles is noted for those men who delight to take money to work for the police and act as a stool pigeon and turn traitor against their own kind."

My friend has had for years a heavy correspondence with Switzerland, France, and Denmark—and, have met many from those countries—and they seem to have no trace of this prudishness and holier than thou-false Religion, the very hysteria of self-righteousness which makes men become plain clothesmen—and entrap their own kind.

It is this lack of prudishness that makes him wish to live in these countries, France in particular—as he loves everything of France—its history—music—and its art, and gets along very well with French people, who are so broadminded and so very tolerant.

Los Angeles and New York—will never have the tolerance of the Rue de la Paix in Paris—and Los Angeles will never know the live and let live of the Parisians.

We here must try to be better than others, more holier than thou—and, with out hypocrite religions. We persecute and drive to suicide men by the hundreds, thinking ourselves better than they are—as we hide what they feel—a[s] they openly admit and honesty—to their feelings.

The Parisians at least admit it—and do not pose and act so extremely pious and holy—ending with cruelty and persecution to enable them to feel "better" than the next guy.

I await your reply, and thank you.

Yours truly,
G. D.

8 April 1961
Midsize town in southeastern Pennsylvania

Gentlemen:

Would you be willing to send me some information giving your side & your views?

1. When a man goes to see a doctor, tells him he is emotionally inverted (likes men instead of women), is the usual procedure for the doctor to give him a strong drug that makes him mentally ill?
2. Is there a weird drug or substant that people put in such a man's coffee, soda, etc. that makes him mentally & physically sick? What is it's name? Of course, they don't inform him that they've done it.
3. Is it true that they give poison to effeminate men? Will you please tell us the laws relating to this? Is there a death penalty? What is the "curare cure"? No doubt laws differ in different States.
4. Do laws prevent even doctors from talking to a patient about this problem? Is there a Federal law? Do doctors harm & exploit them when they come to them?

I actually don't think you'll disclose this information, but I thought I would write out of curiosity anyhow.

(PLEASE USE OTHER SIDE FOR REPLY.?)

R. D.

23 May 1963
Houston, Texas

Dear Friends:

The May Magazine has been received and read and, as usual, thoroughly enjoyed. Especially fine are the contributions by Frank C. Wood.

The lead article on "The New Nazism" is good, and contains much truth. But I sometimes fear for one thing. It seems, from my observations, that some are all too inclined to develop a sort of exaggerated police phobia, in which state of mind the police are the very embodiment of all evil, the beginning and the ending of all brutal schemes and rank injustices. I'm sure Mr. Kearful didn't intend this narrow an approach: but the reading of his article prompts me to speak of this situation, which has made me feel sad at times.

It must be remembered that the job of the police is a difficult, or impossible one, at best. They are placed between officialdom and the public—and often also squarely between opposing factions of the public. Of them everything is demanded: and credit for good is seldom granted in their behalf. If they shoot, they are murderers: if they don't they're cowards.

Speaking specifically of the persecution of the homosexual element: it goes without saying that there are men on the various police forces who enjoy going out of their way to trouble the gay set. But it seems at the same time a very safe bet that every organized campaign against the homosexuals has had its roots much deeper than with the boys who do the dirty work. It just doesn't sound logical to think of the vice squad boys for getting together and deciding on a queer hunt for the week's main attraction! No—they are hired to do as they're told—and if they didn't want to, they wouldn't be on the force, they'd be doing something else.

I'm speaking from inexperience in the above—please pardon if I appear to be over-zealous in the defense of the police! But really, it seems all human problems should be faced with a mind open to all sides—or better not faced at all! In recent weeks, I've had the experience of listening to the woes of an ex-Houston policeman, and an ex-Florida queen—not acquainted with each other—both equally embittered about life in general—and it's both amazing and amusing to note the similarity of the complaint! At times, when recalling a bitter outburst regarding some past happening, it is hard for me to recall which person made the statement! All of which proves—we are all victims of one thing and another. But let us strive not to be victims of bitterness and narrowness, whereby our usefulness and happiness are destroyed.

Thanks for giving the compliment of quoting a few lines from my letter to the Houston Chronicle on the matter of censorship. Specifically there are two bills introduced concerning obscene motion pictures—the second only dealing with the commercial showings in theaters, and perhaps not as serious as Rep. Miller's. The paper has been filled with legislative news, have been watching for word about these bills but have seen none recently.

Gay life in Houston seems relatively trouble-free as nearly as I can tell from my somewhat aloof perch (I don't patronize bars or attend parties or socialize much). A newly opened bar a few blocks distant is attracting great crowds on the week ends, with cars parked for blocks around, and always police watching especially toward closing time. The gay folks I meet seem delighted, and gloomily prophes[ize] that it is too good to last—I haven't heard of any trouble so far though. Percentage-wise it seems to me this area has fully as many gay folk as any area in any of the larger cities in the North and West. Don't know of any other part of Houston where gay life is concentrated, though, except for a cheap theater downtown where the rough trade operates in amazing quantity and frankness—but could hardly call that gay life!

Enough for this time—forgive the rambling chatter!

Good wishes always!
Oscar

~

Published in *ONE* magazine,
May 1954, 28
Washington, D.C.

Editor, ONE:

The following is from a letter I addressed to SEXOLOGY magazine:

Reviewing a play on homosexuality, the writer says, "The law still marks homosexuality as a crime." This is absolutely wrong.

To the uninformed public, homosexuality means perversion or sodomy. No state in the Union has a law against homosexuality, but against Sodomy, the Crime Against Nature, Buggery, Bestiality.

Dr. Franz Alexander tells of a young man who said he had homosexual acts with a woman! This shows the ignorance of people.

Dr. Hirschfeld (Encyclopedia of Homosexuality) states that 40% of homosexuals practice fellatio, 40% mutual masturbation, 8% pederasty and the other 12% Platonic relations. By common law definition of Sodomy (still on the books in some states,) only 8% are punishable, while in other states where fellatio is also considered Sodomy, 48% of the homosexuals are considered "criminals."

But Sodomy is by no means a monopoly of homosexuals. Even a husband and wife are punishable under the law for such acts.

[no name published]

Florida Crackdowns

Police crackdowns against homosexuals were rampant in Florida in the 1950s and 1960s. *ONE* magazine documented a series of Miami police raids in 1954, noting, "The Miami story illustrates what trumped up hysteria can do in a few weeks to any city in the United States. Corrupt politicians and opportunistic demagogues can endanger any community that permits itself to be herded into pogrom."[6] These raids foreshadowed a later episode of antigay hysteria in Miami-Dade County when Anita Bryant and other antigay activists in 1977 successfully worked to repeal a newly passed ordinance that would have banned discrimination against gays and lesbians.

∽

16 September 1954
Miami, Florida

Gentlemen,

Are you aware of the degree of persecution that homosexuals in Miami Florida have been subjected in the past six weeks?

I assume you have read of some of it in your press. It all began with the murder of an Eastern Air Line Steward, William Simpson on August 9th of this year. The enclosed newspaper clipping shows briefly the state of affairs that has developed. In politics from the local level all the way up to the state it is popular to yell war on homosexuals and every Tom, Dick, and Harry is jumping on the bandwagon.

Eastern Air Lines is conducting a private investigation of homosexuality which has already caused the resignation of a considerable number of its stewards and it is in its early stages.

My reason for writing you is that I, with others, am ready to fight back, however I do not want my efforts to be futile and wasted. I have read several of your publications and remember that you sent a representative to New York to help in organizational work.

The situation in Miami is a challenge to every homosexual in America and I trust that we will in a concerted move make our voices heard all over the land.

Yours is the only source of leadership I know to turn [to]. I believe I could get as many as fifty people together for an organizational meeting if I could get some help or leadership.

Please answer me promptly and if you are in contact with "Mattachine" please see if they can offer us any assistance.

Hopefully,
Charlie

～

Published in *ONE* magazine,
August-September 1956, 44
Key West, Florida

Enjoyed your article "Miami's New Type Witchhunt."
Really nothing to what is happening here in Key West.

Everyone who is suspected of being a deviate has been warned to leave town. The usual hue and cry was raised by the Chief of Police.

Many have been arrested and charged with "vagrancy" which carries a fine of from $10.00 [up] to and including $150.00. This charge has been placed against the native-born, employed, and wealthy, as well as against visitors.

It is hardly safe for a deviate (male or female) to be seen on the street, not to mention the bars or restaurants.

Mr. F.

～

26 November 1963
Fort Lauderdale, Florida

Dear Friends:

The article entitled, The Inquisition, in the November issue had a rather profound effect on me. Little wonder, though, as I once found myself sitting in front of such a venomous animal as Clayton Jarvis. I have always been sort of a sitting duck for these types of inquisitions and the likes of them. I guess it is because I am considered to be too beautiful for a boy, and I'm constantly being taunted and suspected by various witch hunters, and believe me we have them here in Florida. I have learned to live with it, though, and unlike the poor soul in the story who hadn't the backbone to fight for his rights, I'd like to meet the SOB who could force any confessions out of me. I will fight to my dying day for my rights as an American citizen, which, in my opinion, include the right to go to bed with whatever, and whoever I please.

        Sincerely,
        Barry Ross

PS You can print my name if you wish, I have nothing to hide, and do not lead a double life.

~

        29 January 1961
        Small town in eastern
        Massachusetts

My dear Mr. Pedersen,

I am a Danish house-boy, in the home of an accomplished doctor and scholar, and the other day I found the December copy of your interesting magazine, ONE, on a coffee table, and that evening read your excellent Editorial. Since I have been in the United States, I have gone to a number of churches of different denominations, not out of any need for this organized "religion," but mainly out of curiosity, and I must take issue with you in one of your statements. Near the bottom of the first page you say that "homophiles (are) conspicuously unwelcome in most churches—Catholic, Baptist, Unitarian, whatever." It has been my experience, widely, since it has been my lot to travel all over this country and over a great part of the world, that the Unitarian people have made me the most welcome, even when they definitely knew my taste and preference. European Catholics, I have also found much more tolerant than the Baptist, Methodist, Presbyterian, Lutheran and of course the large number of obviously limited Catholics in this country, although one is more apt to fine [sic] all sorts of surprises because few Catholics follow out the rituals they give lip service to in their Masses and Confessionals. Many of the Irish boys,—and girls too, for that matter seem to know very well how to wink at the "rules." But I do think the Unitarian attitude is generally very broad and tolerant towards non-conformists. I remember being in your State of Florida a few years ago, at Miami, when there was quite a to-do there, when the mayor went rather berserk on a "clean-up" campaign, and there was a lot of arrests and trouble. The only church which did anything to help toward a fair and balanced judgment was the Unitarian, who opened its doors to a series of evening lectures and forums, giving each side an opportunity to be fairly heard, and these were very well conducted, and should have made the mayor quite ashamed, but he may not have had the awareness or sensitivity of the matter to understand the actual situation. I find this often the case where there is too unfortunate[ly] a small degree of emotional maturity.

Now, all this because I just could not sit by and fail to give credit to the many splendid, fair-minded Unitarians it has been my privilege to know.

I think you and your colleagues are doing a splendid and wonderful work generally in having such a magazine as you bring out, and I am sure it must take a great deal of courage to so openly face so much limited knowledge, intelligence and emotional immaturity.

cordially and sincerely yours,
William

27 August 1960
Los Angeles, California

Dear One,

I have been reading your magazine for over a year and find the stories, poems, and such, all very enjoyable.

Both your July and August, issues of much interest as:

I came out to Los Angeles, from Miami, Fla. July issue

I was in the service. August issue

I lived in Miami, Fla. for five years and in coming to Los Angeles, what a change.

Gay life in Miami, is nothing like Los Angeles.

In Miami, the kids stick together, such things as parties are not raided or are there any vice cops snooping around. The Miami kids carry on just as much as Los Angeles kids and get pick up just as fast. But, most of the Miami crowd know when and where to carry on. Out here these kids don't.

In Miami, you don't find the kids stealing from one another and you don't worry about leaving people in your home when your out.

Here in Los Angeles, not the city so much but Hollywood, there aren't very many kids you would want in your home because they would steal you blind.

In Miami, there aren't many kids who would bother to sponge off another person. They have too much respect for themselves.

Not so in Los Angeles, here everybody sponge's or work for nothing in coffee houses.

Kids, with cars in Miami do not run taxi service. Everybody chips in for gas and expenses and there is a better feeling when the driver pull up to a gas pump.

Here in Los Angeles, if you have a car see how many offer to chip in for gas.

There are quite a few gay kids from Miami out here and they find the Hollywood crowd phonie and most of the kid cheap and untrustworthy.

Of course your readers are thinking why in the H— don't they go back to Miami.

Answer to that is that Miami crowd want to see if they can't do something for this mix up city but mostly Hollywood.

Maybe we Miamian's are sounding a little high and mighty but we do feel Hollywood could be made over a little bit. They are putting in new sidewalks in Hollywood, why not put a new feel of trust and respect in the Gay crowd. Stop street corner shows for tourist and police.

Respect the police and they will start to respect the Gay crowd a little more.

You might find them staying away from parties and not writing in their notebooks so often.

In your August issue of One, your articles on the Homosexual Servicemen were exquisite.

I myself was discharge from the service because of being a homosexual. I was given a U.D. or what is known as a Gay discharge. I of course thought my life was ruined. I didn't know how I was going to explain away my years on a job sheet.

Well I got a hold of myself and found by using the excuse of school I could make out quite well until I had a job or two under my belt. To explain away the 4-F draft card was easy with a bad back which no one can prove different.

It should be explained I entered the service when I was 17, and discharged at 19. I am now 23, and in a managing position with a small company here in Los Angeles. I have met quite a number of young men who have gay discharges.

Most have stop worrying about their discharge and done something for themselves. But, there are still some who are afraid to try and get away from the past and look toward the future. I'll grant with such a discharge you can't work for the government or civil service but there are plenty of jobs which don't ask for service records and as long as you have filled your time in service they hire you.

When I was discharged I was one of 350 other men so there must be a lot of men with U.D. discharges running around.

All this talk of homosexuals could be stop in service if the Sec. of Defense would correct an order written by the Sec. of Defense during the last of President Truman's term.

Many good men have been discharged because of the order mentioned. There is no need to dismiss men from the service because of their sex preference.

A homosexual probably knows how to handle himself better with a spy or enemy agent than a straight person and would be more loyal to the government than what we call a straight person.

I myself would have gone to my commanding officer and take orders from him how to handle a spy.

The War Department should know by now it can't rid homosexuals from the service and as long as they don't cause trouble let them be.

Like a friend of mine who was a WAC was to tell me.

The WAC's never ask whose gay in the barracks but who's straight.

There are a number of doctor's and lawyer's who lobby in Washington for us. Let's get behind them and get a few of our laws change so a homosexual doesn't have to be afraid of what he is or what his sexual need might be.

Pat

Postal Harassment

The fear of having mail seized by postal authorities—and the unwanted attention such a seizure could bring—weighed heavily on the minds of many *ONE* readers. Some of them refused to subscribe to the magazine through the mail, preferring to buy it at a newsstand instead. The letters here highlight the dangers of sending *ONE* or other mail with gay content across international borders.

∼

Undated
Pasadena, California

[. . .][7]

You will understand why I do not give my name, as I have children to think of, and the position of ONE is so open to attack from the misguided that some day even its correspondence may be seized by 'McCarthy-ists.' In answering, just copy my post office box VERY

CAREFULLY (so your letter won't fall into other hands!) and your reply will reach me.

[no name]

~

29 April 1958
Hamilton, Ontario, Canada

Gentlemen,

Well now the ax has fallen here in Canada, the United Stated Supreme Court may have declared One magazine <u>not obscene</u>, but that does not go for Canada, so I found out today.

Yesterday I received a notice from the Customs Postal Branch here in Hamilton that there was mail from Los Angeles there for me. Today I went up there, mystified as to what it could possibly be, and there the familiar envelope appeared which the customs inspector had to open in my presence, and One magazine was there, I only got a fleeting glance of it, but so did he and went away to investigate the matter. Returning he said that he was sorry but One magazine was prohibited in Canada. So I said, since when? Apparently since last September. So I said again, how come it's "hot" all of a sudden, since I've been receiving it regularly for about 4 years every month and that it had been investigated and found to be OK by the U.S. Supreme Court. Well he said "it's on the prohibition list here and I cannot understand it how you've been able to get it since Sept. and how we slipped up; well anyway this is orders and I cannot give it to you." "Yes," I said, "but it is harmless, there's nothing obscene about it, no sordid pictures or literature of that kind at all. I cannot understand it." He also said a little later on, "well maybe they'll soften up the laws around here a bit." I had to sign the original postal notice and he attached it with some condemning papers (I suppose) and said that now it would go to the Post Office itself who decide further what to do with it, most likely to be burned. I asked him about this and he said that they have the right to open all kinds of mail if they think it necessary, but in the presence of the addressee or to his order.

Well when I got outside I got good mad at these stupid laws over here and it spoiled the rest of the day for me. Anyway this is what happened and I thought you might like to know about it, maybe you've heard it from others already about this Canadian Prohibition of One magazine.

A likely explanation of why the Customs Inspectors hadn't caught the One magazine before is, that only recently the Prohibition list has been changed and that before One was somewhere at the bottom, since at that time Peyton Place was on top with a few other which are OK now after investigation, so One may not have been so easily identified.

I phoned up my lawyer and he suggested to wait until there'll be more of a to-do about it and then it would probably be taken up automatically by the proper investigations committee which may take some time mind you. I doubt he would take it to court anyway, if it ever came that far. Well I'd like to do things quickly, yet openly and honestly, but if this needs some stronger action I'll do it too.

Last year I traveled thru Europe for a 3 months vacation and I met many people whom I told about One and its actions in America, [and] never did I hear of them having had trouble with their mail. And so far I have not had any trouble with various European h.s. magazines coming to me for also about 4 years now.

Well this is my story for what it is worth, could you give me any advice as to what to do if anything. If you have extra charges because of this correspondence or if you want to try something which involves money, as long as you don't go overboard without advising me, just charge it to me and I'll pay up.

I'm afraid this is a rather long letter to burden your department with, but I had to bother somebody with this problem.

No matter what happens, I do want to keep up my membership, I guess I needed this jolt by the customs here, to realize that I look forward to One's magazine, always, but not quite realizing it that way.

       Cordially,
       Steven

∽

       22 May 1958
       Hamilton, Ontario, Canada

Just received your note of the 20th, so thanks for answering my epistle, 'though you couldn't give me any bright news yet.

Last week history repeated itself, another One magazine was stopped at the Customs office and labeled as "Prohibited." Obviously using the different sender's address of Box 15692—L.A. didn't fool the customs clerks either. I had a good mind to grab the magazine from the clerk's hands but of course that wouldn't do. I guess I'll never see these issues now, and now I'm even more curious as to what all devilish things could be printed in them. Now that it's the "Forbidden Fruit" it makes it more in demand.

Anyway, to heed further One magazines from the Post Office fires in Canada, I'd like you to mail the mags to a friend of mine in Chicago where I hope to spend a short vacation there, this August.

So, the address would then be:

[. . .]

This goes, as long as you haven't any other idea of how to get the mag to me.

Don't hesitate to call on me for any help I might be able to give on an "all-out onslaught inside the enemy lines," as you call it.

Needless to say that I'm very sorry about the Canadian situation now, also I do thank you for your attention therein.

Best Regards,
Steven

P.S. Do you think it might be an idea to change envelopes to a regular white business size, fold the mag. as done herein, a piece of paper around it so that no printing can be detected thru the envelope, the address in writing, just as if it's a letter, also possibly mail it from a neighboring city. I think the envelopes are a give away now. Why not try this?

∽

22 December 1960
Chicago, Illinois

Dear Sirs:

Early in November I sent in a subscription to ONE: and now I'm a bit worried. It has been just a little over a month since I received the first issue—and I am wondering whether you might be having difficulties with the Post Office Department in connection with the mailing of your magazine.

My reason for this feeling is not primarily the slight time delay, but rather that it has been brought home to me very vividly the way in which the Post Office is working these days. They apparently confiscated a mailing list somewhere which contained my name, or took it from an item addressed to me. I was accosted today by a postal inspector who forced me to sign, and swear to, a statement that I would not receive through the mails anything which any postal inspector might judge to be obscene. (I stated that I was forced to sign the statement—the alternative to signing was lost time from work for a series of hearings in the City.)

Naturally I do not consider ONE Magazine to be obscene, but rather a very wonderful work. But as I pinned the inspector down, in discussion, to indicate which things he meant by "obscene," he insisted that several equally serious works were in that category. I did not mention ONE.

Therefore, by the very broad and completely undefined nature of the oath which I was required to take, I am forced to state that my subscription to ONE must be cancelled if the Post Office adjudges it to be "obscene"! This especially in view of the fact that the inspector informed me that any magazine which did not have the second class mailing permit was to be turned over to the post office!!

Will we ever see justice in our lifetimes?

Very truly yours
Oscar

~

24 March 1963
Midsize town in central
Missouri

Dear Mr. Lambert,

In reference to the subject of our telephone conversation last Monday, Mar 18: Not having the courage of your convictions, I have looked into the Postal Regulations pertaining to the withholding of foreign mail. Article 261.3 states that foreign mail may be withheld on <u>suspicion</u> (sic!) that it contains obscene, filthy, or lewd matter (or a lottery!). The Regulations direct the withholding Office to notify the addressee of the article, and request his signature, permitting the Office to open the article, in the presence of a representative of the Postmaster. It is this first notice which I have received, and about which I telephoned you. I have not responded to it for the reason that the Postal Regulations allow <u>suspicion</u> of o., l., or f. matter as ground for withholding.[8] The withholding Office (Appraiser of Merchandise, Chicago) could easily reply to my letter, if I wrote one, with a quotation of article 261.3. I would then have to undertake the practically impossible legal problem of contesting their suspicion of o., l., or f. matter. This, I'm not prepared to do. I'm a Faculty-member of the University of Missouri, [. . .], a middle-age bachelor, and cannot afford to stir up any hornets' nest.

Article 261.3, or some neighboring article directs the withholding Office to send a second notice to the addressee if the first notice is not acknowledged after 15 days. If the second notice draws no reply from the address, the article of mail is to be returned, unopened, to the sender. I've decided to let the matter take this course. I have, of course, advised the Zurich Office, and requested that they suspend both the monthly and the PS.[9] They have replied, and say that they have had another letter from Illinois reporting the same experience as I reported. The Post Office Department may have more than just a suspicion of the contents of the envelopes from Zurich. I'm afraid I'm not the one to undertake a test of the probable judgment of the P.O. Dept. that the periodical is o, or l., or f., though, of course, such a description seems to me to be beneath serious consideration. My do-nothing decision very likely seems to you to be a compound of irresponsibility for freedom and fecklessness, and, of course, I'm sorry for that, but I haven't the courage to strike a blow for freedom on this field of battle. I'm glad to have had the talk with you, and I'm sorry to appear to have ignored your advice.

Faithfully yours,
Robert

~

Excerpt of Dorr Legg's reply, 22 April 1963: "I get the impression you do not differentiate between 'Postal Regulations' and LAW, concerning mail. These Regulations are pretty much the product of the minds of petty little beaurocrats [sic] who weasel their ways into positions of advantage (at tax payer's expense) and then proceed to throw their weight around, quite irrespective of LAW in any way. Their efforts (whatever their motivations) are effective to the degree that citizens tolerate such behavior."

~

22 October 1961
Manchester, United Kingdom

To./
The Editor, Don Slater.
Dear Sir,

At long last I can write you re—the August issue, so here goes and, what follows is no "snow-job." If you wish to use any part of this letter in your 'LETTERS' feature, you may do so, freely.

The Editorial of the August issue is, to say the least, most illuminating. However, people in the high State Service, and any other important posts need greater protection against the blackmailer. The Laws of various countries tend to <u>encourage</u> blackmail by making oddities of behavior great and grave moral issues as effecting the nation. This should not be so.

Every human being <u>should</u> have the right, on this planet, to a perfectly free and private life divorced from all career and anything else where the sinister and unscrupulous may not enter in. Individual integrity, not collective integration, should be the hall mark of a responsible man or, woman. For any profession to <u>want</u> to control the personal and private life of anyone is a lowering of the standard of humanity—and is there, tending to make of people a common mould, usually, the worst possible shape. The heterosexual and the deviant <u>are</u> targets for blackmail—one when he, or she is married; the other <u>because</u> he, or she does not marry.

See how pernicious blackmail is, who can fight it? No one. And, it is the worst censor of public morality and conscience. Change in the law and selection <u>alone</u> can disarm these hideous traders in the human foible and practice.

A security risk is anyone who is not secure in himself, or herself that is why careful selection is necessary; then, protection for the one selected is <u>the</u> supreme task of government anywhere. We here in Britain have had a case of Burgess and Maclean, the alleged reason for their joint flight was <u>moral</u> degeneracy in at least one of them—but it did not emerge until after they had gone—yet it was supposed to have been known many years before that![10]

Strange that no official action was taken, again, I personally suspect the blackmailer. So much for your thought provoking article.

The leading article is, to a Britisher, something of a surprise, we have no postal censorship here in Great Britain[;] the mails are free and secure, state guaranteed of no violation. A measure of privacy is enjoyed here as nowhere else in the world. The United States therefore, would do well to recognise this perfect state of affairs. How can censorship of any kind be reconciled to the Freedom of the Press, Speech, and Religion? who are these McCarthyites anyway? that seek to dominate the minds of men, and for what end?

Personally, I am always suspicious of anyone, or anything which depends for its existence on ignorance and the suppression of personal viewpoints. The stamp of the mark of the Tyrant is limitation, division and the desire to conquer via control of the mind, I am certain that the United States of America is bigger, and much more intelligent than to allow for one instant such antiquated jugglery as this sinister postal interference.

True, youth <u>must</u> be protected from seduction from such sources as pornographic literature, photography and the like—but is it protected in this way? Explain the incidence in the States of youthful drug addiction—<u>that</u> merchandise doesn't go through the post! Obscenity and pornography are sore points, but what is obscene? who is to judge?—what in life can be classed as obscenity and what, indeed isn't. Is Sex a dirty word? or is it all a natural function? or is it really the mainspring of life and the seed bed of all creative, productive effort?

I set the test questions, how are you to answer them dear reader?—but, <u>PLEASE</u> do not answer if prejudice is your only storehouse of knowledge and ideas.

I believe the Puritanical way of life—is based on a corrupt view of life—and, possibly, it is the worst movement ever to assail man. Since when was it immoral to laugh, make merry, dance, make love—and enjoy oneself? Cromwell, on reflection, must have been somewhat cranky. He certainly was not human, in the flesh and blood sense. He was historically, cruel.

But, alas, as Shakespeare has so well said, before him; "the evil men do lives after them." How very, very true—but Shakespeare is not recognised as a prophet—at least he dealt in truthful inspirations.

The Right to know, which implies the freedom to find out, should over ride all forms of censorship; les[t] we blunt the human mind in its' desire to grapple and delve for truth, knowledge, experience and light.

Still on the August issue, your case is startling.

How could anyone hound anyone else, like this, for whatever reason? the nursing profession has a fair number of deviants in its ranks in this country, and, they rival the female nurse in skill and the art of nursing very well; without any trouble at all. A man, or woman, doing a useful job—rendering useful service needs encouragement rather than insults, for such people as John are very scarce these days. Tenderness, concern for others is dying, it needs agencies like <u>ONE</u> and agents like John to ensure that humanity be constantly lifted up rather than trodden down. The late Senator McCarthy was hated this side the Atlantic and his sudden demise <u>was</u> a relief, in Britain at least? we do not want his kind.

John like many more, has proved and is proving that, the homosexual <u>can</u> work hard and honestly, does desire a decent, useful and worthy life;—and, who dares deny him, or her this much? no one but a demon who is wicked enough to deprive anyone of life anyway.

The 'TANGENTS' feature is excellent and proves how virile is the deviant group activity—and I am sure, no one is outrage by them and their search for happiness. And certainly the profit margin in these places justifies the acceptance of the trade and custom—the dollars, I'll bet are very welcomed, even if the PERSONAL side: through prejudice is resented.

I can see from this feature life proceeds in the States very much the same way it does here.

Speaking mainly for Manchester, I will, from time to time, keep you posted with the rendezvous and gay spots in and around the city. We have at least six gay gathering spots, two of which are mixed—but, co-existence (PEACEFUL OF COURSE) seems to be working.

All in all my friends and self have found ONE most interesting, stimulating and a sense of oneness, of belonging on a wider scale gives life greater meaning and broader horizons. Fear and despair, not that I am personally beset by these, must consequently decline in favour of greater hope, an expanding happiness and reverence for life par excellence.

The "Lady Chatterly" case of course, was farcical, Lawrences' book, English has been available, from Belgium for years. And, if you had it in your PRIVATE collection you ran no risk whatsoever.

However, Penguin Books were courageous in taking the stand they did—and its still selling well, although not my cup of tea, or is it coffee? I like both.

The readers letters section is very good and of human interest. I may say we have learned something in the letter from Mr. D. of London, Eng: "Man and Society" is very undercover we in the North have not seen it yet.

So ONE has my support, at any rate.

Yes Sirs, you are to be congratulated and respected for this service you are rendering to all deviants everywhere.

Later on I may need more SUBSCRIPTION BLANKS and the BUFF COLORED folder. Count me as ONES' CRUSADER in the Old World on behalf of the minority the NEW WORLD life giving inspiration—at least we are on the side of LOS ANGELES.

           Yours Sincerely,
           Edward

∼

Job Anxieties

Following the lead of the federal government, many state and local governments, as well as private companies, screened their employees for homosexuality and fired them when homosexuality came to light or was suspected. In this section, two short letters from women, letters that eloquently capture the era's employment anxieties for lesbian and gay workers, frame a lengthier letter that describes an anti-gay purge at a hospital. In this letter, the correspondent believed that hospital investigators secretly sympathized with their gay victims, but were too afraid to provide any assistance to them because of the pervasive McCarthyism.

∼

9 January 1958
Los Angeles, California

Dear ONE,

I learned of your magazine from Cory's <u>Homosexuality</u>.[11] I bought my first copy today, and read every word with great eagerness. The name alone repels me. It is filled with such awful loneliness. As for content, I would like a page devoted to questions and answers.

Would someone be kind enough to advise me what could be done about a threat to expose me to my employer as a homosexual? I have been promoted to management level, and I know my reputation is such that no one would believe him, yet it does worry me. If you need further information, I will give it to you.

Enclosed find money for a subscription and a small contribution for the magazine. Please do not publish my letter.

Thank you.

Marian

∼

27 October 1958
Santa Monica, California

Dear Bill,

I have thought considerably about our conversation on Saturday, and felt that since one matter we discussed has gone on troubling me I ought to write you about it. It is that I don't feel comfortable about our exposing or making any sort of attack on the investigating officers at the hospital.

Granted that these people are doing a very cruel work and that their methods are so low and nasty that they can only continue under cover, still I doubt that the over-all situation can be improved or that they can individually be encouraged to change by our putting pressure on them or by our threatening them. Certainly if we were to retaliate in this way we would be following the standard and quite acceptable code. But I wonder if this code has ever worked very well. One thinks of Ike, troops and Little Rock, or of Dulles, ships and Quemey. Of course it will be a long time before "we" can have troops or ships. And one could only hope that by that time we'd know more about power and how to use it.

In my interview with the investigators I acted on the assumption that the best experience for them would be to encounter a gentleman who can be frank about his homosexuality and who is neither angered nor frightened by their attack. I assumed that they are very fearful people, which means that they can only be made worse by being frightened or by being allowed the impression that they can frighten others.

I believe we have in "us" the capacity to understand the investigators (official or otherwise) well enough and that we can be confident enough of our own position that we can deal therapeutically with them. But it is not easy to keep clear about the fallacy of punishing a sick man. And that is particularly so when that sick man is running loose. If he were hospitalized, we'd know we must not attack him or his irrational behavior. We'd begin by winning his trust and confidence, by coaxing his reason to life by demonstrating reason in our own conduct. But when this fellow is an investigator, and seems to have power over us—well, it's not so easy to remember what his position and condition really are, and what role we ought to be playing.

So far the situation at the hospital has gone quite well. I say this because: the investigators are obviously disturbed by their own performance when a victim refuses to justify it; many (to all appearances a great majority) of the persons in charge at the hospital (doctors, supervisors, etc.) are now informed and are anxious for relief from this sort of thing as they never have been before; and among other personnel there is quite an amazing awareness of the problem and open expression of sympathy with the homosexual. There is a healthy ferment. With regard to stopping this specific investigation, it may be best to wait to see what Karl Menninger can do.[12] He may be in a position to stop the business at its origin. He has taken action to do this sort of thing in the past.

My own sense of defensiveness has so much abated in these last three years, and I know what a change this has made in my own over-all outlook and energy and feeling of confidence in meeting bad situations. Such personal experience does, of course, influence our feelings very much. It makes me wonder if we do the right thing for homosexuals in general to keep before them accounts of the constant battle <u>against</u>. I'm not sure who needs the most help in these situations. I am sure that the first help has to go to the fellow homosexual. But somewhere along the line help will have to go to "these others," the investigators included. Poor dears, they are in such a muddle. In my own investigation, it became obvious that they are as caught up in this mess of prejudice as we are. And in my visits with sympathetic superiors and colleagues, I began to feel I had to encourage them. They felt perfectly helpless. The most logical and apparent conclusion to the whole experience seems to be that to the homosexual who can free himself from fears and doubts there are a lot of other folk who are ready to gravitate with the hope that he can free them, too. Until we can help them in this way, we must not harm them.

Now I have this off my chest, Bill—another of those long letters for you to wade through. It was very kind of you to take so much of your busy time last Saturday to talk with us and to show us about the place there. I will get some items to you, the first within a week, I hope. If in any of these items revision would make them acceptable or more acceptable, I hope you will be free with your criticisms and suggestions. Would love to tackle the thing on teaching, and may attempt it.

We'll be getting in touch with you soon. Next week [Cliff] and I are moving to the front half of [Mickey . . .]'s place. When we get settled, we hope we can get you out this way for a visit with a number of us.

Best wishes to you and to the other faithful ones there. As you know, we are very grateful for your work.

Sincerely,
Patrick and Cliff

∽

23 August 1964
Midsize town on Long Island,
New York

Dear Mr. Legg,

Thank you very much for your answer to my letter. Contrary to your expectations, it had a great deal of effect on me. I am usually able to face such issues quite squarely, and I feel that I am capable of a great deal of growth. However, I have never before had the opportunity to discuss my fears with anyone who was interested in this matter, and who also had some facts at his disposal. Whenever I have raised the topic of "One," or any of the other organizations, they have always scoffed or warned me of the dangers involved in associating myself with any of these groups. I realize that the facts may not warrant this attitude. However, the following questions are of deep concern to me:

1. How frequently do teachers lose jobs because of suspicions in this area? I have read in recent issues of "One" about teachers in Florida who have been having trouble.
2. Would a school give a reference to someone whom they had let go under these conditions? (Assuming that the individual had not carried out any debatable activities in school.)
3. Would this person be blacklisted by other schools?
4. Would such an event be reported in local newspapers?
5. The envelope that "One" is mailed in has a return address. Does the post office keep track of who receives mail from such addresses? (This sounds ridiculous, but I read something in a local paper recently indicating that this is so.)
6. Can any kind of legal action be taken against a person if it is known that that person receives "One"'s publications or engages in work for the organization?
7. Might this information be given to the person's employer?

It would be of great help to me if you could answer some of these questions. I hope that you will be at the New York meeting, as I would very much like to talk with you about these things. . . .

Sarah

~

Civil Rights

As worry, anger, and disgust mounted over the possibility of being arrested, fired, or having mail seized, gay people, individually and collectively, thought about how to improve their situation. In the following letters, *ONE* correspondents shared ideas about civil rights strategies. Some of the questions raised in these letters continue to be debated today: Should gay people seek mainstream respectability, or instead proudly flaunt their differences? How much energy should gay activists devote to cultivating heterosexual allies, such as prominent psychiatrists or political leaders? Several letters were published in *ONE*, thereby influencing American gay rights discourse at an early stage.

∼

>Published in *ONE* magazine,
>January 1955, 42
>Los Angeles, California

Dear Editors:

It takes great courage to do so well the task that you've undertaken; plus immense compassion for your fellow man—to be quite willing to help splinter the moral bigotry that imprisons our so-called "enlightened" society. Maybe if I had known of your publication a year ago, a dear friend of mine would not have taken her own life—if she had felt that there was some slim chance of one day being both understood and accepted.

>[no name published]

∼

>Published in *ONE* magazine,
>July 1953, 22
>Washington, D.C.

Dear Friends:

Received the April issue of your fine magazine, ONE, and liked its make-up very much. It is well edited and has articles interesting to our friends. I am enclosing $10 as a contribution to help you in our struggle to get recognition.

In 1925 I met several inverts in Chicago and conceived a society on the order of that existing in Germany at that time, Society for Human Rights and we published a few issues of a paper, called Friendship and Freedom and even had a charter from the State of Illinois.[13]

But one of our members turned out to be a married man (bisexual) and his wife complained to a social worker that he carried on his trade in front of his children and the social worker found a copy of our paper and all of us (4) were arrested without a warrant and dragged to jail.

I managed to get out on bail and hired a good lawyer but the first judge was prejudiced and threatened to give us the limit ($200 fine) but I got a better lawyer who was politically connected and we also got a new judge, who was rumored "to be queer himself" and he dismissed the case and fined the married member $10 and cost.

I was then a postal clerk and a stupid and mean post office inspector brought the case before the Federal commissioner with an eye to have us indicted for publishing an "obscene paper" although of course, like your paper, no physical references were made. But the commissioner turned it down. However, the post office inspector, even in spite of us being acquitted, arranged my dismissal from the post office. The whole thing cost me all my savings of about $800 and no one helped us, not even the homosexuals of Chicago.

Of course, I see the faults we committed, we should have had prominent doctors on our side and money on hand for defense, and a good lawyer.

I returned to the army in 1925 and am now retired and doing well.

G. S.

~

Published in ONE magazine,
October 1953, 10
Santa Monica, California

Dear Sir,

I have been a great follower of your magazine and the Mattachine Society. However, I cannot openly engage in the activities of the magazine or the Society, as I am a government civil service worker, and at the risk of my job (as a bad security risk) I must refrain from giving you my name.

In government circles I hear talk of both the magazine and the Society in regard to being subversive. The Gov't seems to be very much in favor of the way you approach the problem of homosexuality, but since both the magazine and the Society have not required their staff and members to sign loyalty oaths, both will remain in danger of being declared subversive by Senate investigating groups, until such time as loyalty oaths are signed. It is believed that if loyalty oaths are signed by both groups, success in their undertakings may not be far off, as they can proceed as spotless groups in their undertakings and can well win the public to their side without being spotted or smutted by Senate investigations.

Many civil service employees feel that they could then sympathize with these groups and feel the government would take a different attitude toward this minority group, if they knew the group stood firmly against communist infiltration of this country, and no longer would there be prejudice against this group, such as has existed in the past five years. It seems the attacks against this group are based on poor security risks, and the possibility that this group may be the victim of communist agents. If this group took a firm stand, wouldn't these attacks by Senate committees disappear? Many labor unions took a firm stand, and the attacks against them practically disappeared into thin air.

It is our belief that the Magazine ONE and the Mattachine Society who are pioneering in their undertakings could require their staff and members to sign Loyalty Oaths and obtain nation wide recognition with the sanction of the United States Government in their undertakings to obtain acceptance and adjustment of this minority group into the National Society making them citizens this country can be proud to have.

[no name published]

~

Published in *ONE* magazine,
September 1953, 12
Reno, Nevada

A Reply to R.L.M. in your JULY issue, AS FOR ME:

Who is in a position in this world to require conformity from anyone?—least of all one homosexual from another. The desire to have all homosexuals well mannered, intelligent, courageous, manly, men is easily understood. These are attributes most of us classify as desirable; most humans do, according to the standards of their own society. Is it not the aim of all persons in this country to attain both a personal integrity and equal rights before the law of our society? We as reasonably enlightened, 20th Century individuals are not in any position to slap the bar-fly or to condemn bar-flitting; promiscuity to us is a personal matter; emasculated affection is neither my concern nor another's. The so called "gay life" is not for me to reform and I hesitate to define the "very worst elements."

No! If we must have a crusade it must be for civil rights and equality before the laws of this land, not for conformity to some ideal of personal ethics. I do not care how many "gay" bars exist or who goes to them or what they do there, who delights in emasculated affection or uses perfume; but I do care that my rights as a citizen of this country are nil and I know that getting all homosexuals to act like bourgeois gentlemen is not going to get those rights for me. I am not sure what will but I think ONE might be on the right track.

[no name published]

~

Published in *ONE* magazine,
April-May 1956, 46
Los Angeles, California

Dear Sirs:

We homosexuals are a minority group with generally a much smaller degree of social visibility than some minorities, such as the Negro. We are in for as enthusiastic a persecution by members of the larger society as is any minority, especially if these people are sexually insecure themselves. Unlike most minorities, we do not propagate our own kind. . . . Wherever we do come from (and I refuse to recognize myself as the product of tragedy), the hard fact is that we <u>do</u> increase and there is no more chance for us to resign from our particular minority than there is for the Negro to change the color of his skin. We are definitely not like the reformed Communist who joins the church and begins writing for national publications. . . . Parenthetically, it would seem obvious that any homosexual who echoes the common prejudices concerning other minorities deserves what he gets in society's treatment of him. We can't <u>will</u> ourselves out of homosexuality by any conscious effort of the mind, nor by trying to be super-conformable to society's demands in other respects.

In view of these considerations, I feel it is in poor taste for any homosexual writer to write of his fellows in a demeaning manner, even by implication, unless it be for some specific literary effect. His own feelings of inadequacy don't need to be exhibited for the edification of others, especially the general heterosexual population. . . . I say that those who do will never have that essential for every human being, a certain amount of self-pride.

Once I determined to stop apologizing to anyone for being homosexual, even by implication, I found that it was no longer necessary to hurl imprecations at my parents for getting in there and mixing up all those parent-child images. And a bounty was added when I began to learn pride in my group: a satisfaction of identifying with my fellows, a secret comradeship under the stress of peril, the indefinable thing which soldiers miss when they rejoin civilian society. As a member of this group, it was imperative that I learn the basic truth of all minorities, that stereotypes don't fit. . . . Certainly the homosexual stereotype is the most wildly untruthful of all. The only trouble with stereotypes is that they tell much more about the people who hold them than they do about those whom they concern.

As these truths have been borne in on me, my own hunt for homosexual companionship has become less compulsive and predatory. Instead, I can look for a good, solid, and permanent circle of friendship founded on honor, truth and understanding. The high turnover in homosexual comradeships results largely from the search for a strangely distorted goal; by re-appraising the goal one may have a chance. . . . Let's not be too damn apologetic for our homosexuality. For myself, this life has enough to recommend it so that I would not wish to exchange it.

            Mr. D.

Published in *ONE* magazine,
May 1959, 31
New York City, New York

Dear ONE:

The lugubrious Dr. E. of Michigan (Letters, February, 1959) must carry a very long face among his patients. I wonder, does he ever smile at them? Our fight, if we must call it that, is indeed for a difficult cause, but laughter is a very potent weapon and has won just as many battles as tears and lamentations ever have.

There's fun in "Hamlet" and "King Lear" as well as tragedy and high drama. Dickens is deliciously funny, yet the number of reforms he sparked is well known. Rabelais and Shaw didn't tear their hair out putting their points across. We remember what they had to say though, don't we?

And there's no sense in trying to say that Christianity is a sad religion, if we must turn to religion, which we invariably do. It isn't. In the first place, witness Easter, the essence of joy, if not of laughter. And anyway, God came before Christianity, and He must have a marvelously developed sense of humor. He invented us humans, didn't He?

            Miss J.

ONE's business manager, Dorr Legg (also known as William Lambert), answered most of the letters that were written to *ONE*. Legg was a major figure in Los Angeles gay activist circles from the 1950s to the 1990s. He was intellectually brilliant, but known to have a difficult personality. Sometimes he wrote scathing replies to correspondents who, in his opinion, complained too much. As the following two letters suggest, Legg's replies annoyed such correspondents.

～

3 April 1954
Kansas City, Kansas

Although this is a long letter, please read it to the end.

My dear Mr. Lambert,
Your letter of March 30, 1954, was indeed "severe," but this was perhaps no more so than my earlier letter. It was clear, of course, that I had angered you. This was not my purpose in writing to you; therefore I extend to you my apology. Undoubtedly, I shall have angered you further by my letter a few days ago to Mr. Dale Jennings. If, as you say, "we cannot accept further registered letters," my letter to Mr. Jennings may well be returned to me undelivered. This would be the better alternative.

At the risk of burdening you with still another unwelcome letter of considerable length, I take the liberty here of writing what may offend you to an even greater degree. I regard your letter of March, 30, 1954, as ill-advised and in poor taste.

I have emphasized before that I wish an impersonal, business relationship with ONE, Incorporated. Your conclusion that I am, thus, uninterested in the problems of the corporation is an unwarranted one. Your implied accusation that I am a "child of fortune," innocent of the hostilities around me and protected from the realities of attacks from without, is a presumptuous one.

Because of my impetuous behavior, I found myself a number of years ago unwanted at a succession of universities, in spite of the fact that I had achieved an enviable record of high academic standing. I had to experience years of unceasing battle to win recognition once again at a university from which I was once expelled. I assure you that the somewhat provincial attitude in this section of the United States did not make my struggle an easier one.

At a time when severance from government employment because of deviation is a matter for prideful announcement in statistical reports and in newspapers and magazines, I find myself employed in a professional capacity in a government agency. I have direct responsibility for the distribution accruing of a very large amount in federal, state, and local funds derived principally by appropriation by the legislature from tax revenues. I am under constant attack by the recipients of those funds for justification of my decisions with respect to the distribution. I am a public representative with all the vulnerabilities that such a position entails—<u>save one</u>. I am not afraid because of my personal life. I respect this courtesy from those who do not have the same standards of moral behavior as I have, and I have accepted the obligation of cooperating with them by maintaining absolute integrity in my professional relationships. It has been necessary also, that I be unrelenting in expecting equal integrity on the part of my associates.

Although I am young in years, my experience has been fairly broad and understandably harsh. I have felt the wounds, too, caused time and time again by the man or woman who may have written me a congratulatory letter [about] one or another of my successes, but who can no longer feel comfortable in speaking to me on the street. I have fought my own battles, and I have won my own campaign ribbons. I am proud to wear these ribbons for what they are—and no more. I resent your assumption that I am a casual observer, and not a veteran, too—along with you. I hope you appreciate that I cannot take at this time a public stand in this matter; for, to do so, would be to fail in my obligations toward those who have prejudiced their own jobs and the respect of their friends and families to give me freedom from fear and freedom of action. But, nonetheless, I <u>am</u> "with you" in a very real sense and in a very urgent manner. Your goals are mine. Your battles are mine. Your heartaches and disappointments and rebuffs are the ones I have met already or may well meet tomorrow. Truly, I am "with you"—to the very depths of my being.

Recently, I had the occasion to complain to <u>The Saturday Review</u> about an error in my subscription account. I received a prompt reply satisfying me that the error had been corrected. This was all I asked from you.

Recently, I sent to the Encyclopedia Britannica Corporation a number of letters—all by registered mail. I did not receive a reply charging me with "a lack of good faith" on my part. You are too sensitive to imagined reflections upon you. If you have integrity, then you need not react so unfavorably to my own methodical way of completing my records, else you make me wonder whether or not "the man protesteth too much" by you not confusing a complaint about an error in business management with an imagined allegation of moral deficiency? I meant only the former.

May I not say that it is senseless for us to strike out at each other. We owe each other the support of standing together—and this is far more than a mere courtesy. So long as each of us maintains integrity (and perhaps even otherwise!), we are bound to each other in a way beyond destruction. I hope it is not trite for me to say that I do realize that an injury to you must make me "die a little." I did not write to you earlier out of arrogance, but in dismay. Your reply was written seemingly in the vein of the former. This was hardly fair to me. Surely, though, we can reconcile our differences; for, mistake it not, I am with you devotedly.

          Sincerely Yours,
          Alton

~

         3 June 1964
         A suburb of Los Angeles
Att'n.: Mr. W. Dorr Legg, Vice Chairman
Re.: My letter to you of 14 May 1964
   Your reply of 26 May 1964

Dear Mr. Legg:

Your letter of the 26th was read by me with much disappointment and an equal amount of bewilderment and frustration. I was indeed, very disappointed that you were unable to give me information about the viewpoints held by the various candidates for partisan and nonpartisan offices in the Primary election just past. If this is your organisational position, then I cannot dispute it with you.

Your reply made it abundantly clear that ONE is a non-political and non-sectarian organisation, and as your letterhead states, concerns itself only with "education, publishing, research and social service." These functions, of course, are very valuable and I in no way wish to detract from your organisation's usefulness to the American homophile community within the limitation you have set for yourselves.

Nevertheless, I must seriously question the social effectiveness of an organisation which holds itself so aloof. Do you honestly feel that you are doing the most you can for homophile betterment by maintaining this position? All the time I have lived in Los Angeles I have never seen an advertisement about ONE in any of the metropolitan area newspapers, nor have I seen any editorial mention of the work your organisation reportedly carries on.

As a vivid contrast, the Dutch homophile organisation in The Netherlands, CULTUUR-EN ONTSPANNINGSCENTRUM, has much publicity in the press there, nearly every weekend. In addition, the

"C.O.C." maintains a lobbyist on behalf of the Dutch homophile community in the national parliament, to say nothing of their endorsements and condemnations of various candidates for political and judicial offices. With their active participation in Dutch politics, religion and the judiciary the "C.O.C." has made its influence felt quite heavily upon Dutch society and the resultant freedom for the homophile community has been really enormous. In light of this, perhaps it would be wise for ONE to re-examine its functions and make itself over into a more vigorous and governmentally active organisation.

The CULTUUR-EN ONTSPANNINGSCENTRUM was founded in 1946 and in the eighteen years of its existence its influence has been felt by every element of Dutch society; it has become a faction to which all politicians come for endorsement. The "C.O.C." on the occasion of its twentieth anniversary is scheduled to be officially recognised and endorsed by the Dutch Royal Family for its valuable contributions to the betterment of Dutch society; twenty years is the minimum time in which an organisation may receive such recognition by The Crown.

ONE was founded in 1952 and in the twelve years of its existence is still virtually unknown even by members of the homophile community in Southern California. I wonder if this is not because of the attitude of aloofness which ONE maintains! In the twelve years of existence, precisely what has ONE accomplished for American homophiles in securing additional personal freedoms, and more importantly, understanding by the heterophile majority?

In my opinion, it would be much less a chore to make great social achievement in the U.S.A. on behalf of the homophiles than it was in The Netherlands. The U.S.A. is a new, vigorous, dynamic and socially pliable society whereas Dutch society is tremendously resistant to change and the changes that do take place usually take much longer and require much more dedication than is necessary here. Yet the "C.O.C" has made Holland into a haven for homophiles within a span of eighteen years—truly the freest country in the world. Will ONE be able to say as much for its work and accomplishments in this country upon the occasion of its eighteenth or even twentieth anniversary?

Finally, Mr. Legg, I wish to reprimand you personally for the unwarranted sarcasm contained in your reply to my letter. There was nothing in my letter to you to warrant insinuation that I had written without first "reflecting" upon what I intended to express; in fact, my letter was written as a sincere and honest inquiry to an organisation I expected to receive at least a sympathetic reply from. If you answer all inquiries in this manner you will succeed in alienating everyone and will simultaneously cease to have any usefulness to the homophile cause.

Yours sincerely,
A. V.

~

Organized gay rights activism first emerged in the late nineteenth century in Germany. In the 1930s, the Nazis shut down most European gay rights organizations, but by the late 1940s, about a dozen European homophile organizations had reemerged. The following letters highlight the international character of gay rights activism in the 1950s and early 1960s.

~

Published in ONE magazine,
December 1955, 28–29
Philadelphia, Pennsylvania

Gentlemen:

Enclosed is a money order covering two subscriptions. . . . I spent this summer touring northern Europe by bicycle with an American Youth Hostels group. Because of my short stay in each city and impossibility of telephoning a post office box, I missed the group in Brussels and Amsterdam, and the man in Paris was away at the time I was there. I did reach a gentleman in Hamburg but it was a brief visit for I was there overnight only. However, I had time to write ahead to Copenhagen, Stockholm, and Oslo. There was no reply in Copenhagen, apparently the mails were slower than I expected. . . . Copenhagen is so fascinating in every way.

On my arrival in Stockholm I was contacted and taken to visit some of the members of the organization there. They were extremely friendly and hospitable in every way, and I so enjoyed my three days in their beautiful city that I am eager to return. As we parted they gave me some money and asked me to see that they receive a subscription to ONE. It's a small return for their kindness; that's why I am especially anxious that there be no errors.

Again in Oslo I had a wonderful reception! There I met only three of the group but I was most cordially treated and made lasting friends. They gave me a pin used by their organization and spoke hopefully of having the symbol adopted for others and the ICSE [International

Committee for Sexual Equality]. Both groups told me that very few foreigners bother to go out of their way to visit them—perhaps this is why they were so genuinely glad to see me. I will never forget the wonderful people I met everywhere in Scandinavia!

Some of the groups I wished to meet I found no longer exist; Ganymedes Samfundet and the Internationalt Forbund for Sexual Lighed in Copenhagen; the I.F.O. in Bremen and the organization in Frankfurt am Main; the Friends-Club in Gothenburg, Sweden. Someone also mentioned that "HELLAS" is no longer published but of this I am not completely sure.

Miss B.

~

31 May 1957
Amsterdam, The Netherlands

Dear friends:

Reading in and about ONE is like looking into a strange and sometimes curious country of a—you might excuse—fairy tale. I appreciate your courage, initiative, phantasy and hard working will, but—BUT I think (from my own European, typically German and Non-American point of view) you might as well do good or even better by doing less and perhaps lesser than you think you should do. Even if there are fine things like your Social Service, your Book Service, your Educational Program—you can put those things aside, for there are many things still to be done and many, many years to come.

But I forgot you are Americans, and this means more optimism than realism. You just haven't got the courage to put things aside which offer themselves to you for being organized.

Founded in 1951 we find ourselves in a much lesser developed status as international organization than you as national organization. Our board of directors is spread all over Europe and we find ourselves confronted with a mass of work, problems and things to do, but we just do what we can, following the devise "The most one is the possible one." (I have nailed this phrase on my wall!)

When I came here first early in January this year I knew merely one thing: the name ICSE [International Committee for Sexual Equality]. It was set up as a committee dealing mainly with scientific work to be stimulated in an unorganized body of scientists all over the world known to us whose ideas we use to represent in socalled international congresses. For that purpose we received [an] annual fee from single members (some two hundred) as well as from 12 organizations including your group.

In membership figures we should talk about some thousand ICSE-members, but this is untrue due to the fact that organizations usually pay much lesser than they should pay according to their actual membership figures and due to the fact that we cannot force our single members to pay their annual fee.

From the money brought up that way we pay a small salary for one person (last year was the secretary, this year the editor), rent a room and cover current costs like postage, paper, printings, telephone and transportation expenses.

We should have a printed magazine, but we have only one badly mimeographed, we should have large national and international meetings, but we haven't, we should make money, but we spend and lose—in commercial terms—most of it.

As to ICSE-PRESS for instance we found someone willing to pay the costs, but we have not had a single reprint since October 1956, except a bad critic in "Salzburger Nachrichten," Austria—you might call "bad publicity." But we still hope the service keeps its value plainly in terms of information the press of both Germany and Austria obviously is lacking. Only recently I started as a "Versuchsballoon" the first issue of a news service while ICSE-PRESS until then mainly was published as a monthly correspondence.

From our seven men/women board of directors three are living in the Netherlands, one in Belgium, one in Luxemburg, and two in Denmark. These seven only meet once a year, but the three named first meet more often in connection with the 10 COC delegates to the ICSE. As you probably will know every member organization can send one delegate for every 250 members (and lesser if they are less than that) into the general assembly of ICSE. So the Netherlands with some 2.000 "light" (and some 1.000 "dark" members, so called by their paying fee) members may have at least 10 delegates which meet every month. You receive the then edited "protocolls" in German language, made out by the undersigned. This meeting [has] been used as [an] advisory board and discusses all things attached to the office.

So there is only one full-time man in the office, while the other two are quite busy with their jobs (one is salesman, the other international translator mostly outside the country, now in Nice). This one is performing several functions:

1. answering letters and correspondence
2. shipping material required

3. preparing organizational meetings and new developments
4. editing the three publications
5. shipping them too
6. busy getting new ideas from himself and elsewhere

The COC headquarters is working with three full-time workers: the president, one managing editor and one administrative personnel. There are usually two and sometimes three half-day-helpers, some unpaid. The ICSE lacks in such assistance for the simple reason that we cannot pay another man. But we have thanks god one who helps at least two times a month half a day paid.

FULL TIME in ICSE terms then means: working in the office usually six hours, working at home usually six hours at night and two in the morning, make 14 per day plus some weekends and holidays. For this I receive a salary of hfl. 60.—per week, which is fair to little in Dutch living standard terms. But the handicap lays more in the too less of money for postage, paper and office budget. We are quite aware that one currency unit per years and member is much too little for the member organizations, but they are all struggling leave alone Holland and the friendly but not connected KREIS. (The Skandinavians pay regularly, the Germans mostly not. Their groups are very small. We are now busy in getting their exact figures.) The some two hundred single members do not pay either. The results of the Lottery were fair to good, but the money has been spent already within the frame of our office budget. Copies of NL and KURIER are often accepted for granted where the[y] are actually for sale.

And still we certainly know that we offer too less for what we receive. Now the idea of building an "interior" branch has been born out, some people do not think this is within our tasks. Although everyone expects us to act like general headquarters of all homosexual organizations in the world, we just do some concentrating of the scientific work. The contacts between ICSE and its member organizations are very few and only necessary ones, sometimes only with our directors or with the head of the organization. In this respect you cannot actually speak of ICSE as an international organization center. But it ought to be done that way, I at least think. Hope that out of our Frankfurt meeting will come out any good and profitable.

Our first and mainly trouble is that of finding good translaters. We know that our English is very pour [sic], that we really should publish sometimes things in French and that we do too much for Germany at the moment. But here we are: amidst in a country where almost everyone educated speaks at least two if not three and more languages: Dutch, German, English, French, and some Italian. We have some who speak Scandinavian. But they are all not able to write it without faults and errors not to speak of a good style. And good translators or correctors we would have to pay for. Again a money problem.

I will finish, hoping that you at least have gotten the idea and the point of view. If we move together things will be easier but at the same time more complicated. If we do too much at the same time it means doing less.

Hope we could meet in person very soon.

In friendship yours,
Jack Argo, editor ICSE

∼

28 June 1957
Zurich, Switzerland

Dear Bill,

As this is more or less a private letter I'm not even using our office-paper. You asked me why the CIRCLE [DER KREIS] isn't a member of the ICSE? Well, Rolf has, as long as he has edited the monthly, maintained the fact that the CIRCLE isn't an organisation but a loosely connected number of subscribers to the monthly. It is the same with our "Club" over here—if the CIRCLE did not exist we could not have a club like the one we have had now for as long as the monthly exists. Both—the magazine and the club—complement each other. Rolf has never in his life sought any publicity but has preferred to work and fight quietly—and one must not forget that he worked for our cause already at a time when even in Switzerland the old penal code was still valid. The change for us is just about 15 years old, a fact easily forgotten by people.

In my own and private opinion—and please don't quote me anywhere, as I disagree on this point violently with Rolf—at the ICSE there is a lot of talk and of organising and the such like—but what has been done does, in my own opinion, not amount to too much. In a recent letter from Stockhomsavdelningen av Förbundet av 1948, Postbox 850, Stockholm I (the official Swedish organisation) their leader raised in an open letter all sorts of questions connected with the work done by ICSE—and I should advise you to write to them and get a copy of that letter and have it translated (it is written in German)—it may tell you in great detail how things at the ICSE are. Personally speaking—I do dislike people who are fond of opening their mouths far too far—I think there is still so much <u>practical</u> work still to be done that we could leave all the big speeches etc for some latertime. Added to that is in opinion the mistake they make in trying to organise Germany from the Netherlands. That's one thing Rolf has always—and rightly refused—to act 'officially' for Germany. On the other hand our whole German section of the June-issue was dedicated to German problems (again I should ask you to find someone to translate these articles as all of them might be of great interest to you too.) In my own opinion the ICSE is vastly over-organized and takes far too much (or tries to) on his shoulders and what so far has come out is surprisingly little when you think of the big words which have been used in advance. Well—as I have said, this is definitely my own personal opinion on which I would not like to be quoted. I am all for work and not at all for 'Big-Mouth, Inc.'

Yours, as ever
Rudolph

15 June 1956
Novara, Italy

Dear Sir,

Thanks for your letter of June 1956. My Novel LA LINGA NOTTE DI SINGAPORE, have win the Gastaldi National Prize for the Novel, 1951, but was published only partially (all the scientific interpretation of the diary was not published) and so I think it is not a useful book. It have only served to start a scandal.

The Han Temple Organisation do not like to be much known till 1975. The President of the H.T.O. is saying that the public opinion is not prepared to hear about our work. So all the achievements, after the failure of the Muthu Colonies in Chieng Mai (Thailand) and Indonesia, are strictly a secret.

The late Dr. Lindner was in communication with the H.T.O.[14] In your publication you may only mention, that the Han Temple Organisation is working in the Asiatic Countries in a cover[t] way till 1975. The H.T.O. is based on some teaching of the Buddha-Shakti Sect of Thailand. At this Organisation are attached the HIGH ROOMS of Macao, the MOON FLOWER ROOMS of Hong Kong, the SONS OF MAUNA LOA of . . . Hawaii, the MUTHU ROOMS of Singapore, Malaya and Indonesia. A publication will be forwarded to all Occidental Organisations in 1958 by a Committee of the H.T.O. studying the world situation now.

In Italy there is only a Section of the I.C.S.E. In Naples, there is now a scientific publication, quarterly, dealing exclusively on the homophile problem: QUADERNI DI LIBRA ANALISI (Edizioni Martello—Via Mergellina 226—Napoli) 600 lire each number.

SESSO E LIBERTA is no more published. The magazine TAGES was never published.

If you need some information, please note that I will leave Italy the middle of next month for Baghdad and Teheran, and I will not be back until the end of September. After the middle of July my address will be: Bahrain Hotel—Prior Road MANAM / Bahrain Islands / or: Poste Restante—G. Post Office BAGHDAD—Iraq.

With kindest regards and good wishes for your task,
Sincerely,
Bernardino Del Boca

And Finally . . .

Published in *ONE* magazine,
March 1960, 32
New York, New York

Dear Sir or should I say She:

I happened to come across this magazine today. I found it in his belongings. There's no doubt about it I have a brother who is homosexual, and I hate his guts for it. He never tried to pull anything on me and better not. I read one of his queer magazines and think whoever publishes it and everyone who reads it has to be a queer! I think the stuff you write in those books is a bunch of B.S.

I met a few homos not too long ago. They tried to take advantage of me. However, I got in a struggle with two of them. I had a chain and wrapped it around both of their queer necks.

That's how I feel about fairys, queers, homos—whatever you want to call them. How can a man have sex with another man I'll never know and don't care to know. The same for the women. If I ever meet up with any more I'll use my .38 on them. That's what they deserve.

A Straight Guy

P.S.: I'll expose you all! Ha, ha, you queers.

4

Incarceration

Most of the letters in this chapter were written by gay men incarcerated for homosexual crimes.[1] *ONE* correspondents who were arrested in the 1950s and 1960s usually avoided prison sentences through plea bargains, but several of them served time in prisons or mental hospitals.

Prisons

The first group of letters is from men imprisoned for homosexual offenses. In these letters, the correspondents described their alleged crimes, their dealings with the criminal justice system, and their experiences in prison. Several letters show that one of the most common ways to end up in prison was because of the testimony of another gay person. Reflecting the national hysteria engendered by McCarthyism and the associated paranoia, gay people were often pressured to "name the names" of other gay people in order to avoid exposure or incarceration themselves. Similar to blacklisted Hollywood screenwriters, many gay people faced the choice of personal ruination or destroying a colleague's, friend's, or lover's reputation.

Being arrested and stewing in a prison cell could awaken a civil rights impulse, especially if the victim was a military veteran. Imprisonment, ironically, often reaffirmed one's gay identity and the right to live as one saw fit.

3 April 1955
Midsize town in central North Carolina

Dear Sirs:

Inasmuch as there are several things I wish to tell you I shall number the paragraphs in this letter.

1. I was a one-year subscriber to ONE last year, having received two or three copies before leaving Charlotte on June 9, 1954. Two copies after that were sent to my home address and the others not forwarded. You will please check your records to make sure that the copy is not still being mailed to: [. . .]
2. My present address, [. . .], N.C., will be changed on or about May 1, 1955 so please do not send any more copies to me at this address, as I might not get them. I am not sure just when your copy is to be received. I received your February 1955 issue yesterday. Is that about the right time?
3. Your magazine is serving a very great need to many people and I only wish that I were in a place or a position to be of help to you. I am at present an inmate of the N.C. State Prison Department serving 18-36 months sentence for that "infamous crime against nature," as it is termed in this state. I am going to enclose a brief history of the cases in which I and a good many others are concerned, for any purpose to which you may wish to put it. Since I am not sure just how you would like it, I am going to put it in a chronological form like your English statistics of several months back.
4. As a brief explanation I know that I made many mistakes in the course of the matter to be discussed, but I sincerely believe I have learned a lot from my experience which I hope to be able to put to use. I am as interested in the welfare of prisoners now as I am of homosexuals. I allowed myself to get into a position to hurt the position of homosexuals, I suppose, and only hope that I can help in many ways in the future. If I had adhered to the advice published in ONE many times last year, I would most probably not be here. Being rather naïve I felt that telling the truth would help me, which it did not.
5. I am in a rather fortunate position in the prison set-up at the moment, which will explain the letter, subscribing to ONE, etc. I am in charge of the office and store box at a Negro camp, being white myself, and enjoy a large number of "privileges."
6. By way of explanation of my ownself the following biographical information: I am 30 years old, a veteran of 3 years U.S. Army service in World War II, a graduate of [. . .] College, Class of

1948 with an A.B. in Pol. Science and History, with some postgraduate work both at [two prestigious Universities]. Living with my parents in Charlotte, N.C., when convicted and not certain where I am going to locate when I leave here the end of this month. For my own information I should like to know if I could get any help from any of you people if I decided to locate there this summer. I do not mean that I want any financial assistance, but I would wish to get some help, perhaps, in getting a job should I come that way. I have been offered a job by my cousin who operates a men's clothing store here in Charlotte as his office manager, but do not plan to accept that. I had spent two years as a loan processor and real estate appraiser before being convicted, and before that a year as a furniture salesman, and a while before that as an office manager for a brokerage office in [. . .], S.C.

7. I hope that the information I am enclosing, and the newspaper clippings will be informative if not too useful. I would appreciate also hearing from you in the near future in reply to the question I posed in 6 above. I would like to locate where I could help you with your magazine if you would want an "ex-convict" as I now will be to help. There are certain persons like Dr. McCormick of USC who are doing lots of penal work, whom I would like to consult in Southern California also concerning certain prison reforms which I intend to work for.

Hoping to hear from you in the very near future, I am

Sincerely yours,
Leroy

~

8 June 1964
West Chester, Pennsylvania

Chester County Farms
West Chester, Pennsylvania

REGULATIONS: Persons corresponding with inmates must observe the following: Mail to be forwarded to address in blocked area.
All inmates are permitted to write one letter every two weeks and receive visitors every week.
VISITING HOURS—EVERY SUNDAY 8:30 A.M. UNTIL 2:30 P.M.
VISITING TIME LIMITED TO 20 MINUTES DURATION, ONLY 3 VISITORS OVER 16 YEARS OF AGE PERMITTED.

Inmates are permitted to receive: Daily and Sunday papers and approved magazines MAILED BY THE PUBLISHERS ONLY; apples, oranges, and bananas, total weight five pounds; also money and clothing, razors and blades. NO EXCEPTIONS.

∼

Dear Sir:

I have been in this prison nearly a month now, with <u>at least</u> 4 more to go until I have a trial—all this simply because I can not afford bail or an attorney. It's a vicious cycle—I must stay in jail because my relatives and friends have forsaken me, and they have forsaken me because I am in jail. I have lost everything—family, friends, job, probably even the house I was purchasing with [Darren]. I would not bother seeking help or sympathy—<u>if</u> I were guilty of any crime. But the truth is, the charges against me are completely false; I am waiting to be indicted of assault and solicitation to commit sodomy, when in reality, it was <u>I</u> who was solicited, and it was <u>I</u> who was assaulted. Since this is a censored letter, I don't know how much I can tell you about my case, but I will try to be as detailed as I can under the circumstances. Over 3 weeks ago, I went to West Chester via bus from Philadelphia with Darren Wilcox (with whom I was living for a year, and with whom I was purchasing a home) for the purpose of visiting some college friends before the summer vacation. We spent Saturday afternoon at the college here, then decided to take the train back home. While we were walking to the station, a group of college kids <u>called us over</u> to the car in which they were sitting; it was Darren who spoke first: "Are you guys just driving around?" But it was [Ray] (who had Darren and me arrested), who then said, "Do you guys want cock?" They then said that if we wanted what they had to offer, we would have to pay for it. They asked us how much money we had—Darren said we were broke and had to catch a train anyhow, so they drove up about a half a block, and stood waiting for us on the sidewalk. When they refused to let us pass, one of them asked us how old we were (Darren is 26, I'm 20) and where we went to college. When I said that I had attended W. Chester, one of them must have become scared, because he punched me in the stomach and kicked me in the face, while Darren yelled for the police. Finally they left, and Darren and I ran to the train station, when we were picked up by the police and taken to H.Q. It seems the "hustlers" realized the seriousness of what they had done, and in an attempt to protect themselves, they told the police that it was Darren and I who solicited them! I, who had only said two things to them ("20," my age,—"West Chester," my college) was now accused of solicitation! And I, who was beaten and kicked, was accused of assault, for it was said that I placed my hand on the rear of one of them. I won't even mention "police brutality" because I know it would be censored, but they (the hustlers) were given the privilege of pressing charges, which they declined, but after the police talked with them in private, they were persuaded to change their minds. Consequently, Darren and I are waiting in this prison; waiting, but we don't know what for. Naturally, we've lost our jobs, and while we're waiting, we're probably losing our house and furnishings—all because a bunch of college hustlers won't tell the truth! And we're outnumbered—there were 3 of them, and only Darren and myself. We won't be appointed a lawyer for several months, and then it will be a half-interested public defender. Things look very grim for us, indeed. As we may write only 2 letters a month, this is my second. My first plea for help went unheeded, as will, I am sure, any further letters I may write. My family never wants to see me again—there is no one Darren and I can turn to for help. Then I remembered ONE; it was worth a try. Even if only to tell someone where we are, and why we are here; even if only to have someone on the outside worry about us. But what we are really hoping for is help to fight this case—a most profound injustice!! With financial and legal assistance, Darren and I could prove our innocence (isn't this uncanny? Here in America—we must prove innocence?) We will gladly submit to any lie detector test, truth serum, etc. in order to prove that we did not assault anyone; we did not solicit anyone. Now that you know that we are in prison for a crime that we did not commit, I can only beg that you will do anything possible to help us. I never really believed that minority groups in this country were oppressed, but now I know better. Please, sir

Richard

Two months later, the editors received this follow-up letter:

25 August 1964
Midsize town in southeast
Pennsylvania

Dear Sirs,

Back in May my lover and I were arrested in Chester county and detained there for approximately 90 days to await trial. While we were there Richard, my lover, wrote a letter to you explaining that we had neither lawyer or ready cash to pay one. You were kind enough to get in touch with the Janus Society in Philadelphia who in turn procured for us a very good attorney that handled our case on credit. We were released without having to go through trial on a writ of haebas corpus.

At the hearing our attorney stated that the states witness is the one that should have been in our position and the judge concurred. Richard and I did not and are not pressing charges.

Thank you very much for your assistance in this case. Without your help we would probably still be awaiting trial without legal council. Please let Richard and I know the cost to you for your communication with the Janus Society so that we can send you a contribution in excess of your cost.

Thank you again, and <u>please</u> keep up your good work in the homophile movement. You and the Janus Society surely have two active supporters.

Sincerely yours,
Darren

Like the gay couple above, the writer of the following three letters believed that the criminal justice system was treating him unfairly because he was a homosexual.

20 March 1961
Wilmington, Delaware

Gentlemen:

I have just returned (March 3rd) to Wilmington from "Florida's Finest Finishing School" (Raiford State Prison, Raiford, Florida) after serving a three year sentence for the usual charge. Since my return, I have been busy doing two things: (1) looking for a job (most unsuccessful); (2) catching up on more than two years of back issues of OUR magazine.

I have reached one conclusion: IF a homosexual has a problem in finding or holding a job, then a homosexual with a prison record has the same problem multiplied a thousand-fold.

Three years ago if anyone would have told me that I would be unable to find a job it would have been unbelievable. I have a somewhat unusual work background in that I am a graduate nurse, with post-graduate work in mental health, operating room technique and surgical procedure, and have completed a two year post-graduate course in anesthesiology from one of the best schools in the country. In addition, I have completed a business management course (in prison) and am a fast and (fairly!) accurate typist. Still, no job is available in this area. I left the Jacksonville, Florida, area because I did not wish to continue the possibility of seeing anyone that I had known in prison.

Being without family, friends, or funds, I had been in contact with an experiment known locally as "Half-Way House." There was some difficulty in that "because of the nature of your crime and the fact that you are a known homosexual" I was precluded from entrance into this program. It was finally agreed that "because you are a manly homosexual and not likely to cause trouble" I would be accepted.

This place is interesting. It is a large, three story building which has room for sixteen "guests." It is fully integrated and the capacity is maintained with a waiting list. We have but two rules: NO WOMEN above the ground floor, and NO ALCOHOL. We have a constant series of interviews with social workers, psychologists, and TWO psychiatrists. Each Tuesday night we have a "House Meeting" when all the problems relative to running a place such as this are discussed and the work assignments are distributed. Each "guest" is expected to give ten hours of work each week to the house while not working and IF he finds a job, he is expected to give five hours and $10.00 per week. This is the only mention of money. Breakfast and lunch are on a "do it yourself basis" and one leaves the kitchen the way one found it. Dinner is prepared by a professional cook and is superior.

Community living such as this is an interesting departure for some of us here and I think it is a bridge that has long been needed for the man released from a prison to assist him to again resume a place in society. I do not think that it is the complete answer, or even that it would work in many places. I do know that something should be, and indeed, MUST be done for the homosexual that is finally released from an injust place; i.e. the prison.

During my prison career I was an administrative aid to the Director of Education. My work consisted of the usual correspondence, interviews with prospective students, records, and assisting the Director in obtaining his Masters Degree from Florida State University. For the first four months in prison I was not trusted to have a good job and was rejected to work in my own field. Finally, through the good works of one of the free-men instructors who was (to be kind) very sympathetic to me and to my "problem" permitted to transfer to the Department of Education.

It is unfortunate that I am not in the Los Angeles area. I feel that your Social Service Division would be interested in my case history. You might recall (by checking through your files) that I am the same individual that wrote you some three years ago about the "witch-hunts" in Key West, Florida which ended up in my receiving a three year sentence.

My work here in "Half-Way House" is in the office and I find that there is very little work to be done. I visit the employment agencies frequently and get the usual answer—"Don't call us, we'll call you"—from most of them. Therefore, I find that I have plenty of time on my hands. If you feel that a case study (or resume) would be of interest, I shall be glad to supply one. I believe you would be interested in the homosexual life as lived in the Florida State Prison (beyond belief!) and in the manner in which the average homosexual is arrested, tried, and sentenced in the State of Florida (also beyond belief).

If you have the time, I should appreciate a letter from you. Anything that I am able to do in any field outlined in this letter will be done promptly. Anything else (short of money, of which I am fresh out of) you might suggest will also be appreciated.

Incidentally, is the work field as closed in California as it seems to be here in Delaware?

Best regards to you and to the good work that you are doing. Oh yes, I should like to congratulate you on the fine magazine. As it has been more than two years since I had seen an issue (it is NOT permitted in the prison) I was greatly impressed with not only its format but with it's content. Seems MUCH improved.

Please let me know if you would like more details re the above.

Very truly yours,
Timothy

∼

24 June 1961
Midsize town in northwest
Illinois

Dear Mr. Lambert,

Please forgive me for being so remiss with my correspondence with you. It has not been that I have been so busy but many things have happened (see enclosed clippings) since my last letter to ONE magazine.

There has been a terrific scandal in Delaware and the main character (an instructor in history at the University of Delaware) has attempted to involve every person possible. As you will recall, I was released from the Florida State Prison on 3rd March and I immediately went to Wilmington, Delaware, where I had been offered a place in the program of [. . .] (a "Halfway House" sort of thing). While in Delaware I had great difficulty in obtaining a job of any type. I was precluded from returning to my own field (I am an anesthesiologist) because of the lack of a current license. Finally, I obtained a job in an office thru "Manpower, Inc." an employment agency that supplies workers by the day. This job was apparently satisfactory and I worked for more than a month without difficulty. <u>Then</u> one bright day I was called to the Security Gate of the plant and there was met by two detectives that forced me into a car (would not permit me to call my supervisor or anyone else) and hauled me off to Police Headquarters (State Police). I kept demanding to know if I were under arrest and if so, on what charge. No answer except to say that I was not under arrest; I was merely a witness and no criminal charges would be placed "at this time." After arrival at Headquarters, I was placed in a small room made of ceiling tile and there was told to wait. So, I did, and waited and waited.

Finally one of the detectives came back and started to ask me all types of questions about lower Delaware. Please remember that I had been in prison more than two years; lived in Key West more than three years before that without a single return to Delaware.

At last, out it came. [Bill Harding] (see clippings) told the police that they had no right getting rough with him because he KNEW that a State Trooper had had an affair (in uniform yet) on at least one occasion with a homosexual (me) and that they could just lay off him. This really shook up the troops; just think—one of their lily-pure picked men had stooped to having an affair with a pervert! It was just too much for them.

This, then, was the problem: they (the police) would not do anything to me if I would admit having had this affair! Having read the relevant laws of the State of Delaware very carefully before my return, I <u>knew</u> that they could do nothing with me over this case (Statute of Limitations is three years). Naturally, I said that it was all a lie. The trooper involved (Harding had even given his name) is now married and has two small children and a perfect record in the State Police. As soon as I said I did not recall the "incident" things got rougher (nothing physical—just vile talk and half-threats) and several members of the staff took turns questioning me. They simply could not (or would not) believe me when I said that I had been drunk (I have never been drunk in this country) and that just another man in uniform would never make that much impression on me. Also they could not understand that I did not ask name, rank, and serial number before throwing someone in bed.

I was very anxious to find out how I had been located and was told that they had been looking for me for three weeks. Their contact in Key West said they "understood" I had gone to Alaska (!) but finally a "friend" of mine said that I was back in Delaware and working for Manpower. That did it.

To cut this sordid tale short, the constant questioning lasted from 11:00 AM until 5:00 PM in two different locations. One of the "girls" in the office (a friend of long standing from well before I even went to Florida) had immediately gotten on a telephone and called everyone she thought might help. One of the first persons she called was the Program director of [the halfway house]. He immediately went to Police Headquarters and attempted to see me without success. All this time I kept demanding to use a telephone but this was not allowed.

At long last I was told that if I would submit to a lie detector test I would be allowed to leave. Now, for years I have had what is known as essential hypertension and when my blood pressure builds up, a sort of half halo of light appears around any bright object. Blood pressure! It must have been 300 mm by this time. I told them to run the test and get it over with. As I knew before they started my pressure was so high that a reading would be impossible (my half halo of light was two full circles by this time). Such was indeed the case. The test was completely inaccurate and it was attempted even without the blood pressure cuff. At 6:00 PM I was returned to freedom with a severe warning NOT TO MENTION THIS AFFAIR TO ANYONE!

Much to my surprise, offers of help came from all over Wilmington and a lawyer from Philadelphia phoned and said that he had a client that was interested in this "pick-up" and could he assist me in anyway? I felt that the best thing that could happen was to have the whole thing forgotten because I certainly am not going to give any information that would hurt in anyway the Trooper involved. Actually, I had "known" him over a nine months period and not for just the one time mentioned by Harding. He was a very nice person; it was fun; we both fully enjoyed our relationship so why should I now cause him to be fired from the Police in disgrace? I just won't do it, now or ever.

Immediately following all the above I received a letter from the administration of a hospital here in [. . .], Illinois, who was interested in having me join this staff. I explained that I did not have a "current" license and let it go at that. Apparently the Hospital Board thought that I had just forgotten to pay my dues or something because they offered me the position. Do I have to say that I jumped at once? So, here I am in North-west Illinois [. . .]. Fortunately, I had done my post-graduate work in Chicago so the men on their staff here are familiar with my instructors and background. I hope it works out well for me at long last.

Only one person in Delaware knows my present address. I felt that if the police were going to harass me there, they might try it here so if my location in unknown to them perhaps they will leave me alone.

Now that I have a job I should like very much to start receiving "our" magazine again. I don't remember what the subscription rate was, so if you will let me know, I'll get a check in the mail at once (a "check"? much more like a money order!) to cover same.

I have found a very nice apartment in a good section of town and so now I am busy trying to make like a housewife (widow, that would be).

I don't know how I am going to like living in a small place (15,000) like this but I am going to give it a real try. It may not be good for "social life" as there are only four low-type bars here but at least I have a job and a nice place to live and I can always hope that the happiness side of life will suddenly appear around the next corner.

I still have your questionnaire and I shall complete it and return it very soon. I shall also send you the complete story of my arrest and conviction in Key West and my prison experiences.

Best regards, Mr. Lambert, and do let me hear from you soon.

Sincerely,
Timothy

~

2 July 1961
Midsize town in northwest
Illinois

Dear Mr. Lambert,

To complete my promise made you in my letter of 24 June, here is the detailed story of my arrest and conviction:

I was chief anesthetist at [. . .] Hospital, Key West, Florida, for more than three years. Shortly after my arrival I met a sailor from one of the ships stationed in Key West and we immediately formed a good relationship. I do not think that I am effeminate in any way and this man felt much the same. I was introduced to his ship-mates, his officers, and to his brother who was serving aboard the same ship. To the best of my knowledge there was no talk about us even though he moved into my house and drove my car daily. We frequently entertained members of his crew for dinner or for general gatherings in my home.

After one and a half years he was released from the Navy to return to school. (Note: He will now leave this tale of woe but I should like to say that throughout my period of arrest and imprisonment he kept in contact with me. He is now stationed in Alaska (on missile research and development) and he has many times asked me to join him there. He has sent me several hundreds of dollars, a letter authorizing a car dealer to supply me with a new car, an unlimited gasoline credit card, and last week a TWA plane ticket from Chicago to Anchorage. I feel that any close associationship that we may reform can only hurt him due to the nature of his assignment. He also states that he has purchased a small house there and he "needs someone to be his housekeeper." I still think it would be better if we remained apart. Immediately after he left active duty he married a bar maid; had a child; lived a very unhappy life. His divorce is now final. He said that he married his wife during a drunken weekend—and this I believe.)

Following the release of the above mentioned individual his ship was transferred from Florida waters, thereby cutting all contacts with his friends.

Some weeks later while returning from Miami, I picked up a hitch-hiker who turned out to be a life-guard at the Main Station pool. He was a member of the weight-lifting Body Beautiful Club and, needless to say, I fell like a ton of bricks and was off and running. This relationship was good, too, although the temperament of the two men was as dislike [sic] as night and day. This one ([Bob]) was a very beautiful person with a truly wonderful body. He liked very much to display it and it was (for a time) a joy to buy him clothing and uniforms. This one, too, I made no secret of and even became so bold that I took him (upon invitation) to visit ranking Naval officers with whom I worked. He was referred to as "Tim's Boy" and frequently invitations would arrive which said "And bring along your Boy." This may have been because of his physical beauty (God knows it was not because of his mind!) and the women present would fawn over him and he eventually made several sexual contacts with either the wives or daughters of the officers he had met with me socially. He would tease me and ask if it upset me to know that he was out with females and it was he who became upset when I said that if he did not want a woman once in awhile I would not want him either.

Through this man I eventually met many other sailors that were stationed with him. I do not like to "cruise" bars and my contacts were always made by introduction. My home became a real gathering place for the athletics of the Navy in the area and each night would find the house full.

During this period I was appointed deputy Public Health Officer for the Port of Key West and through this appointment "met" several members of the Coast Guard Establishment and several members of the Marine Group (including the entire basketball team) stationed in Key West. I realize that the foregoing sounds terrible but actually the activity (for the large part, at least) was that of running a very good restaurant, bar, reading-writing club and all for free. Also during this period we started taking pictures (yes, the kind you think) and developed a large collection.

As you can see, I did not have homosexual (as such) friends. I was approached by a laboratory officer and along with him, his friend, a preacher, and asked if they could "visit" me. The lab officer was a real wild one (strictly "female") and the preacher would only have sexual union with another homosexual and then only in the female role. He was especially interested in big bodies with abundant hair and he immediately proposed union with me through the lab officer. After a few visits the preacher left the scene of the story. Not so the lab officer. One day when he came to visit me he found Bob (wearing a few beads of sweat) and immediately he started pawing the ground. This session broke down into a three-way split and that, to me, was that.

Also, in the meanwhile, a young sailor was visiting me that wanted to really get married, BUT, _he_ wanted to be the wife. This was too much for me on a permanent basis but when he met Bob he wanted to know if Bob would be Daddy—at least once. I asked Bob and he said he would if "I would not get angry." I was delighted! The affair was set up and it was too much for words because it also turned into a three-way parlay. Following this, there were two other occasions when three people were involved.

Approximately a year had now passed since I met Bob.

One night he came to my home and found that I had a guest, a member of the Blue Angels (the Navy crack flying team) that had "known" me the year before. Each year this flying team comes to Key West to practice in our perfect weather. This seemed to upset Bob very much and he stormed out—and away.

This did not distress me, however, because I knew he would return when he got over his mad. He did—and how.

Two weeks after the above, I had attended the International Orchid Show in Miami (yes, I _also_ raised orchids; had about 800 plants) and returned to Key West before midnight (because I had the duty at midnight). At about 1:45 AM (this was 22 February) I received a phone call which said the <u>police</u> were looking for me and that I should leave the country <u>at once</u>. The information came from an excellent source so I immediately called my top superior (a rear admiral) and told him the entire story without omitting anything. He clucked at me and advised me not to run because he was certain that it would all blow over. The next chapter happened at about noon (I was making rounds in the hospital) when I was told that two men wanted to talk to me. They were two detectives from the Sheriff's Office and they asked me to step out on the lawn with them so we could not be "overheard" (in view of the article in the newspaper the next day, this was really funny). Anyway, the crux of the matter was that I was charged with "crime against nature" with three different sailors—one of whom was Bob! (I did not know the other two by name but it turned out that one of them had been mixed up in our three way plays—with Bob— and during the entire mess "he" had kept running his hands over Bob's body and <u>insisted</u> that the lights remain on—draw your own conclusions. The other one I had never seen and certainly did not know).

    I was told that I would have to go down to the County Jail and "check-in" and that I would be released promptly. One of the detectives drove my car and they allowed me to stop by my house and take off my uniform. We got down to the Jail and I was asked for my name, age, address and telephone number. With that a guard was told: "Lock him up!" I gave a howl and was told that I would have to stay there until I produced $6,000 in cash. They would not accept a property bail (this was, you will remember on Sunday, Washington's Birthday).

    Late that afternoon "my" admiral arrived and said that even he could do nothing for me that the Navy had removed all three witnesses from Key West and he did not know how to locate them that day. He left. A few minutes later the Marine basketball team arrived (in a group) and they told me the same story: the three men had been sent from the Key West area. The following day I was visited by a pair (one from CID and one from ONI) and filled in (somewhat) on the story. Seems a fabulous faggot in Miami had been giving a party which was raided and "there were more than thirty members of the Armed Forces present in various stages of undress." Included were several from Key West. These men were told that they would <u>not</u> be prosecuted if they would inform on homosexuals in Key West and appear against them in Court! Both Bob and the other one jumped at the chance and the third one (that I <u>did</u> not know) went along. Many harsh words were exchanged at this point and I was asked about the young sailor, the lab officer, the preacher, etc. Naturally, I did not know what they were talking about and they left in a huff.

Bail was arranged and I saw my lawyer who gave me the good news that he could not handle my case (he was also a commander in the Navy) because it involved Naval personnel! Much frantic search for a lawyer. The newspaper hit the street and I appeared (front page, no less) as a combination of Bluebeard and Elmer Gantry. It seemed that I stood on a corner with a tambourine and lured poor innocent sailors in my den where they were forced into a life of sin! At this time I was informed that my connection with the [. . .] Hospital was severed permanently and all its staff members was warned to have no contact with me upon pain of dismissal.

I got in contact with a friend of mine in the Navy in Washington (by public telephone) whom I had known from World War II. "She" is still going strong and "she" said that if these three witnesses were still in the Navy "she" would find them. She did.

I was taken into Court where the charges were read against me ("- - - that you did take into your mouth the sexual organ of said witnesses and perform the detestable and abominable act of Crime Against Nature —") and, this was repeated three times! Never has anything been so upsetting to me. I pleaded "not guilty" and was told that I would be held for a jury trial. In Monroe County a judge will not hear a case where a plea of "not guilty" has been entered. Trial was set for 5th May.

The longer I waited the more panic stricken I became. I finally ended up with a lawyer who was known as a "fix" expert. His initial fee for talking to me was $300.00 with an additional $500.00 retainer. There were several other lawyers consulted (five and not one of them would risk going into court for me) and they all agreed that the best thing to do would be to change my plea to "Guilty" to escape receiving the legal statute (6 months to 20 years) on each charge. This I would not (at this time agree to do) allow.

Finally my trial date arrived. I appeared in Court (which was packed due to the newspaper stories which appeared frequently) and there was much legal hassle. The judge asked the Court Reporter if she would just turn the recording machine on and leave the room "because of the nature of this case"—and she did. I wanted to take the one to trial first that I did not know so that IF I beat his charge I would be in much better position. This was not allowed. The Navy had all their big guns there because they "wanted to make an example of this man (me) and show that conduct of this type could not be allowed in the Key West area." My fix lawyer, prior to the start of the trial had gotten another $1,000.00 and he told me to bring what cash I could get "because you might need it." While the screaming was going on, my "fixer" asked if I had $1,200.00 in cash. When I told him that I did he spoke to a prosecutor (who had been yelling about giving me 60 years in prison) and then asked for a five minute recess. It was granted. He told me that the case was hopeless and that I would be found guilty on all three charges and sent to the prison for the limit of the statute. However if I would give him $1,200.00, change my plea to guilty I would receive a total of three years. By this time I would have admitted anything to escape the thought of 60 years! The exchange was made, the plea changed, the judge lectured me ("you have been made no promises of any specific sentence or treatment, etc.") and then gave me three years. He also threw me a foul ball in that he said: "You have been sentenced on only one charge but you have entered a plea of guilty to all three. Therefore if you ever dare return to Monroe County while I am still on the bench, I shall return you to prison for the limit on the other two charges." This was not in the agreement but my lawyer said he could do nothing about it at that time. So, there I stood: convicted and facing three years in prison. My lawyer told me to do the three years and I would be allowed to return to Key West (More about this later).

I was returned to County Jail (this was 5th May) to await transportation to the Florida State Prison at Raiford, Florida (about 750 miles or more north). My treatment while in jail was excellent. The jail was new, clean, cool and the food was good and abundant. We slept four men to a cell (a total of about (I think) 20 men in the entire section[)]. Regulations were lax and they did not care who slept where as long as there was a bed for everyone! Lights went out at 10:00 PM and there was no check by the guards after this time. I was allowed private visits each night and was allowed to have anything sent in to me (with the exception of alcohol and food) that I wanted. I was really treated very well.

Finally the 9th of June arrived and I was taken (along with three other convicted felons) up to Miami. During this trip the good treatment continued (i.e. we were allowed to buy soft drinks and sandwiches, etc.) and so we arrived at Miami's Sky-Scraper County Jail.

We were taken up to (I think) the 26th floor and there jammed in a large day room which was full to over-flowing. The dirt and filth there was beyond description and the least said about the food the better.

The next morning we were taken out at about 4:00 AM for shipment to the prison. Transportation was by pick-up (I think it's called a pick-up truck) truck and my name was called and I was given a seat with the driver rather than inside on a wooden bench. So we left Miami.

There were three of these trucks that traveled as a train. During the trip (which lasted until 4:30 PM) we were allowed several "comfort stops" (right along the road in open country!) and we stopped and were given a hamburger and coke. I was also permitted to buy ice cream, candy, and cigarettes for the other men—none of which seemed to have any money. Our trip resumed and finally we passed under a large arch which said "Florida State Prison." We were driven inside the prison (which has three large wire fences around it) to a receiving building and there inside were stripped, given a brief physical examination, a shower, and a pair of cover-alls. We also had the prison regulations read to us.

We were given dinner and assignment to a bed in a huge dorm.

Here I was—a prison inmate. Date: 10th June.

I shall next send you the story of my period in prison. I believe you will find it unusual and I hope to have it to you in a week or so.

Incidentally, is this the sort of thing you had in mind? All the foregoing is true, and I should only like to point out one or two additional things:

The men with whom I was involved were all adults.

They were promised protection if they would testify against me (what actually happened to them was that my friend in Washington got Bob a dishonorable discharge and the other two received undesirable discharges on a Departmental level—this means that they can <u>never</u> be exchanged or reviewed.

I was <u>not</u> caught in any homosexual act nor did I bring any disgrace to myself or to the hospital.

Please write soon.

Sincerely,
Timothy

~

23 August 1960
Small town in central
Pennsylvania

Dear Mr. Slater,

I want to thank you for your prompt and encouraging reply to my letter. As I wrote in my letter, I was dismissed from the Army after about sixteen years service. I was accused of and pleaded guilty to several acts of homosexuality. The two fellows I had my relations with enjoyed the experience. I am sure and needless to say I did too. However, someone reported me and the two fellows got scared into making statements and I got tried and convicted. I pleaded guilty in order to avoid a lot of embarrassment for me and my friends. I was sentenced to a Dishonorable Discharge and one year at Fort Leavenworth. D.B. [Disciplinary Barracks].

The ironic thing is that several other men were guilty of similar behavior in another outfit but they were just transferred to other units. My Colonel got excited and threw the book at me but when the other fellows were accused, saner heads convinced him to use less drastic measures. Everyone was amazed at the deal I got inasmuch as I had an outstanding military record. I have the Silver Star, Purple Heart, Eleven battle stars, served in World War II and twice in Korea during combat and had outstanding units as a 1st Sergeant. My behavior was strictly non-aggressive and had no effect on my efficiency or the efficiency of my company. So Mr. A. you can see that I am still a little bit upset. I got out of the disciplinary barracks on 8 July this year. I served nine months. I actually believe that the Court Martial Board was influenced by the psychiatrist's report. He stated that the different behavior tests were inconclusive but attributed that to high I.Q. He also stated that I had homosexual tendencies (who doesn't?). Of course the idiot knew that I had entered a plea of guilty, so his statement seemed silly. Anyhow I am now out of the Army, out of a job; out of circulation and most of all I am out of my restricted addresses and all my male nude photos which I miss terribly. I either destroyed the addresses and photos in order to keep the "normal" investigators from using them as evidence against me. I could have gotten five to ten years. So I wonder if you would do me one or several favors?

I live in a very small town. 1800 population. Everyone knows everyone else's business. As far as I can find out after returning home there are no fellow and kindred souls near. Inasmuch as I just got out of the D.B. I am maybe overcautious but nine months in the Army D.B. with no contacts and no good reading or looking material I am really in a bad way. Could you give me any addresses in any of the cities where I could find friends? Pittsburgh, Pa, Johnstown or Altoona, Pa or anywhere in Pennsylvania west of Philadelphia? Gay bars, although I don't drink, clubs or anything. Also could you send me some addresses of nude photo outlets or maybe some pictures to get started again? I had remembered one male nude studio in Washington D.C. but mail was returned with "Box closed" stamped. Today I bought an English book "ManAlive." It is exciting but falls short. Do they handle the male nude on one of the pictures as shown? (who ever made posing briefs anyhow?)

So you see Mr. A. I have problems. I enjoyed reading the copy of "One" which you so generously sent. As I stated earlier in this town (95% Catholic) I couldn't risk subscribing to "One." I will have to wait until I can get a job somewhere away from here.

Perhaps Mr. A. you have been in a situation such as mine and I hope that you never will be. It is hell! I miss things so much. In the D.B. it wasn't so bad for obvious reasons but now that I am out it is pretty tough. I am glad that I am not the violent type. I can definitely control myself but I need to meet friends soon and at least get some snaps to look at.

Can you help in any way at all? I am going to stay around this town until about the 10th September so there will be quite a few lonely nights. I sure will repay you if you can do anything for me. Addresses, books, stories, pictures, anything to help me.

I promise to help regularly foster and expand the ideals as set forth in your literature.

So long.
Dan

Mental Hospitals

Since homosexuality was widely considered to be a mental illness in the 1950s and 1960s, many judges, legal experts, and psychiatrists believed that sending people convicted of homosexual crimes to mental hospitals was more humane than sending them to prisons (not unlike sending a drug offender to rehabilitation instead of prison). In practice, however, incarceration at a mental hospital was usually very similar to being in prison, and it could be much worse depending on the facility to which one was sent.

In the first letter below, a judge gave the writer a choice between spending one year in prison or 90 days' "observation" at a mental hospital. The mental hospital seemed like the logical choice. Not only was the term shorter, but the man writing the letter believed that he was going to be sent to a particular hospital in Southern California with a progressive reputation (meaning they would not try to "cure" him of his homosexuality). But for reasons beyond his control, he was sent to a different institution instead, and he quickly regretted his choice. The letter writer was an occasional *ONE* magazine contributor and volunteer.

He addressed his letter to Jim Kepner, another member of *ONE*'s staff. The letter is reprinted in its entirety to show how an arrested gay man might pass the time while being "observed" in a mental hospital in the 1950s. The correspondent filled page after dense page with intellectually astute observations about poetry, literature, film, and art. Writing this letter was a strategy for staying sane in an environment in which he was completely out of place and did not belong.

> 19 January 1955
> Atascadero, California

> Sat. 1-29-55

Dear Jim,

    I gave Bill all the dope (I had his address but forgot yours) to give you so I hope he did. I am allowed only 2 letters a week at the hospital's expense, which I've already written, so until I can get at my money, I thought I would signally [illegible] you by accumulating momentous data meanwhile.

    It is OK to send and receive mail here, by the way, should you be worried, but I don't expect you to answer unless and until you feel like it. These exercises are only to keep busy, since I am in isolation, until they are certain my T.B., arrested for 4 yrs. now and negative, is still so, by tests and by checking with previous records from L.A.

    First, I endorse (I hope I remember to) a list from memory of those items in my "library" which I think could be written up or quoted in the magazine. As you can see, nothing remarkable is listed, mostly "old-hat," but none has so far been printed there and therefore is possible material, I think. I also included some items I wanted you to see, whether printable or not, if you haven't already. I think most are already marked by turned down pages but are further identified, if possible, from very faulty memory.

    If I can get such out when (if) I leave, I'll probably attempt some writing and drawing. As you may know, I'm here for 90 days' observation, after which the court will decide what further penalty is called for. How they can be so free with my time (for only, after all, a misdemeanor) I am trying to get my attorney to determine and do something about. He, with my cousin (boss) and family, however, are just the kind of "fuzzy-minded liberals" (using H. Hoover's favorite phrase), (politically liberal only), who accept "authority" (I know one of the "psychopathic tendencies" is "rejection of authority") in any field outside their immediate area, especially in art or science, and, being, of course, disturbed no end by my "situation," have infinite hope in "Science's" miraculously bringing about the cure they are sure is indicated. So you can see I can hope for little incentive from their direction, in case I need action in this situation. Just in case Bill doesn't get the info to you, or incompletely, etc., Jan. 13 I appeared in court to hear the decision based on the recommendation of the 2 psychiatrists. The first, McGinnis, of the Co. hospital, you may have heard about. At the time of the report to the State legislature by the Langley-Porter clinic on sex legislation, he, among others, also testified. Do you remember it? According to the News account which I think I sent you, our boy, De Rivers, was also there, as usual, with his usual "recommendation": mandatory shock treatment and brain surgery for deviation (he also identified "criminal" and potentially "criminal" types by "facial characteristics," you know).[2] Maybe, whatever happens to me, I'm lucky to escape him. (Unless he's director here, or something, do you know? O irony!) Anyway, McGinnis testified for confinement of all deviates, as I remember, with no details. (Are there any, if you see the article?) My attorney promises to send me the complete reports of both gentlemen (McGinnis and Wires). Until then, I can only guess about the guy. In the interview, as I may have told you, for whatever motives, he sympathized completely with my position, called the legal situation in connection with it, unrealistic and probably unconstitutional, etc. So I can only assume he rationalized that, however unjust, until it is repealed, the law must be observed. Therefore, like most authorities I know of, he used the term "psychopathy" in a strictly legal plainly non-scientific sense (as do Lindner, Kinsey (Pomeroy), Karpman, etc.[)], i.e., that an individual failing to adapt himself to social requirements to the extent of conflicting with the law in a certain manner and area of behavior, must be "constitutionally" unable to adjust himself, and thereby is probably, from that point of view, compulsively driven, etc., and psycho. Significantly, such repetition, etc., in other areas, such as most types of non-juvenile heterosexual activity, larceny, etc., is not so considered. As you can see, and as Lindner pointed out in an exhaustive (and somewhat Marxian-oriented) analysis in "Stone Walls and Men," such a definition is strictly superficial, social, and cultural; whereas in any social context or culture, T.B., for example, is still demonstrably pathological, physically, or syphilis, etc., in one culture a form of sexual behavior, or any behavior pattern, may be normal but abnormal in another. From this, as you know, Lindner apparently progresses, in his next tome, the "Prescription," to condemning our entire cultural system as abnormal, particularly the sexual area (I quote, I believe, verbatim and not out of context, "Our society is unique and probably abnormal" sexually), and therefore the so-called psychopaths, who have not "adjusted" (Lindner's dirty word) to this abnormality, are the only healthy ones, potentially, left!

Anyway, McGinnis, from whatever motive, rendered a decision of psychopathy, I am told. From the interview, I guess further he recommended some kind of "psychotherapy" to attempt some kind (I couldn't find out what specifically) of "adjustment to society." He definitely disagrees with attempting heterosexuality, I'm sure he frowns on De Rivers' techniques, and he admitted repression of homosexuality was undesirable—so what's left? Curbing "promiscuity" (or reducing activity) involves some degree or kind of repression. Perhaps he means to teach how to become "safely schizophrenic," as a way of life, maintaining a "balance?" between homosexual drive and "sublimated" behavior??

Wires, on the other hand, you probably know, has been working with the Kinsey group at Norwalk (where he's the director).[3] Apparently, he agreed with most of the good doctor's theories and rendered his decision, in my case, of non-psychopathy. Incidentally, as I mentioned, both Pomeroy who I think is the psychologist of the Kinsey crew (if not Gebhardt) and who handled my second and recapitulative interview for them, and Wires made it absolutely clear, if there were any doubt left, about the strictly legal and non-scientific definition of psychopathy. (I know I am protesting too much, but it's a hell of a situation to find oneself in!) In this instance, the director himself admits that many of the inmates, and most of the homosexuals, at Norwalk, are by scientific, psychiatric standards, normal, and are, by Pomeroy's famous (I hope) quotation "there, as you or I would be, if found with a 16 yr. old partner." If this is so, I want to expiate upon the report given at that research meeting that night by Guy, remember? I did, and I assume everyone else did too (did you?)—accept his use of the phrase "psychopaths at Norwalk" to refer to people in need of actual psychiatric treatment. Therefore, his report on the UCLA test we took, as showing a pattern similar to the Norwalkites, would require a totally opposite interpretation, no? (that is what Pomeroy told me when, indirectly, without mentioning specific details, I mentioned a "rumor" of such a report to him, during the interview, but I didn't quite grasp the import at the time.)

You remember also I tried to find out from Guy exactly what, besides adjustment to environment, was standard to an opinion of psychotherapy in the test. He didn't specify but from Lindner and others I think it resolves itself down basically to that. Lindner goes into detail about other facts from the psychs, personality—among them various "infantile" qualities such as indiscriminate response to sexual stimulus, and immediate satisfaction and release on a physical level, without interest in the sex object, or intellectual involvement, foreplay, and what he calls "paraphernalia," etc. Now all these are exactly what Kinsey analyzes as characteristic, not of infantile, necessarily, as opposed to mature, personality, but of "lower class" as opposed to "middle or upper class" behavior! If so, again we have a very dangerous tendency of explaining basically social qualities by psychological causes.

Thus, an individual from the middle economic and educational level will behave as he does because, to oversimplify for comparison, he has, let us say, a steady job and income, money in bank, insurance, property, and therefore a future of expectancy of the continuation of such. He will therefore feel less compulsion to satisfy needs as opportunity presents itself. What he misses today, he can count on being even better able to afford (being a saving man) tomorrow, etc. Similarly, his educational background will be such as involves a certain handling of intellectual situations (relatively more so than at a lower level); he accepts the religious and moral ideas of his social context relatively more seriously, etc. (See Kinsey's chapter on Social Levels in the Male Report and a brilliant analysis and expansion of this in the paperbound book on the report, by Greenberg of Columbia U., I believe, really something). Anyway, it should be evident that, in contrast to such a middle level, the lower level individual would have an expectancy of being out of a job and income by the morrow and therefore possibly in jail for vagrancy and in any case without means of gratifying needs and pleasures. For him not to seize upon immediate, as against "delayed" satisfaction and opportunity, would be unintelligent behavior. Similarly, the generally lower educational level and less dealing with intellectual, as opposed to situational and personal, kinds of contacts, would influence his behavior correspondingly. And it is such lower class behavior (which in a middle or upper class individual might be illogical, compulsive, or escapist, because contrary to his habitual conditioning), that is legalized as "psychopathic" for the whole population.

The reality of such social classes and the differences of behavior between them I think is pretty generally conceded sociologically. I don't remember Kinsey specifying percentages here, but Herman Harvey of USC (on Psychology on TV) recently gave as sociological consensus (recent) absolute minimum proportions so:

Upper Class	5%	
Middle	45%	Total US Population
Lower	50%	

Each class was further subdivided into Upper and Lower, without figures being given. So that we have over half the population being forced into behavior set by less than half (the Upper and Lower both varying from the middle behavior), since most of the political, educational and communicational elements basically derive from the middle, and almost all the legislation. (The <u>control</u> the upper group actually exercises economically, etc., is another and, I think different question.)

Now, you know all this, or disagree, etc., but whatever truth may be in it, is certainly painfully relevant to the problem in hand, especially since, as Kinsey emphasizes, some of the worst offenses in such thinking come from psychiatric fields in our society. I think Lindner is somewhat aware of this, and Harvey. But how many more?

So much for psychotherapy! Anyway, I drew a "split decision"!

Sun. 1-30-55

Resuming, you lucky boy, you; I hope you appreciate the honor.

Well, as I said, it was a split opinion. The probation office recommended referral to a third authority, but the court, in what it itself called "legal blackmail" (joke!) allowed me the decision between a jail term and 90 days' observation at Norwalk. My lawyer said this was an advantage to me, Wires' favoring my case: the jail might involve up to 1 yr., Norwalk would probably decide to let me go free (I was not told at this point that after the observation period, the court would decide what penalty to impose further.) Very reluctantly, I agreed to both the lawyer's and probation officer's advice.

This was Thursday. I was to be moved from the Co. jail to Norwalk either Friday, or "definitely Monday." As you know, I waited 13 days instead. And instead of Norwalk, without warning, Atascadero was assigned. (Too late to contact lawyer, etc.) Now the legal situation was that I could choose jail or observation, psychopathy not being officially determined. I made my choice only on condition the commitment be to Norwalk; any other institution would have determined my choice otherwise. It therefore seems to me that something illegal is involved here. My lawyer I haven't yet heard from about this; if I do, I doubt he would do anything about it.

As yet, of course, it's too early to tell what practice or theory obtains here. Physically, it's all very expensive: new buildings, "modern architecture," all the "conveniences." To me it's too close to "1984," however. From gossip of those who have already been in such places, however dependable that is, the prospects can be damning. For example: even at Norwalk, under Wires, although this might apply only to actually psychotic patients (but I don't think so), it is assumed you have a "problem" or you wouldn't be there. If you are well-adjusted and deny any problem but the obvious legal one (or only the usual schizophrenia modern man must endure), you are "uncooperative." So you are if you disagree with the authorities in any other way, also. Since, as I've already done, you sign an agreement upon entering allowing any and all treatment the authorities shall decide necessary, excepting, it specifies in bold print, sterilization, (failure to so sign is the first sign of "uncooperation"), technically anything, from that of indefinite confinement to shock therapy to brain surgery (what else is there?), is possible. Such a realization of Huxley's Brave New World or Orwell's Big Brotherhood so soon is to me alarming. If I am unreasonably alarmed in my situation, I think others may agree that the problem of non-conformity in the sexual or social sphere is not too far removed from the political. If so, what an opportunity! (Lindner is properly alarmed, by the way, in his Prescription.)

Well, I hope there is evidence left behind that I was, I think, a tolerable but much more promising painter, and maybe (at least in verse) a possible writer. What I may be if I ever emerge is too variable for prophecy. I'd think, however, the day of fertile non-conformity is pretty much over: imagine someone like Marlowe (in the religious, political and sexual spheres he rebelled in) or that wonderful juvenile delinquent, Rimbaud, functioning untampered with in this society today.

I guess I've protested enough, especially as I'm sure you agree with me in the first place. But there is always the possibility of doubt: plain jail in this situation is tolerable, even honorable, in a way; but "commitment," even for observation! I suppose the authorities are right after all! One thing seems certain from here; return to my family will [be] impossible. They always worried that I preferred books and my own sex to sports and the female variety. In typical upper lower class reaction (lower painfully aping the middle and therefore more insistent, self-consciously, on the middle-morality), this will only prove it.

It's now after dinner, so I might as well make you sorry again you ever knew me.

Naturally, I brought nothing with me but what brain I have left (for a while). They're supposed to have a library here, of whatever kind, [but] I still don't have access to. No papers or any decent quality or quantity of magazines. So what I remember of the Genet poem I've resumed working on (translation). I've been at it about a year now, or more; out of 29 stanzas of 4 lines each, I've gotten six down somewhat decently. These I've reworked over and over (the possible variations, subtleties of sense and form are seemingly almost infinite and quite a problem.) The greater refinement the farther remove, possibly, from the original material. Admirable as I think that original, I now see that, for my command of the language, too great formal subtlety is not among its outstanding qualities. Thus, one of my conscious considerations right now, in verse (if not prose), is avoidance of repetition in expression (unless intentional, of course). While I realize this is a virtue only in certain styles of writing, and Genet's may not be one, it is a necessity to me at this stage. So here I am with results almost too smooth for the vigor I feel in Genet and I am becoming discouraged about the whole thing. Besides, I want to do my own, but do not feel free to handle material here I might require for the kind of thing I want to do.

Tough no?

To show how much of a pest I can really be (if you've read this far by now, you probably will have less time of your own than when on the magazine), what do you think, if you can of getting John Schmitz's address for me (the "Voices" film guy)? This may only prove my "alienation from reality," etc. but you know I have always been pretty naïve in personal relations, as to when to stop in such matters. I have, however, rewritten part of a "scenario" I've long considered for a 16mm thing on the Genet (again!) I'm sure that's all that Schmitz needs right now, but if I ever got out, I know I'll never get the time or nerve again to do it, so I thought I'd try. The theory of the film is my own derivation from Cocteau's esthetic and I don't know how sympathetic Schmitz may be to such, not having been able to see his "Voices." The idea of the particular sequence I have in mind was first suggested by a friend (hetero) who was doing modest 16mm work of his own in N.J. Very liberal in attitude on art and sex, he begged me for ideas and my work on the Genet suggested a visual realization of such (I admit being that lazy both for material (Genet) and technique (Cocteau)). I do think the material and process I suggested very practical and inexpensive for such small resources. The particular form the sequence took was obviously influenced by what my friend had on hand: a young soldier from Ft. Dix near him, a horse on an isolated farm, his wife and that's all. The only difficulty to my inexperienced self is the chief virtue (if any) of the idea: as close and absolute a photographic control, frame by frame, of every visual detail—tonal contrast, texture, composition, etc.—as possible. Without, it is hoped, too badly impeding motion and rhythm. Anyway, Cocteau's method, especially in the Bloody Poet, of analyzing motion, from the frank still shot through slow-motion through normal speed to high speed motion, varied by reverse action, and by negative printing, seems to me formally impressive. And not only formally. Notice his use of the still, plastically composed, as climactic, or emphatic, punctuation at the end of a sequence (not only symbolically), and as a sort of apotheosis (the last arrangement of the reclining Muse, among her limbs and draperies, in the Poet, or the rather strained attempt at such in the final scene of Eternal Return—the two lovers side by side in a great temple (from a humble fishing shack.))

Well, the N.J. friend never got around to doing the amount of work he contemplated. Besides, an alienation of affection occurred—although "tolerant," he proved not sufficiently so when I very stupidly tried to demonstrate my theory to him. To do so I only suggested it was likely he, like most heteros, had repressed a homo. potential in himself, etc. This he must have been aware of as standard psychoanalytic theory but for me to associate the possibility with himself (whom I judge as a pretty overstrenuous imitation of conventional heterosexuality—nobody is that typical), was stretching friendship too far. (Maybe his marriage, to a German girl about 10 years older than himself, was causing him doubt about the success of his imitation). Anyway, as all things must—etc. So here I am with a brand new (slightly used, rather!) scenario in hand—. If you don't have Schmitz's address, does One? Don't worry too much. I probably won't ever get around to doing anything about it, if I did have the address.

Mon. 1-31-55

Here it is Monday, tomorrow will be a week here. 11 weeks to go! If I'm not psycho now, I may be by then. (I say 11 weeks to go, then there is the sentencing—for how long? In a purely criminal case, there is a limit for misdemeanors, but if they judge me socially menacing, mentally, I suppose the commitment can be indefinite? It looks to me that anyone admittedly a "confirmed" and "active" homo can be so declared!) (O no? This is California, chum.)

I got to thinking about the "tolerable and promising" painter boast, above, and then considered the examples you have thereof. I'm sure you appreciate the honor bestowed by my concern for your opinion, etc., but I must repeat again, please do not judge thereby. As I recall, there are only 2 small oils anywhere near finished and exhibitable in the bunch—the small baseball pitcher and the small sailor head (H.C.), not the flower-in-the-ear one. All the others are mere tentative, unfinished essays and doodles I never got around to throwing away. Also all the notebook material (some of the matted (framed) w. colors are somewhat decent). I like to think "even Rembrandt" (as the saying might go) could not be estimated on the things he was lucky enough to throw away before being rendered unable to. (Besides, canvas is expensive, and if I never got up the nerve as contemplated, to point over such, I probably could not just throw them anyway. You don't know how lucky you are to be a writer. Equipment: 1 pen, some paper, and you're free to flee. Consider my equipment and the canvasses, etc., and then remember I was formerly a sculptor (stone, yet), and realize my need to get up and go.)

Well, while I'm at it, still bored, I might as well continue. (Just shaved.) Seriously, although I know such may be taken (again!) as psychopathic symptom, (forgive me, please), I do think some of the w. colors the best done in the country so far, and I include Marin and Homer and Eakins (the latter two of whom are mostly technically outstanding only). Some of the best of Don[g] Kingman are superb compositionally while [Charles] Burchfield I think too vulgarly "aesthetic." Some of Cezanne's better, more abstract washes, and possibly some early Chinese things (which I think somewhat and somehow related to his) are, frankly, all I know on a par with yours truly's. Now in self-defense to what I am sure is an almost inevitable objection from you, I will pull the old bromide (still, I think, true) that essentially "literary" values (or pictorial values influenced by literary conceptions on a basic, not superficial, level) are pretty difficult to separate from what I call "purely (shall we say) visual" values, in our culture. By that I mean that our thinking in our kind of "literate" society is apt to influence, subconsciously and by reflex action almost, our thinking in other fields, without a tradition of visual art, such as the other, non–Anglo-Saxon cultures have underlying and even predating their periods of more "intellectual" development—the abstract disciplines of mathematics, science and developed "atypical" prose. I suppose this will appear an easy excuse and defense against almost any criticism, but it is still an important possibility to allow for, I think. (I think John Dewey, in his Barnes patronized period, did some good thinking on the subject. Do you know his writings on aesthetics? I don't, too well, but I do know they emphasize the different kinds of intelligence (abstract, literary, plastic) in a way I consider pretty thorough and logical.)

Have you gotten around yet to Hart Crane's letters? I hope you will. Not only is he a hero of mine, on several levels (our greatest after Whitman, and maybe not too far "after," either—you can have Eliot (T. S.) with all his admitted purely historical importance, ditto Pound, whom I like a little more), but he has much to say of relevance to us there—and for you, his sojourn in Mexico should be especially fascinating. Let me know, huh?

How about Hadrian's Memoirs (and Rome and a Villa [by Eleanor Clark])? I know if I keep this thing up, if you do not read it through, struggling through the hen-tracks, you'd have little time left for reading anything else.

Have you seen the Italian "Romeo" film yet? If so, what? I know the director, Castillani (no?), is highly thought of. How was the poetry read? I don't know if I'll be in a position to see "Picnic," "Rose Tattoo," or "I am a Camera" when they come out. But such a harvest is maybe significant, no? So many at once. (You know about Inge (Picnic), I suppose?) In Tattoo, how can Magnini fail to impress, even in Hollywood. Ben Cooper is physically, anyway, appropriate for the sailor. But Burt Lancaster, even dyed brunette, as a Sicilian? His height is a factor too. From the play, although his virility is emphasized, one imagines the character as small and compact, even shorter than the Magnini character. (If they make him speak in a J. Carroll Naish "Italian accent" now—!)

Speaking of the Italian "Romeo," do you know the several reviews Agee did of the Olivier "Henry V" when he was reviewer for either the New Republic or Nation? I think I have at least 2 issues containing such among the stuff you have. (He is rhapsodically enthusiastic). Also one or two columns on Chaplin's Verdoux, fiercely defensive (that I don't think I have).

While I'm at it still, if you've not already found them, there are several copies of what was that Fleur Cowles' magazine of several years ago? Flair? Anyway, you will note a long article by Genet, mostly non-critically "poetic," a sort or mutual admiration society's—one sided—contribution, on Leonora [real name is Leonor] Fini, with a couple repros, very interesting, at least for me, searching as I am for such treatment of such material. An article by Proust's housekeeper, I believe, with photos, on Proust. And the first printing I know of T. Williams' "Resemblance Between Violin Case and Coffin," that I think is in "Hard Candy" and you read there. Not bad, no?

Well, I just had supper, after finishing the above and swearing by Priapus (my special deity) to leave you alone for at least the rest of today. I am still on my scenario kick, however, and was wondering about the attempts I am sure you've made in that direction—imagining naively they would be very sober, clear, expository (of some theory, formal or dramatic) (or political), etc. (Scenarios, that is). Because believe it or not, my taste runs in that direction (toward sobriety, clarity, and at least formal exposition and analysis—mostly, I suppose, in compensation for qualities I lack). Therefore, the worst excesses of "romanticism": Wagner, Dali's ptgs (not drawings), Richter's films, etc. I condemn and try to be impartial about those qualities in works I otherwise admire, that are admirable in spite of such qualities—such as the phoney further of "uncooperation," etc. Anyway, you see how I can end up here indefinitely. The courts apparently depend entirely on the hospital's recommendations and the rumors I've heard indirectly from patients (being isolated from direct contact), again, however, dependably, seem to indicate a "playing safe" policy and "protecting society" at the expense of the individual. Naturally, I am allowing for the possibility my case may turn out less drastically but I am beginning to appreciate more readily the poignancy of Kafka's "Trial" (do you know it?)

Everyday, outside my window, sheriff's cars drive up with more "incorrigibles." I wonder what the quota is here? At the rate I judge, I don't think mass production of the conformists is achieved yet but nothing is beyond "American efficiency;" give them time.

Last night, announced on the intercom, tryouts for a production by patients of—guess what—Mr. Roberts! Also something about a "music appreciation" class, basketball tryouts, etc. As an isolation and observation case, of course, should I want to, I couldn't indulge. I do wish though individual radios were allowed. Somebody, somewhere, was playing Mozart and reminded me of what I'm missing.

Wed. 2-2-55

I gave you a break, I think, yesterday and kept my trap shut. Hope you appreciate same. (No, I've just rechecked and seen I did write yesterday.) How is yourself? And the ulcers? Still on the capsule diet? Reminding me you have your own troubles. And here I am assuming the situation may have bettered a little between you and the magazine. At least, not worsened, I hope? I'm curious if they printed, or plan to, the 2 things I submitted (a poem (old but innocuous) and the book review of Hadrian). I asked Bill and haven't yet heard from him, and may never; and he's supposed to send me your address, so you (o fortunate!) may never get this. I do want to know if they'll print my things, though, first, because I understand and hope (correctly?) I'd be given a subscription renewal in payment (am I right?) and secondly, because it will influence my enthusiasm for submitting others. I have a couple already tentatively written and several more contemplated, pending such information.

Fri 2-4-55

This time I really did spare you, yesterday. Nice of me, no?

Still nothing from Bill, so I guess you won't get this, but at least it is still a device of confession, etc., for me, so I might as well continue. Rereading all the above, however, reminds [me] of how, among other things, its self-absorption might strike you. Also, its "name-dropping" (or "idea dropping") of which you complained to me in connection with Gerald Heard. I suppose this tendency may be somewhat abnormally in evidence, right now, as a reassurance, at least to myself, of intellectual probity, although I know very well, it is logical coherence and especially "mature," as opposed to "infantile," thinking, that are standard in the situation (that just such display may seem indicative of "immature" exhibitionism, etc.) O well!

Now, verse No. 9 of the Genet. No, am not that fast a worker. As you'll guess parts of the poem have been half or tentatively outlined for a year. This is merely the finishing touches stage.

Do you remember the preface in "Window" magazine that I lent you, of Sartre's comment on Genet's poetry? Sartre's preference for "opaque," as against "didactic," verse? Well, Genet's certainly is, to its glory, and I wanted to bring this up because Sartre is certainly, in all his stuff I've read (novels and essays (no verse yet)), didactic and demonstrative, but an extraordinary perceptiveness and taste, I think, make him one of the greatest critics (no, I will say the best I've read, including Shaw) (forgiving that forward to the Genet plays we read). (You should read his essay on antisemitism and that part of "Intimacy" dealing with a similar subject. Devastating.) So that when I think he talks of limiting such a tendency to its proper medium and style (certain expository prose), you can respect his opinion more readily, perhaps, than someone else's. He would be referring then to that difference in <u>kind</u> of intelligence that I have harangued about before.

Personally, I think I tend to the didactic type myself but I share others' opinions on the legitimacy of such tendency for certain types of verse, such as S. Johnson's now returning to favor, or Pope's, or Milton's, on a certain level. So I am particularly wary, I think, of what I judge misuse of "opacity" in verse, as I am what I consider "romanticism" (sentimentality, etc. too) in any art. But its true and proper usage (Shakespeare, of course, Rimbaud, Dylan Thomas) (— Auden I think essentially didactic) I can respect and envy (and I think occasionally achieve myself).

However true it is of all such expression, I think it may be true of some at least, that apparent "opacity" may be only tremendously condensed "exposition." Take a line from this Genet. It's pretty corny to say of a love object, "Your voice is sweet," which is roughly a prosaic expansion of the idea. Expanding into verse expression of the kind discussed, you proceed to simile, still as equally a prose as a verse form, such as "Your voice is like honey"; thence to relatively stronger a verse form, the metaphor, in which the comparison, indicated explicitly by "like" in the simile, is made directly, more briefly, as "Your voice <u>is</u> honey." Still readily plain to everyone (no one likely to take such literally). Now, it is still easy to proceed from this to the next, but the process should exemplify more "opaque" examples also like "Bees go to steal your honey of echoes" (my rendering, pretty literally, of Genet's line). (Aside from meaning, here, of course, the possibly even more important formal quality emerges—beyond the rich semantic sense of the phrase, in the French, the phonetic, accentual, etc. qualities are superlative, I think: "Va l'abielle roler de miel de leus échos.")

All of which you probably agree with. But immediately I am struck with the theory of cinema of Cocteau (in Poet, especially) and (I guess) [Kenneth] Anger, which I interpret as an almost direct (and therefore literary, cinematically impure?) transposition of this process from poetry to film. Instead of tracing the development, or explaining it, from "prose meaning" to "verse condensation" (or "image"), the image itself is directly offered, without introduction, to the observer. (Would an image, or brief sequence, flashed on the screen, of bees gathering honey—in context of praise of love object, as in poem—be as clearly* and acceptably "opaque" as Genet's line is?) Anyway, that's my justification of many "unsuccessfully symbolic" images in the Poet, although of course many others remain unrealized, or inadequate.

And now comes the inevitable. That is what I intended in my scenario too. Here, of course, the images are already given by the poem; how to realize them on film is the fun of the whole thing. As in the "Poet," I think greater "reality" (and thereby "truer poetry) is achieved as a result of technical and material limitations, judicially employed. The smooth (slick?) precision, technically, of Orphée, compared to the Poet, is almost, I think, a disadvantage to my view. While in Poet, the idea or image is dragged through the material (paraphernalia, medium), accumulating all sorts of appending and fertilizing "debris," (how striking appear constantly the unexpected solutions to seemingly unpromising situations!), Orphée perhaps, as a

---

(*I see the irony here—clearly "opaque"!)

virtue of its particular style ("speedy," "thriller" technique), moves so rapidly and efficiently from one image to the next that practically no "drag" or accumulation can follow (it is all "story"—almost, or at least apparently so). Am I clear? Anyway, at this stage of my "development," I certainly do lack technical and material free, so that I am interested in the Poet style more than in that of Orphée.

What do you know. Actually a letter from Bill. With your address, so I'm finally blessing you with all this. Can you forgive me?

I'll try to write more later (unless I wise up by then). All the best.
                                                                Cyrus
PS Bill says (dependably?) the review (2 books on Hadrian) is "going ahead, the poem not." Milennium! (Etc.)

Like the previous letter, the following three letters concern a young man sentenced to a mental hospital after being arrested for homosexual activity. His case involved a minor, earning him the classification "criminal sexual psychopath." The correspondent was younger than 21 himself at the time; the two men's ages were probably only a few years apart. Whatever the hospital's plans were for him, he had no intention of "straightening" out. Upon his release, he planned to move to Los Angeles, where he might find a more vibrant gay community, or to Illinois, the one state in the country where homosexuality was legal at the time.

∼

                                                    23 June 1964
                                                    Westville, Indiana
Dear Sir—

I have recently acquired a copy of "One" for March, 1964. Your mention of the Social Service Division came to my attention. Will you please forward this letter to the person or agency you feel is best suited for me.

I am a "patient" at the Norman Beatty State Hospital (State of Indiana). I am here as a homosexual, and legally classified as a Criminal Sexual Psychopath (C.S.P.)

The fact that I am a homosexual does not embarrass me, nor am I particularly proud of my alleged "pathological" condition. This factor has existed in my life since a very young age; I am not aware of living in any other manner, nor do I feel that I care to live otherwise, however, regardless of my personal opinions, I am obliged by state law to remain here "until such time that the psychosis has been permanently removed."

Let me relate the chronology of my case to you. Previously I worked for the [. . .], Indiana Bus Station as a night auditor. While employed there, I met a young man with whom I became very attached. Unfortunately, the relationship was very one sided, unknown at first to me. Because of various circumstances, which I shall relate to you later, should you be interested, the young man, (a minor by the way), revealed our relationship to his parents who in turn notified the police. Exactly one year ago, on 6-22-63, the [. . .] Police Dept. registered me and took me to [. . .], Indiana, the county jail to await trial. The trial came in October of the same year, and I was committed for "observation" to the hospital. In December, the "observation" was finished, and I was returned to [the county jail] to await regular commitment. Regular commitment came on February 14, 1964. As of that date, I must spend a minimum of two years and a maximum of life here at the hospital. Is it necessary to relate my experiences at the county jail? I have never in my life been a prostitute, either by force or by choice. At jail I was subjected to all sorts of humiliating and in some cases, terrifying experiences.

A few details about me—

I am 21 years old, my birthday is Sept. 24.

I am a H.S. graduate, in 1961 from the [. . .], Indiana school system.

I lived for 1½ years in Chicago, near-north. While living in Chicago I worked for the Chicago Electric Co. and the B & O Railroad as an auditor and clerk. I was discharged from each of these positions when my sexual habits were known. In [. . .], I worked for 9 months at the Bus Station before my arrest. My hobbies include playing the piano and organ, (not very well) and collecting records. My collection of 850 L.P. classical records was removed to God-knows-where-when I was arrested.

Here at the "hospital" (really!!) I have been assigned to work in the laundry. In my spare time, I go to a psycho-therapist 3 hours per week. I also play the organ for the Catholic Mass on Sunday, and occasionally for the protestant services. My religion is Unitarian; I am a member of the Preston Bradley's Peoples Church, Chicago.

How can you be of help to me? I believe that with the proper legal counsel, I would not be here. I believe that with the proper legal counsel at this time I could be dismissed. I must clarify one important point at this time. I am unable to pay for any services at this time; I will very gratefully pay for any services you are able to render me when I am able to do so. My desire is to move to California, around the L.A. area.

I would also desire to have literature from "One" sent to me, however this is impossible because of censoring of the mail. This letter is being mailed to you by a relative who visits me. When you write to me, please do so through her.

I hope that you will be able to help me. If you desire to contact me, please do so according to the procedure as follows:

Through the mail: Please write to [. . .]

Please mark envelope—"Personal"

"Please Hold for Pickup"

Please use plain envelope.

If you desire to have someone in this area contact me personally:

Please visit—Mon—Tues—Thurs—Fri—2:00 PM-4:00 PM

Sign visitors register with name and in relationship space—"Friend"

I realize that I have no right to ask that you help me without any charge. If you feel that you can be of no help to me please let me know by mail at the above address. If you wish to help, please write the above address and let me know when you intend to visit.

This is necessary for me to know when to expect you.

Thank you for your help.

Yours, in the Brotherhood,
Warren

P.S. [. . .]

The hospital phone number is [. . .]. I <u>am not allowed</u> to talk by phone. Call if you wish additional details from hospital personnel.

22 November 1964
Westville, Indiana

Dear Mr. Slater—

I have just now received the October, 1964 issue of "One," with your excellent editorial and appeal for funds.

I am in the State of Indiana Mental Hospital, "being cured" of my homosexuality among other things. I would not be here today if I had not been so gullible to the claims of various public officials, "We want to help."

Needless to say, "One" magazine is strictly contraband here. I definitely can not receive it through the mail, which is censored, and so must rely on my outside contact to bring them to me. Hence, they are about 2 months late arriving, since my contact lives in Chicago and cannot visit often. I owe a debt of thanks to you for having established this contact for me through Social Service Division a few months ago. He has visited several times, and is at present working on some legal aspects that may get me out of here. A homosexual employee of this hospital is also doing what he can to make necessary outside arrangements.

I am enclosing my cigarette and coffee money for one week as an answer to your request for funds. I will not go into the details of the "Wheeler-dealer" tactics I had to use to obtain the funds in cash, since the "patient's" canteen funds are usually paper transactions, handled on the bookkeeping records only. This amount is all the state "who is trying to help me" allows me to keep.

Will you print this letter in your "Letters" column as a message to all those in circumstances such as mine. Do not give up. I have not, and am not about to do so. Good luck to you in your efforts.

Sincerely yours,
Warren

Please!! If you use any of the material herein, please delete reference to [. . .], Chicago, State of Indiana, and homosexual employee, as well as my name and initials. If you care to answer personally, please do not use a return address, and be very general in the content, writing to the address below. Thank you!

~

23 August 1964
Chicago, Illinois

Dr. W. Dorr Legg
[. . .]

Now onto Mr. Robert Gregory's letter to me of August 13, 1964.

I visited [Warren] 22nd August for about two and a half hours. His grandmother, Mrs. [. . .] hadn't brought him my letter yet, so I was a bit of a surprise to him. He appears to be genuine, very intelligent, and worth any efforts to help him. He did all the talking and to the best of my memory related the following story. He was employed for the [. . .], Ind. Greyhound [bus station] as night clerk. Two acquaintances of his (the minor referred to in the enclosed letter) were drunk this particular night horsing around the depot. So as not to have to tell them to leave, Warren went out for coffee after locking up. While out they broke in taking $800. He called the police telling them about the money being stolen. A few days later two detectives came in to take him to the police station without naming a charge or having a warrant. He went with them on account of the scene being created. Upon arrival he was handed a typed confession and told to sign it. It said to the effect:

1. Do you know "such-and-such" (the minor)? Yes.
2. Did you commit sodomy with him? Yes
3. Did you take the $800. Yes

They forced him to sign, although he did get them to change the third question to no. At no time was he permitted to call a lawyer. He was jailed. Still under 21 years old at the time himself. Later on the charges concerning the $800 were dropped since the boy gave back the money working out some deal with the police so as not to have to go back to the reformatory where he was on probation from. So the whole business presumably was crooked depending on who could pay off the judge, police, etc. At his trial he wasn't permitted to plead not guilty or for that matter, say anything. He has another year to go at the hospital depending more or less on their whims whether or not they feel he will repeat his offense (homosexuality) and go straight. I ask him what could be done to help him. He said to obtain a lawyer to reverse the illegal records, etc.

He said he'd like to live in Illinois after getting out of there. And to make it his mission to warn others of falling into the same traps. He asked that if you write to him to send it to me for forwarding. Also if I would come to see him again; I said that I would.

That about covers it for this time.

With warm regards,
Charles

P.S. Your editorial on the Life Magazine article was very good.

The following letter, written by a young African-American man in New Jersey, tells a remarkable saga. The correspondent fell deeply in love with his pastor. They had a passionate affair. Then the pastor broke it off, explaining that he was reuniting with his wife. The letter writer, in response, attempted suicide and his mother committed him to a mental hospital.[4]

29 January 1964
Midsize town in northern
New Jersey

[Cover Letter]

Dear Sir:

I have been male born. I was raped at the age of 7. I didn't know what the act was call. Later I grew up and read lots of books etc. I let a person try the act with me wance since then. But I jump up and ran. I have many girl friends. I don't twist or make a fool of myself. I was and honored graduate of 61. I am the type of person who loves homosexuals. But will only play the male role. I met a person and I just didn't no love could be that way. I would like to join your organization. Here is the story, I write. I told my Mother, which was wrong I was in love with this person. Since I am out once a year. I am Lonely I am Lt. Complextion. I can't love colored male anymore, but I will play male with any other race. I am afraid if I don't find someone or if I can't, I will try and kill myself again. My Mother humiliates me and now we have terrible arguments. I had lots of bills to pay. Please answer this letter quickly as possible. She threatens to call the law on me because we have such arguments. She doesn't want me to bring home no friends, I can't talk to no one unless she knows and likes the person[—]women of 65 or 75[.] So if you think you can help me please do. Here is some pictures of me and my story.

                        Sincerely
                        Donny

                Main Letter

        Love Died in My Heart The Night I Died
        No' No Let Me Die. Why I wanted to die?

    All I ever wanted out of life was to be loved, have who I wanted. And above all understood above that was my crave. Yes I fell in love at first site. Being young and nice looking for my age. I learned fast I could charm the birds out of the trees. All of this brought me heart broke. To live with the rest of my life. Trey was a preacher I knew that he was gay from the start just to look at him. I am not a homosexual I just happen to be young and loved to find out everything was to be known. In the big city of Atlantic City, New Jersey. Now in the town I thought I would try out male postitution. So I watched wow every move he made in the sermon, it was pure lure sex. I was still in high school at the time. I came from Richmond V.A. at that time only to work the summer through. After that Sunday I only wanted one talk with Rev Trey to see what it would be like. So I kept the program with his name on it. So I had to soon leave for school in Richmond so I said good-by to all a deathless summer. Soon it was summer again and I was an honor graduate. I returned to new Jersey I had forgotten all about Trey. I am a natural male and I dont know what on earth came over me. One day as I was at work a tall dark guy looked at me in the department store where I was standing, and turned up his noise [sic] at me. Well I said to myself that's a boot to you. Later as I was going down stairs that evening he looked back over his shoulder and said Hi. I looked at him sartically how do you do sir I replied? I knew that from the look on his face he was embarrassed. So I soon got ready to go on home from a hard day. I never saw the guy anymore so as I was coming home one day, some one yelled at me. Hey' say you still work at Greenes? I turned a round and I started to curse him out. But I stopped . . . he said pardon me for inturpting you so rudely but you still work at greenes. Why yes whats wrong with it? Oh nothing I quit. Why did you I asked. The work was to hard and it didn't pay enough. I am sorry I called out so loud. Well I said you were lucky but I guess its ok. When I saw you I said to myself their goes look like a nice intelligent young man. I think maybe I could be friends with. So you think I am nice do you. Well thanks for that much. Really I said you don't know me. I am the type who loves to Live fast, Love fast and die fast. Oh are you from New York now? No but I always wanted to live their. So I see. I have lived their but I dont like it that much I love to party. Oh by the way my name is Robert. Whats yours? Donny I replied evenly. Really I havent lived here long. Well how do you like our town. Well it stinks out loud like all the rest I guess, we both laughed. I like New York better, Why because their is where all of the happings is. I can run get losted in the crowd. Run from one pair of arms to the next ones. I see that you are sort of like myself. Come up to the house sometimes. Well ok I guess. Because I am gay are you. I wasnt hip to this talk so I said I suppose so. I went and knocked on the door. He came down and I thought that maybe their was a girl or mother around. So I said you live here all alone? Yes a friend of mine and I. Then I caught the message so I played dome to learn what it was all about. I got to fix supper for my friend. Then a light old looking guy with thick mustaches came in. Oh Freddie I want you to meet a friend I work with donny. So like whise I said hi. I didnt know Robert played to role of the wife, and Freddie the husband. So we talked right on so after quite sometime I got up and walked behinde Robert and started to try out this thing. Child' no thats my friend in their. Oh I am sorry I said. That's all right I will forget it. I dont cut out on him. Well I guess I had better be going. No child you need'nt rush. I will help you find a nice friend. The next day on my way home from lunch here Robert called hi child. Hello I replied I must keep this new mix up I am in away from my mother. Then I would go to Roberts house to find out more about this buniees. So this evening I dressed extra carefully. So I went to Roberts house and he said chile I am taking you to meet some more of the sassies. So I went on to see what it was like. I went to this house then

the first little cheep Bright skin creep was named Johnny. I Thought
the kid was nice at first. The[n] I met bart who was the wife of Ralph.
He was dark short hair and nice looking. Then they begain to put on
the act. So since Ralph was the man well I talked to him. So I learned
Ralph was the panist in the church and this notorious Johnny was a
hair dresser at the beauty solon. So its about 1 oclock in the morning
when I went home and went to bed. I met dis[as]ter with mother the
next Moring. Youd better come home and stop staying out so late at
night she warned. Ah rats I said to myself I am a big boy now. So as
time went by he finally took me to the man I wanted to meet. But to
me surprise I didnt recognize him. Then I met Trey, Richard was their
also. But Trey was Gay and richard was gay. But Brent was supposed
to be going with trey. But Trey only wanted to play and tease him.
Also Michael was going with trey my I thought these gays aint worth a
dime a dozen. A spanish guy was living at treys to. But those spanish
will do anything and want to still be called a man. So further in the
small conversation Trey said yes I preach. You mean you preach at
Temple? Yes I am the assistant pastor. Well at last I said to myself. So
I left treys and went to Chucks. Chuck was another gay who lived all
by himself. He was tall and dark. A very nice person you wouldnt
want to meet a nicer person as a gay being a gentleman. He liked art
such as Mexican pictures and hats and stuff like that. So that is how it
all begain. So the next Sunday Robert came by for me I was busy
putting on my clothes to go out. So I went to church with him and
came back. I went home about ten oclock their was a knocking at the
door. Hi child I came to get you to carry this money with me to treys
house. I started putting on my clothes rapidly. Child don't hurry take
your time. Then he said to my unckle you sure have some dreamy
eyes. My unckle only smiled. You will take us to Treys house? My
Unckle said maybe sometimes. Well I am available at all times. Let's
be going I replied before he gave his self away. Look I said when I got
him out in the streets you are starting something now. Child I will
always keep a spare cause I dont never know what might happen.
Well I said he dont like no dam gays. Well I was only teasing I didn't
mean no harm. So that night I went back to Treys house. I started
teasing he said Donny to my surprise I thought that you were quiet.
Oh come on trey you can think of a better one than that. So Robert
said lets go. Oh I will be on later I replied. I was really enjoying the
company of Trey. So when Robert left I told Trey the trick that he
tried. So the next Sunday I went to church as usual but I never went
to Roberts house anymore. Because I knew his kind three cents on
the market. So that next Sunday he came up to me whats the matter I

havent seen you all week. Oh I was tired I lied thought I had better get some rest. So I brushed him off lightly. I will never know what promp me but I went to Treys house. Then I met the guy who was going with Richard his name was Desmond. I knew Desmond but I never knew he liked gays. So their was always laughter and lots of fun whenever I was around or Desmond. Then that night Trey got on the bed and laid down. So I will never know what got into me but I went and laid beside him. I didnt love him I only wanted to exprince and see what it was like. So all of the gays came to his house as a meeting place. I later met tucker He was dark small and in the service but came home every night. Tucker was a nice friend to me he was gay but we had a broth[er]ly way about each other. So later Trey turned on his back then I begain to cress him and kiss him madely. Then some one walked in. It was the spanish guy Alberto. No Donny please dont some time when Alberto and no one is around. I see you stop playing round and means business. So one day I caught him alone and I made loved to him with a passion that I never knew I possed. Lots of men started coming round. But finally one night I became angry. And cursed him out, Look Donny I didnt tell them to come here. So one night the old flame he used to love came Emmanuel. But Trey pretended to be unhappy. So later on in the year things begain to work out. I often told my mother I was going out of town. And she fussed I had to be carefully about Trey because although he was a minister, and was married but wife left him. I wanted to make everything just right. So one night we went to a party even all gays from everywhere was their. Something happen that night I will never know what it was though. While the music played I got close to him and let that charm that I possed fell. It did the trick too I knew from that moment on something happened to me. When we got home that night I practically loved him all night long. How can you explain something like this. Soon it was xmus and I had to meet his family. He was empressed so was all of the rest of them. So after xmus I always stop by to find out how he was and come back later. I went and to my surprise in the chair laying was a spanish boy name Gustavo. I then realized how much I loved him. [S]o good thing Gustavo worked day and night. And that made trey mine anyhow. What the hell is his I asked Trey by himself. I knew him before you and I didn't want to take him in but he had no place to stay. So I made sexual relation to Trey sometimes for spite. So I had a girl friend in New York als[o] Gustavo. Gustavo was never home on a Saturday night only came Sunday night about 11 thirty. So I noticed gustavo. Trey liked him but he was in love with this Spanish girl and I could tell. So one day Gustavo left took all his clothes and went. Trey liked him for only looks but when it came to the bed and talking while dressed he didn't stand a chance. The[n] Trey promised me he would love me always no matter what. But I always told him I dont believe it and that it wont last. I was too beautiful. I gave up my girl friend and the daughter she bore me for him. When we went to the movies the drive in of course. We held hands. I reposed his body with over powering love. This was Saturday mother was why don't you go out with your unckle this and that. You are hanging out with a bunch of no goods. I liked my mother She didnt like my girl anymore and didnt want me to go to New York. So I guess I made my vows no one will stop me. I went to Treys that evening. This is for you darling. An engagement wedding band. Donny I love you Donny pleas[e]. I am going back to my wife you know that. But I will see you, ho god it's a beauty. Take it back and get your money out of it. No I shall keep it regardless to rem[em]ber you. We went to East Orange that night. Our supposed to be wedding night. When we returned home Richard was jelous of Trey and I. We went to bed as usually. So it cracked, and sque[a]ked, while we made love [. . .]. Then all of a sudden Richard ran in the room he slammed that door. No one slamed no door Richard. Well I have to get my durn rest, because I have to work in the morning. Look here dam punk I said Trey had gone to the bathroom. You are just jealous of Trey because you used to go with him and now I do. You can have his name if you want to but I have his heart. No that's no[t] it. I havent touched him since you all started. Then he turned and went started with Trey. Then Trey and I was alone. We went to the park together and everything any normal person could think of.

    I shall never forget Easter sunday. We went to the park. Seem as if the sun said to us its here, so devine and beautifully. So when we returned home I said promise me you will never leave me. And that their will be no one els[e]. I promise he replied in his soft voice. So I came home that night early. So I and Trey was supposed to go to the movies that Sunday night coming. At church that night I was eager for the sermon to get over so I could leave. Finally church was over and at last I would be with Trey. I waited and waited he did not come out. I became very angry so I played smart and went to his house. I knocked politely on the door, but got no answwancer. Then I saw all kinds of devils, I had it why not walk down the streets to the other parking lot. In the parking lot their set his car. I walked up their stairs with fury burning at my heart. I then called "Trey" "Trey" open this dam door.

Because I know that you are in their. Then he cracked the door then said yes I am home. Then he slapped me in my face. My hand was in the door. Now will you please go home Donny. I shoved the door open and flew into him like a mad man. Although he was larger and older, but in my state of panic I was like insane. "Why you dirty rotten son of a bitch. I spent money on you Ill kill you.["] Please stop it Donny this is enough of this foolishness. I will carry you any place you want to go. I didnt know that blood was on his clothes and mine until I got to the street light. Fix up your coat Donny the cops might arrest us. When we got to the car god damn it get in. Then I pulled out my dagger when he started running. When I looked he was too far away to catch. So I started to walking home. I cried I dont know what or how I got home. Maybe if I told my mother I loved him she would let me have him and be free. I marched up stairs then I hollowed Look' at me see me mother. Yes all of those times I said I was away I lied. I love him mother dont harm him if you do I will kill myself. Mother looked like she had just seen the ghost of Dercular. Go to bed she said. Who is he? You'll see tomorrow. I went to sleep it was like a sleep of death. Finally it was mor[n]ing get up Donny and go to work. Mother please don't make me go to work. Yes you must go to work. I got up and look[ed] at the gray cloudy sky. It hit me all of a sudden. All the things you wanted in life and the fun and all you[r] mother will never let you have them. I must die I said in a wisper. I wrote in my Dirary my funeral arrangements and my farewell notes. Good-by I said to everything. Then I wrote Trey a letter and mailed it, this was death day.

May 4, 1962

Dear Trey,

I will be dead by the time you recive this letter. I never ever thought that you were such a no good person. But as a man was to a woman. I was true to you And you told me that you would never ever leave me. Like a fool I believed every word that you told me. But we made a bargain that if I died before you you would have a seacret moment with you. So please let me rest with that promise you made me before fill. I will love you to my grave. Life is no good without the ones that well we love so well. So I shall always cherish Sunday. I have swim the ocean blue just to prove my love to you. You will find no loved you like I did, Care for you as much. What more could any man do. I hope your family back together. Never to know the

days that pass, sweet will be the flowers and grass. Think not
of me if someone ask, when you work at your task. Only the
fut[u]re and not the pass as you go a long the greener path.
In my sleep of death good by.

>Sincerely Yours"
>Donny

Then I got up and went to work. Good by everything I said.
Everyone asked me whats the matter kid. Nothing I lied to be left
alone. $1.00 he called the kid abbie Donny you kiss me you can have
it. Now you know that its not that serious.

So finally I made the day until 4 oclock. My head was splitting. I
took 3 aperins. Any how I took twelve. I could feel my heart beating. I
took another box od aspirins. Soon it was 5.30 time to go home goodby
I said to myself. By I said to the flowers as I passed and everything.
Its only a matter of time. Before I have no more worries. When I came
mother was dressed. Are you ready yes. Why not let me go pick up
the radio. Just tell me where the house is and I will no. I want to you
hear everything that he says. He was at his cusion house. So I took
my mother their. Mrs [. . .] you may as well know. I didnt know what
donny was after when he came to my house. He is to finer boy to get
messed up like this. Yes said mother he is and do you know that he
is my only dam son. Lay low mother I said you promise no voliance.
I am going back to my family. Trey even told the small things I told
him people said about him. Mrs. [. . .] I slapped Donny but what did
I get. I got the worst end of the slap a black eye. Tooth bleed all night
long. Busted lips I couldnt even go to work. Let me tell you this dam
much you keep away from my son and I will see he never bothers you
again. I am not angry with Donny or anything. I will always speake
to him. How I wished I could died. Good day Mrs. [. . .]. Bye Donny.
Goodbye forever I said. I my minde I said you will never see me again.
I went to the store on the corner and bought me a bottle of sleeping
pills. I looked in the mirrow he never said he loved me like I did him.
I took 10 sleeping pills. I fixed my room extra special. I put my smile
on like I knew a secret after I had written mother a note. Soon sleep
came like sweet dream. In my sleep sometime later I herd mother say
My "god and ran out. But still I was in my dream of everlasting beauty.
In a haze I saw the doctor the policeman. I was sleep. Donny whats
the matter wake up. ["]No no" I want to die let me die. Then I saw
light. My body was shaking all over convelson. I open my eyes in the
hospital the doctor said what the matter no no I said. When I awoke

the next morning I was in a small private room. I cried but no tears came. Then I started shaking all over again. Then nurses came I was all right in about 8 minutes. That evening mother came and my uncle. I said take me home. Not knowing they drove and drove. I look out then I saw Lions the Va hospital. I said to myself this is a mental institition. Ho well, they will see that I am not crazey. The doctor asked me what was the matter? Did you try to kill yourself. I failed I replied but the next time I wont, I wont. I shower routine I thought. Say goodbye to your mother. Hate and fury all came in me. Good bye I said with all the hate I could look at her and pour out. I stated in reception one month. Then I was taken to cottage. Mother visited me regular I hate the site of her. This physologist asked me why. I said cant you see she took everything away from me. What have I to live for only sweet death. That will be all for today Donny. I walked out. Three weeks later I had shock treatment. The agony black outs but when I came to I rem[em]bered everbody and all of my reason for being locked up in a cage like a monkey. I spent three months in their. I have been out now 3 months. I could slip to see Trey if I wanted to. Now I still have all my problems. All the pills and needles, shock treatment still didnt do no good. I have become a male postitute. I will go out with any old rich woman, or young or man if the price is right. If you were born a homosexual please stay away from innocent boys. Now I cant love or pity nothing. I want to hurt like I have been hurt. I know Trey loves me but I could never like him. One day he will need me and I want to come back. I will be able to see him like a begging dog. The birds of the air have nests. The fox of the ground have holes. But the sole of man has nothing, to shelter his sole. Boys stay away from Gaeys. I will never forgive my mother for doing this wrong to me. By locking me in an institution. And love well I sold my heart to the junk man.

5

Representations and Stereotypes

Long before *Will and Grace* and openly gay celebrities such as Ellen DeGeneres, gay people have been interested in how mass media depicts them. The letters in this chapter provide a range of gay perspectives on popular culture. Unsurprisingly, many of these perspectives are negative, but *ONE* correspondents sometimes found affirmation in unexpected places, such as tabloid magazines, the *Tonight Show*, and even a low-budget movie about Vikings.

Attaining openly gay media visibility has been a hard-fought struggle. A letter from two men describing their Herculean efforts to place a tiny classified advertisement for *ONE* magazine in a Kansas City newspaper is a reminder that even the smallest steps forward required persistence, creativity, and courage. Such small steps accumulated over the years and gradually created a more affirmative media climate for gay people—despite the persistence of many negative gay and lesbian stereotypes today. *ONE* magazine played an important role in this process and pioneered an openly gay press in which gay men and lesbians could express themselves honestly and unapologetically.

>24 May 1955
>Midsize town in northern
>New Jersey

Gentlemen—

I am enclosing some tearsheets and clippings from the July, 1955, issue of "Hush-Hush" magazine which I believe will be of interest to you.

"One" magazine is included as an example of pornographic literature in an article by one Ed Sinclair.

Will you note on page 46 the reference to the Mattachine Society as being publisher of "One" magazine.

There is a special reason why I am sending you this material. The Picture Detective Publishing Co. also publishes the trashy "exposé" magazine called "Top Secret." There are also other associated publications called "Dynamite" and one I believe called "Parisienne" which is a vulgar "cheese cake" publication.

In the No. 13 issue of "Top Secret" there appeared an article by a David Seins Houston entitled "The Sex Book That Out-Kinseys Kinsey." It exposed a "pornographic" book by one Marshall Charles Greco called "Group Life."

The item interested me particularly not so much as a question of its being accurate or not, but rather the publisher's "crusade of morality" appeared so ridiculous in view of a newspaper item which appeared shortly before I happened across their "sensational" exposé.

About six weeks ago there was a newspaper report in the Bridgeport (Conn.) Post or Sunday Post concerning the arrest of an individual who had in his possession obscene literature. The striking coincidence (?) is that the newspaper listed the publisher's address as the Charlton Building, Derby, Conn., which is the same address of the Picture Detective Publishing Co. I inquired, but received no reply. I am not saying that they were the one and same organization, but I believe that some research work into this matter would prove to "One's" distinct advantage in retaliation for their treatment of "One" magazine in the July issue of "Hush-Hush."

If you desire I send the newspaper clipping or a photostat of it, I will gladly do so on my next trip to my home in Connecticut.

I am also sending two clippings of ads run in the July issue of "Hush-Hush." One concerning Repsac's older offering for sale "Shapely Pin-Up Book," "Raspberry Cushion," and "Ris-K Hula Girl!" These ads offering such trashy items are typical of those found in "exposé" and detective and "cheesecake" publications now under scrutiny by law enforcement officers in many states.

In Connecticut a law is pending which if passed would make it a criminal offense should these questionable, and often very sexy, magazines are displayed so that they can be purchased or seen by minors.

Cordially Yours,
Wayne

20 February 1956
Kansas City, Missouri

Dear Bill:

Thank you very much for your most informative letter. [Doug] and I were pleased to hear from you, and to receive news first-hand of your big meeting. I can well realize how busy you all must have been through it all. We would have liked nothing better than to have been able to attend.

Also, many thanks for writing to [Larry Carter] in [. . .], Kansas for us to recruit him to help us in our united efforts for ONE. We talked with Larry on the phone last night . . . [and] have not had the opportunity to meet him just yet but was very favorably impressed with his sincerity expressed in his desire to help and genuine concern about ONE. I believe that he will prove to be a good worker and welcome help.

Well, we must give you the big news before we go any further. You will recall that some time ago we wrote to you asking what you thought about us inserting an ad in the "Personals" in the newspaper here. And you fore-warned us about the possible complications in providing direct contact here, etc., and that it might be better if we were to have any inquiries directed to you all there.

Doug and I gave considerable thought to how might be the best way to try to get an ad in the paper; considering the possibilities of refusal, etc. Here in Kansas City we have only one big newspaper which is the "Kansas City Star-Times" (the "Times" in the morning and the "Star" at night) and they have a pretty firm monopolistic hold in the newspaper field here with no-one being strong enough to buck them with another paper.

Generally, the K.C. Star is very conservative and doesn't go in for the sensationalism that is found in the papers in L.A. So therefore we were wondering just what the right approach might be to try to get an ad about ONE and mentioning our cause of homosexuality.

This last week the play "Tea and Sympathy" played here for four nights with the touring cast with Maria Riva.[1] We had long been eagerly awaiting the date when this play would come here, as we had purchased a book of the play from Donald Webster Cory in New York soon after the opening of the play in New York, and with reading the play found it most appealing.[2] As the time for the play to appear here drew nearer, we eagerly read the reviews and preceding notices about it. For four Sundays prior to the opening of "Tea and Sympathy" here, there was a very nice sized article in the Amusement section showing a picture of Maria Riva—but the articles were so mildly worded that if you positively hadn't known what the play was about, you wouldn't have found out from what they told you about the forth-coming play. In these four articles the word "homosexuality" was never mentioned . . . they stated instead that the boy in the play was accused of "bad tendencies"—then another time they went so far as to say that it dealt with the very delicate subject of "moral irregularities."

Then the play opened last Monday night. In the morning "Times" there was a fair article reviewing the play which spoke favorably of the play and even at last came out and mentioned homosexuality, but very very discreetly.

Then in the Tuesday evening "Star" on the Editorial Page appeared this very fine article depicting the play and homosexuality as portrayed. Doug and I, and another buddy attended the play and enjoyed it most thoroughly.

In fact, after seeing the play and reading the excellent article in the paper about it; we came to the conclusion that perhaps the time was now ripe to try to insert our ad for ONE in the Sunday paper.

So, on late Friday afternoon I went over to the newspaper office, with the ad all typed out as we had thought it out so as to try to present our interest with discretion but at the same time to be sure that the readers would know what it was about.

I presented the ad to one of the women ad-takers, and she read it over and then asked to be excused a minute to talk to the Supervisor of the Want-Ad Dept. Then, the ad-taker came back and she said that they could not accept the ad the way it was written to include the word "homosexual"; but if I would take out the word "homosexual" that they would run it with the part in about "Tea and Sympathy Friends."

Well, to this I just told her that I didn't see anything wrong with the wording of the ad, and that if I took off the word of "homosexual" that most readers certainly wouldn't know what ONE magazine pertained to and that to just mention the part about "Tea and Sympathy" would go over the heads of most readers, particularly if they hadn't seen the play. Therefore, that they might just as well not run the ad as it would serve no purpose. After a little pro and con discussion with this woman, she just finally said that frankly she didn't care but that on such matters it was up to the woman that was the head of the want-ad dept. and that this woman had turned it down, unless I reconsidered and changed the wording.

Finally, then I told this woman that I would not consider changing the wording and that there was no legitimate reason why they could not print it as is, and that was what I wanted. Then she told me that I could talk to a man that had complete authority over what went into the want ads, and that this man had the final word over her boss, which was the woman that refused. So I said, "Okay, let's talk to him about it then."

Well, this man was not in at that time; so I just told them that I would come back later to see him. About an hour and a half later I went back, but this man was not yet in so I just waited for him. In due time he appeared and I went over the whole situation with him; to which, his response was "I'm sorry, but we just don't cater to that type of an ad." To which I replied, "I don't see any reason why you can't run this ad." Then he stalled, something about that there was no place in the paper for an ad of this type. I told him that we weren't asking for a special hearing for this ad, that it would be perfectly agreeable to run it in the "Personals." He said, that it was not suitable to run a business ad of this type in the "Personals," that it just had never been done.

Then I told him that there were certainly a lot of business ads in the personals every day. Then I thought, well I'll just come right out point blank—so I said, "Do you object to the use of the word "homosexual" in this ad." Then, he was flustered a little, and stammered some and then finally said, "Well, no they didn't object to that word." Then I told him that if he didn't object to the use of the word homosexual that there was certainly nothing else in the ad that would be offensive; and there-fore that they could run the ad just as it is. Then he said, "No, that they just couldn't accept it. That they didn't solicit that type of business."

I felt determined to keep trying, and thought of the article just a few days prior about "Tea and Sympathy." So then I asked him, "If it's a matter that you don't think that you can print it . . . there have already been a number of articles in the paper from time to time that mentioned homosexuality (there had been about Oscar Wilde and Walt Whitman but I didn't mention any names to him), in fact just the other night there was a big article on the Editorial Page about "Tea and Sympathy" that had headlines in big print mentioning homosexuality. Then he asked, "Just what paper was that?" So I gave him the date, etc. and he looked it up. I then pointed this big write-up out to him, "See, there it tells all about "Tea and Sympathy." Then he asked, "Just what is this "Tea and Sympathy" business?" "Well," I told him, "It's a Broadway Play that has been playing here the last few nights." Then the reply was, "Yes, I guess I have heard something about it."

Then I pointed out the use of the word "homosexuality" in bold type at the heading of this article. To which, he said, "Yes, I can see it alright." I said, "There you are, that's certainly a big article on it and my little ad would be nothing compared to that." Finally, then at long last, the words came that were music to my ears, and he said—"I'll give my approval and you can give the ad to the girl."

So, they took the ad as we had originally written it; and Doug and I held our breath practically until we saw it in print in the Sunday paper. So, we succeeded in setting a president [sic] in the want ad dept.

We were pleased to have succeeded in our first attempt with the contact with the newspaper. We hope that our ad meets with your approval. We took a little liberty in asking readers to write for a free brochure. However, we felt that surely you would have some piece of advertising matter to send to anyone that would be interested enough to write to inquire. That way we thought that perhaps we might get more inquiries from people that wouldn't readily subscribe to anything that they didn't previously know a little something about.

I am enclosing a portion of the want-ad section bearing our ad; also, the article about "Tea and Sympathy" that paved the way for our ad.

Oh yes, incidentally, before this man would approve the ad I had to give him my name and address, so I did. After all, I figured that if it did get in the hands of the police that they couldn't do any more than put my name on a "Suspect List" . . . (I Hope !!). After all, I well realize that you can't stand up for our cause and not be so named. Doug and I are both willing to "stick our necks out" in the interest of providing enlightenment, and only hope that we can get others to follow.

I already know that when I tell some of my friends (gay ones) what we did in getting this ad in the paper that they will tell us that we both are just looking for trouble. Unfortunately, there are ever so many that are quite willing to reap the benefits that we are working to pave the way for, but in the meantime want to sit far out on the back fence to watch what is going on.

Oh, well, such is life I guess! However, we have found that the seemingly depths of despair that we have had to endure . . . have, in the long run greatly strengthened and fortified us in providing a terrific amount of growth and understanding. For this, we are truly grateful.

Well, since this is getting to be quite an epistle—I must get back to the subjects of your letter. We were sorry to hear of the number of returns; maybe we were a little too anxious to build us up an ample listing. However, we are pleased to hear of the good results too. This gives us new hope and encouragement.

Just yet, we haven't had time to check into the newsstands; but do appreciate having this information to present to them. Larry seems interested in contacting some of the newsstands, so we'll see what we can work out together.

Thanks again for the news of your Annual Meeting and Institute. We'll be looking forward to the full published report.

We'll be sending you some more dupli-stickers with names soon; but wanted to get this off to you first . . . just in case you do get some inquiries as a result of our ad. We certainly hope so!!

Best regards always,
James

～

Published in ONE magazine,
May 1958, 31
Brooklyn, New York

Dear Sir:

I read your magazine every month with the greatest interest. Believe me it is extremely difficult for the average woman to find congenial people. I wish somebody would open a club supported by the right group. I believe that older women would appreciate this. The usual bars for lesbians are frequented by teen-agers, as far as I can determine. An older woman, without a companion, feels something like an old granny, and very much out of place.

I have written two novels about the homosexual woman and feel that my books are true-to-life, realistic and interesting . . . that is to the average Lesbian. I do NOT pull that old switch at the end where in most gay books the one girl goes off with a man, thus settling the "problem" of her homosexuality for once and all! This is to me so much whitewash to satisfy the heterosexual reader, and to soothe him into feeling that the world isn't so bad after all, and that, when these bad homosexual things do occur, they always come out right in the end. My novels contain no such lulling conclusions.

Miss J.

～

6 September 1959
New York, New York

Gentlemen,

Have a few things on my mind that have annoyed me. Thought you might be interested.

The first is an article in one of the local papers written by New York columnist Lee Mortimer.[3] In which he stated that in spite of this sniping only one queer joint had been raided. (How sad). In this same column he went on at great length about who was swapping back and forth in the heterosexual world. It is strange, to me, to see whoring and whoremongering—even though they may be of the theater or Café Society—so blatantly, and acceptably, advertised and in the same breath by some one who condemns those who go about their sexual lives in a far more decorous and acceptable manner. I don't know what said Mortimer's particular bitch is, but—the back of one hand to him anyhow.

Also enclosed is an article from today's New York News. I assume things will be tough in New York City for some time to come. All because of police inability to control a certain element which has gotten too far out of hand.

The following is an excerpt from "The Moon of Beauty" by Jorgen Andersen-Rosendal. It is in reference to Japanese plays in which male actors portray females:

"An actor who has specialized in female parts is called an Onnagata, and the leading female impersonators were always the most famous and popular stage performers. Some of them were, of course, feminine men or men with homosexual tendencies. The Japanese know this, but it did not matter. The Japanese accepts as one of the facts of life that some people, through no fault of their own, are born with other erotic feelings than those of the majority. It is beyond them that there are countries where homosexual relations are liable to punishment. It is a private matter, they think, and nobody looks down on people who are attracted by their own sex if in other ways they behave as honest and decent citizens. They do not know of the Western World's slanderous and unattractive persecution of these people. Therefore this problem is so small in Japan that many Japanese scarcely realize that it exists. (pp 75-76)." Come to think of it I know of no Japanese or Chinese homosexuals. Perhaps it is because there are so few of these nationalities in the area.

Now for an incident which did my heart good. I was in a gay bar in Albany on a Saturday night, not too long ago. There was a loud mouth there who was trying to score and not making out. About eleven P.M. a young, very good looking Soldier came in, more than a little under the "affluence of inkahol." Loud mouth wanted to know what he was doing in a joint like that and proceeded to inform him that we were nothing but a bunch of queers. With that the soldier straightened himself up, ran his hand though his hair, and looking him right smack dab in the eye said "So?—everybody's queer one way or another." He was heard all over the place. Loud mouth, having received his come-uppance, left. Why can't I think of answers like that?

A small contribution herewith. Use it as you see fit.

Fraternally yours,
Sincerely,
Bernard

∽

14 April 1961
Austin, Texas

Dear One

Enclosed is a news clipping. No fat gay men? It doesn't say that. But everybody knows that all homos are criminal, and all homo behavior is criminal; so when the learned doctor says that he's never come across a fat man who has committed one of the "crimes"—well what else can one conclude? There must not be any fat gay men.

Another bit of rot. In the March issue of READER'S DIGEST an article by some other smart cookie, called "How to Stop Movie's Exploitation of Sex" pages 37 through 40, has a bit to say, indirectly, about the homo theme.

In complaining about what Hollywood is up to . . . "Efforts are being made to include suggestions—of homosexuality, lesbianism, incest. There is even a report that the 'heavy' role in one great screen classic has been rewritten to make the character a homosexual in order to put an extra 'kick' in the new version." The author is just plain anti-sex for films, period. Of course he is against homosexuality as a theme. Everybody knows it is detestable and abominable and criminal. The poor man then goes on to list several organizations, primarily religious, one can support to stop this terrible situation of showing anything to do with sex in our movies. The article has some points, but is pretty much just another anti-sex proposal. It is true that few films having anything to do with the homo theme are very realistic or true to life, but I do have high hopes that a pro-homo film will someday be made, a film which shows what a wide variety of people and behavior patterns really exist in the gay world, with the hero or heros or heroine, or heroines being gay people, likable and lovable gay people, who, except for their "criminal tendencies," are pretty much like people everywhere. It will never be done, of course. Show homos as nice, likable people? Absurd. There would be nothing realistic about that. Everybody knows that all homos are detestable lechers.

Concerning the March issue of ONE.

I want to compliment you on what I thought were two stories of superior quality, to wit, "The New Butcher Boy" and "The Scavengers." I hope you print more like them. Now to a complaint. What was the meaning of publishing something like "Homosexual Procreation" by James R. Steuart as a serious article, or did you mean it to be humor? Taken as humor, it is really quite funny, but taken seriously, it is something quite the opposite. I do agree with Mr. Steuart on one point, he has gone mad.

In the article "How Homosexuals Can Combat Anti-Homosexualism" by Dr. Albert Ellis, one of the suggestions listed under what he calls the palliative method of reducing anti-homosexual bigotry, suggestion number two is "They should abhor all feelings and actions which would tend to show others that they, the homosexuals, consider themselves in any way superior to or better than nonhomosexuals." Your printing of Steuart's madness as a serious proposal (I still wonder if you really did mean it as humor, but I have a feeling you didn't), definitely is contrary to the suggestion I quoted from Ellis. True, everybody has a right to voice his opinion. I'm exercising that right now, but still, I feel that the article could be detrimental to the "cause" and don't tell me there is no cause. Steuart's idea of a totally homosexual world is just as absurd, more so, than the idea of a totally heterosexual world. Why black or white? And what are the great majority of heterosexuals going to do? Just sit around and let Steuart's world come to pass, when they are so anti-homo in the first place? No, he can't be serious. I am convinced the whole thing is a joke. It's a good one too. Some willing and interested author might take Steuart's idea as the basis for a science fiction novel on a "brave new world" of the future which is totally homosexual. I doubt if it would be published. That might not be such a good idea after all. Straight people may read it, find it completely repugnant, as many people found the way of life pictured in Huxley's BRAVE NEW WORLD, and become more anti-homo than ever, considering it possible that if they didn't get rid of them dirty, lewd, criminals once and for all, why, they might actually succeed in taking over the world, their obvious plan.

Perhaps it would have been better if you had also included an article showing the other extreme, just as absurd. An article by Dr. Bergler, perhaps.

So much for that. Now to a couple of questions that I do hope someone can answer.

Is the Kinsey report on the homosexual out yet? If not, why? It was promised that it would be out in 1960. Anybody know anything about this?

Why is it that in so many of the stories on male homosexuals, one lover is always blond and the other always dark? Why not both dark or both blond, or maybe both red headed? Why black and white? Also, why can't the authors be more descriptive? Blond covers a very wide range/area of colors and shades, some quite different from others. I have been appalled at the shades of hair color that have been termed blond. Many are just short of black. Of course, the word "dark" is more limited in scope. But this thing about blondness disturbs me quite a bit, and I find it very difficult to picture in my mind what the author means when he says "blond." Does this bother anyone else out there? Could it be that the authors are trying to provide at least one character, in a story of a twosome, whom the readers, with their varied tastes, can find especially interesting due to his particular color—blond or dark? Do gentlemen prefer blondes?

I would like to obtain a complete list of the books you handle, fiction and nonfiction. Is there such a list?

Out of curiosity, what are your rates for fiction printed in ONE?

Also out of curiosity, do you have any prepared booklet, paper, or the like showing the breakdown of the number of subscribers per state for the present time? If not, could you satisfy my morbid, criminal curiosity and tell me just how many subscribers you do have for the nation as a whole, and for the state of Texas.

If these questions seem trivial, or if the answers are unobtainable, or if you don't have time to do more than read the letter in the first place, disregard them.

Thank you for your voice in the darkness.

Yours truly
Daniel

∽

11 November 1962
Brooklyn, New York

Dear One:

[. . .]⁴

By the way, I went to a movie today. It was a triple-feature. There was: "The Queen of Outer Space," "The Massacre," and "The Last of the Vikings."

The Queen of Outer Space was a Tension-on-Crotch thing (for heteros). Eva Gabor was the Star making with the "leg" and looking at the blackboard behind the photographer, where she could read her lines. There were three slim-assed astronauts (with nothing in front, may as well be 3 more Eva Gabors), who yapped, "A Who-mahn is ay Who-mahn" at the Venusian Population (all female.)

"The Massacre" got everybody killed, Joel McCrea was the Star, drained and lumpy. The Indians were delicious!

In the "Last of the Vikings" there was a most breathtaking scene where King Howard saves his brother, Gudrum (releases him from being gorilly nailed to a cross, swims him, with much head-dunking across the channel they flop, jiggling, in the wash of the shore, modestly wearing trunks.) Then Howard muscularly squeezes, man flesh on man flesh, his beloved, whom he has just found to have succumbed. Actor Howard really <u>cared</u> for actor Gudrum, the only real thing in the picture. Finally Howard marries, coldly, no touch, no kiss, nothing, noble princess. (Recommend)

Love,
Philip

∼

12 June 1963
Midsize town in northeastern Texas

Dear people of One,

Recently a friend asked me what was your reaction to a piece of writing, "Afraid (fragment)" that I sent you more than a year ago. I replied that I didn't know, that I hadn't heard anything from you about it. Then he asked me whether I knew that you had received the ms. On this point I wasn't sure: did I send the ms. by certified mail or not? So I'm writing now to ask whether you received the ms. in the spring of '62.

You should not interpret my long silence as meaning that I've lost interest in One—I have not. The fact is that after my grandfather passed away in Jan. I was beset with many problems, which are not solved yet. Necessarily my mind has been focused on these problems, to the point of excluding much else.

Until recent months I had watched television only on occasion. I persuaded my grandmother to buy a television set and now enjoy "The Tonight Show" with Johnny Carson and his guests. As a student of trends and symptoms I was interested to see how Johnny handled the queenly Liberace on the show. He was careful not to exploit the situation for "gay" humor; at one point, however, when Liberace held up a bathing suit (one of many gifts people had given him), with musical notes sewn on it, Johnny couldn't resist saying that the bathing suit was particularly interesting around a certain note. Johnny's best humor is derived from the assumption that the audience, Johnny himself, and his guests know more about the facts of life than can be expressed on television. The show is at its funniest when it is teetering on the verge of frank vulgarity. Well, frank vulgarity is not the exclusive domain of the gay—but this sort of wit is perhaps a specialty of the gay. My suspicion here is that the gay mode of humor has invaded television, via the Johnnys and Jack Paars. And where do you think such a trend is leading? I'd say towards more permissiveness.

          Best wishes,
          Albert

p.s. If you have ms. for "Afraid (fragment)," you'll find it under the pseudonym "Edward Denison."

~

          29 June 1964
          Midsize town in western
          Illinois

Dear Friends,

  I have just finished reading <u>Life's</u> "objective" report on homosexuality in America.[5] After that, I am moved to send my monthly contribution to my "homophile organization" a few days early. Others may be afraid to stand with you but I hope that charge will never be leveled at me. So here's five more for truth. I suppose as a homosexual I should be happy that such a prominent mag as Life finds our presence so imminent as to find it necessary to expose us to the public not "in order to condone us but to cope with us." I believe that line rankled me more than any other in the article. The "scientific" tract by Havermann seemed the best of the article but even it had a noticeable anti-bias. A number of contradictory explanations were professed as to why we are homosexual without a commitment from Mr. H— as to the more probable. I assume, however, that LIFE could scarcely become blatantly condemnatory of the existent legal situation vis-à-vis homosexuality. On the whole, I suppose we should view <u>Life's</u> article as a step forward. Ten years ago they would never have presumed to print such an article.

  I will look forward to your comments on the LIFE article in the next issue of ONE. My congrats to Don Slater on meriting a photo in the article and thank God ONE <u>has been</u> disseminating "propaganda" for the past 12 years. Wasn't Dr. van de Haag's answer to his colleague marvelous? Wish some more of these exposes would put more emphasis on the fact that much of the so-called knowledge about homosexuality is predicated upon psychiatric case studies, etc. After all, there are one helluva lot of us who have never seen the inside of a psychiatrist's office and probably never will—

Yours,
Franklin

~

12 August 1964
Pasadena, California

Dear Editors;

I hope you will find the enclosed clippings and articles of some value in your work and fight for our civil rights and freedom.

Of the numerous tabloid type newspapers out now, the "Star-Chronicle" seems to be the most prejudiced, from a gay standpoint, as you can see by the way they delight in printing, with photos, the most lurid and vicious crimes involving homosexuality that they can dig up. They are not content with just U.S. happenings as you see by the Mexican and Argentina cases.

The least prejudiced and more "understanding" (if such can even be said of them) is the "National Informer" (US), and the Canadian "Confidential Flash" isn't _too_ bad.

This new "Photo News" should be watched, not so much because it will have any great national impact, but because it will tend to inflame the more ignorant and sensation-loving individuals who go for this kind of an extreme "sex-trash" publication.

You will no doubt find the latest issue of the Nazi Party's "Rockwell Report" quite startling and intriguing. I am wondering if you ever saw a copy of one of their earliest issues headlined on the front cover "Only a Nazi Reformation Can Destroy this Filthy Cancer"—and a reproduction of one of your editorials coupled with a physique mag. photo of a nude man climbing into a bathtub put together as if they were one and the same publication—with "SHAME" stamped across both reproductions. I had saved this issue, meaning to get it to you, and unfortunately it got thrown out when I moved. You should definitely try and get a hold of this most revealing and horrible publication that shows what kind of life will be in store for all non-heterosexuals after they take power in 1972—as their plans call for. They are counting on increased race riots, internal subversion and

Communism, plus mass unemployment to aid their cause. Don't think it "can't happen in America." A lot of people in Germany used to make fun of Hitler and made the same mistake. It is amazing to me why they aren't content to take on just the Communists, Jews, and Negroes, but are out to wipe out homosexuality as well. A similar pattern evolved in Germany. Part of it is perhaps a "super butch" coverup, as many of the German Nazi's put across the same front, and even if much that has been said about them is hearsay or propaganda, I am sure that they were not all the super "he men" depicted.

As much as I hate to quote that vicious queer-baiter and old time hysteria, gossip and war monger Walter Winchell, it is interesting to note that he has called Rockwell "George Stinkin' Ratwell—<u>Queen</u> of the Nazis." At their headquarters in Arlington, Va. they have a barracks where all their young men stay, both newcomers to the Nazi cause and the more seasoned "Stormtroopers" as leaders and teachers.

In the first three or four issues of his "Rockwell Report," he loved to use the phrase "kikes, Communists, coons and queers," in reference to what most "ordinary Americans" were fed up with in the Government and State Dept. Their official party platform, while calling for a national lottery because "gambling is universal"—demands the "ruthless suppression of prostitution and homosexuality" because they are "<u>not universal</u>." He would seem to have a lot to learn on that score! I think their case is one of protesting their straightness to an <u>abnormal</u> degree of intensity.

If I can ever get a hold of another copy of that early issue I will be sure to send it to your office. It would be of special interest to you because of the reproduction of your editorial on their front page. It was the one on heterosexual propaganda and conformity of a couple years ago. It was really some tirade and said, among other things, that any "normal" man's reaction upon seeing "a queer" would be "to <u>want to kill him</u>." It then went on to say that "perhaps this is too severe" and that they (us) should either be imprisoned for good or "keep their perversion utterly to themselves." Mighty white of him, don't you think.

You could get a copy of their Party Program by having someone there write for it. I used to have one, but unfortunately didn't hang on to it. If you would like, I could write and try to get one or more copies, without arousing their suspicion, although they might wonder why I wanted that particular issue. They used to sell back copies of all issues, but I haven't seen any ad to that effect for some time.

In Shirer's book "Rise and Fall of the Third Reich" he states that <u>all</u> of the original Nazis <u>except Hitler</u> himself, were gay. Whether this is true or not, who knows? I have read where Ernst Roehm was a "notorious" and sadistic type homosexual, and Hitler having shot him for this reason, as Rockwell mentions, it is probably true. Sometimes it no doubt takes extreme methods to fight Communist terror and police state tactics, but I cannot understand why homosexuals have to be dragged into the fight too. The Nazis—or "National Socialists," as Rockwell calls his group also, have an almost psychopathic predilection for the "Christian home and family," child-raising (more little Nazis?), normalcy, ultra-<u>conformity</u> and a super, glorified heterosexuality. They are so convinced they are right on all aspects of life that they feel that those opposing their program are almost unworthy of it (life). Well, we still have 8 years of "3rd class citizenship" left to go. If they and their hoardes of secret supporters are successful with their propaganda, which does appeal to a considerable number of the straight masses, we won't even have that after they take over the reins in Washington.

Queer-baiting and hunting in the State Dept. is given a charming new impetus by the article I'm sending from "Uncensored" on the "swishes" who are still supposed to be infesting the glorious State Dept.—voice of the "Free World." I thought Sen. McCarthy was supposed to have gotten everyone purged who was not a <u>confirmed</u> and <u>obvious</u> lady-lover!

The following articles should also be brought to your attention:
1. "Why Those Gay Boys Travel Abroad"—by I. M. Kamp!—June '64—"Uncensored." (This is relatively mild.)
2. "How Homos Are Ruining TV"—Sept.—"Inside Story." This is filled with typical bigoted and hate type epithets such as "twisted twerps," "frantic fauns," "lavender and lace shirt situation," etc. It shows both Jack Paar, and Dorothy Kilgallen as <u>enemies</u> of gay people as well as the loud-mouth slander artist Winchell, who was described by a biographer of a number of years back, as having committed incest with his own daughter.
3. "Stephen Ward's Homosexual Secret"—July issue of "Naked Truth." Average hate-type smear piece.
4. "Teenage Homos Stage a Sit-In"—Oct. issue of "Hush-Hush"— This article, believe it or not, is quite good and unprejudiced, which is pretty rare for this type of magazine, as you well know. It tells about the situation at "Deweys"—a restaurant in Philadephia's Rittenhouse Square, a la Barney's Beanery in W. Hollywood, only without the "Faggots Stay Out" sign. Somebody should organize a sit-in for this "famous landmark" joint—and test the thing on Constitutional grounds. After all, the Negroes are doing it and a <u>heck</u> (musn't use the other 4-letter word in case the "P.O. Gestapo" might censor me for impurity) of a lot

more. The kids in this article are treated with compassion and fairness.

Hope you appreciate my efforts!

Sincerely,
Paul

ONE Represents the Gay Minority

If the mass media provided distorted images of gay people, then how should gay people represent themselves in publications such as *ONE*? This was a complicated question. What exactly did a "positive" image look like in the 1950s? Should male effeminacy be downplayed, as many *ONE* readers insisted? Why were women so underrepresented in the magazine? Should *ONE* magazine print the word "homosexual" with a small "h" or with a capital "H"? Readers had much to say about these questions.

Ultimately, any opinions about how "the minority" should represent itself reflected how gay men and lesbians understood themselves as individuals. Gay women and men became increasingly aware of the political nature of their private lives after World War II, and they worked in bold and subtle ways to change societal attitudes about homosexuality. The struggle goes on today as gay people continue to assert their fundamental right to liberty, equality, and the pursuit of happiness.

Published in *ONE* magazine,
March 1953, 20
[no city published]

Sirs:

It is with a deep feeling of regret that I embark on the writing of my first anonymous letter, and faint feeling of shame. I have been employed in fairly "sensitive" positions, and may be so employed in the future. For this reason, I do not wish to have any traceable link with your publication. A hint of such activity in my FBI records would be sufficient to put me on the outside looking in, because of our supposed proneness to blackmail.

I enclose a small donation to be used for the purpose of keeping the Magazine going. I have already made arrangements with a friend who has less necessity for concealment to forward the copies of the subscription I entered in his name. Ridiculous, isn't it?

I was very well pleased with the first issue, and am looking forward to the others. There was only one suggestion I feel impelled to make. It is in regard to the editorial policy of the Magazine. Your point was of course well taken about the fantastic, near-psychotic actions of various law-enforcement agencies, when they wish to wipe out, destroy, incarcerate, etc. all persons who may practice any form of homosexuality. This works both ways, of course. The magazine aims to create a more friendly and tolerant attitude on the part of the great mass of "normals" toward homosexual individuals and groups. I should think that one of the most telling ways of doing this would be to try to create the impression of great sanity by keeping the tone of the magazine essentially quiet, reasonable, and calm. Part of the popular legend about us is that we are flighty, hysterical, and intensely neurotic. Of course, there are such people in our group, just the same as any other, but I fear that it would do the group a disservice to allow writings of this sort to creep in. I was favorably impressed by the tone of most of the articles, but there were a few which left me with an uncomfortable feeling of tension, due to the unrealistic ends proposed. Specifically, the idea of expecting any great change of attitude on the part of those officers who are charged with the enforcement of the discriminatory laws. Such people must usually be compelled to act as they do from deep subconscious levels; the error lies in expecting them to change, just as they in turn expect us to change. One is as unlikely as the other. The proper method of attack seems to me to be thru legal channels, thus divesting them of the protection of the law in their persecutions. Certainly it is the height of fantasy to expect exhortation to change their attitudes.

—S. A.

Published in *ONE* magazine,
July 1954, 26
Los Angeles, California

Editorial Staff, ONE:

Your May issue, in my opinion, is particularly fine and thought-provoking.

The art work, as usual, is beautiful—and stimulating.

I would especially like to commend Arthur Krell on his article "We Need a Great Literature." We do indeed. We are bloodless and have no direction because of this lack. That we must make one is apparent. How to go about this is something else again. Krell helps immensely: he points in worthy directions.

I, myself, do not believe really great books about contributions homosexuals can make to society and how homosexuals can transcend their barriers to become finer people CAN or WILL be written by any except those who have succeeded in integrating themselves and are contributing in a vital way to society.

This is a call to homosexual (male and female) professional and non-professional workers to write—and tell how they transcended their environments and psychological barriers to make useful and stable citizens out of themselves. What were their ideals—goals—aspirations? How did they get them? How did they hang onto them?

In the meantime, successful homosexuals lacking tongues, the neurotic homosexual will write.

And his writing is important, too—even if it does only tell us what the bricks are made of that comprise his prison—or what life is like in that prison.

But Krell has helped and I want him to know that I thank him from the bottom of my heart.

[no name published]

~

Published in *ONE* magazine,
September 1955, 26
Los Angeles, California

Gentlemen:

Two letters appearing recently in your "Letter[s]" section have prodded me into getting a few things off my chest. So here goes:

First, may I address San Francisco's letter appearing in your April issue? I assume the writer here refers to the article "In Defense of Swish" and I heartily agree that this was a most unfortunate and ill-advised item. Aside from the falsity of its premise, the results of such an article are unfortunately not amusing or humorous but, as the San Francisco letter so aptly states "tragic and dangerous." Not only does this type of driveling philosophy disgust and estrange and thereby cut off the interest and support of the better type of invert who believes inversion can and should be invested with dignity, masculinity and high ideals of conduct and character, but it serves to further prejudice an already dangerously warped concept and attitude of a neurotically biased heterosexual majority toward the homosexual minority, and this is the most "tragic and dangerous" effect of all.

And now may I address New York City's letter which appeared in the March issue? To this I would say "Amen! Amen!" It so thoroughly incorporates all of my own ideas, feelings and convictions on the subject of the gay bar element and the thrill-seeking crowd whose entire orientation is on the physical.

I, too, care little for gay bars or for the type one inevitably meets there. I, too, would infinitely prefer the company of the thinking individual whose mind is not constantly racing along the grooves of an evening's pleasure. But I, too, cannot be irrevocably condemnatory of the gay bar element of their attitudes because, in asking myself "why is it so?" I inevitably am convinced that these conditions exist to the extent they do largely because of the untenable and chaotic position of the invert in a society where the antagonism and persecution of a neurotically biased heterosexual majority makes his life almost unbearably desperate at times. I am convinced that many of these gay bar habituees were not always thus. Perhaps the majority began with high ideals and standards. They wanted and looked for something better but could not find it through legitimately accessible ways and means. Scratch beneath the surface of many and you will find a succession of disillusionments, heartache and suffering brought about primarily by the stupidity and intolerance of an unsympathetic society in which they have found themselves lost and confused. The inevitable result is the acceptance of what they consider irrevocable, an ever-growing cynicism and the "oh what the hell, devil may care" attitude of taking pleasure as it comes and "what more can you expect in a world such as we have to live in" philosophy. This does not mean that I condone or approve [of] this way of life or attitude, but let us at least be partially fair in placing the major blame where it belongs, namely on a society which sins against the invert more than the invert sins against it and which, in its ignorance and prejudice, breeds the very conditions it so stuffily and hypocritically persecutes.

              Mr. D.

~

Published in *ONE* magazine,
March 1956, 29
Perth Amboy, New Jersey

Dear Mr. Slater:

It is unnecessary to tell you I enjoy your magazine. But I do wish you would print more material covering, and appealing to the female sex. Out of the thirty-four letters printed in the "Letters" department only four are from women. It is quite obvious that most of ONE's readers are males. This is understandable since your articles cover mostly the male homosexual and the "heroes" in your fiction are male. No doubt you have a few female readers too, but I am sure you could have more if only you would include the women regularly in your issues.

People enjoy reading about individuals with whom they can identify themselves. But it is difficult for a woman to identify her self with a man and vice versa. The issue I enjoyed most was the one devoted entirely to the female. But why have just an occasional issue for women? I'm sure you're not prejudiced against us. There must be many who feel this way, so please, don't neglect us.

Miss A.

Published in *ONE* magazine,
June-July 1956, 44
Los Angeles, California

Dear Editors:
. . . I want to thank Ann Carll Reid for her article. She states precisely just what is wrong with "we women" . . . reasons why we don't work together. But, I'd like to offer this thought. Do the fellows want our support . . . our help. Granted <u>One</u> does and is willing to include us. And most of the girls I know enjoy the friendship and company of the "brothers". . . . I can't say the same for the majority of boys. Why is it there has not been a magazine for women before? Why does the Mattachine Review almost sidestep the Lesbian? Why do you not find a greater number of women in the Mattachine Society? I'm <u>sure</u> the women would join, I'm <u>sure</u> they would subscribe and work with <u>both</u> magazines and any organizations . . . IF the fellows would show they wanted them. It seems that their preference for male companionship is so deep-seated that they cannot include in their society women who understand their preference and would help them fight for the right to such preference. . . . I'd like to see an article from one of the men on <u>One</u>, taking some sort of stand on the Lesbian.

[no name published]

Published in *ONE* magazine,
December 1956, 38
Los Angeles, California

Dear ONE:
In looking through a Catholic Newspaper not so long ago, I was struck by a curious stylization. When the press generally (that is, non-catholic) is concerned with the via cruces of Papal adherents in China, they say "catholic." But when the Catholic TIDINGS write about the same incident, they say "Catholic." When Ike is rejecting another

peace proposal by Russia, the press snickers about the soviets. But when UNESCO prints a broadside, it refers to them as Soviets. South Africa passed the apartheid laws to control the colored. But when the National Council for African Affairs fights back it demands equal rights of citizenship for the Colored. It would seem that whenever and wherever national, cultural, or social minorities aspire to, or are granted, the stature of pride and dignity equated with the best in social maturity achievable by society, they are accorded by those who champion them and/or respect their endeavor, the accolade of the Capitalized initial letter.

You may have noticed that I personally always write Homosexual, Homophile, Lesbian, etc., with the Capitalized initial. In doing so I am only attempting to familiarize my correspondents with the dignity with which I feel I am entitled. The more, for instance, I look at your broadside in current and choice book-titles available—AND SEE MYSELF IN SMALL LETTERS—the less I am likely to comprehend my minority as a significant social element capable of unique potentials of community values in coalition or in fellowship with other groups similarly discriminated against.

Let us, then, in counter-offensive, hoist ourselves by our own petards from lower to Upper case. Let us feel that, in doing so, we are re-establishing an honorable historical category (and social identification) not only for our contiguously ancestral Name-heroes but to that even more illustrious, though nameless, legion who in selfless devotion contributed so much to the progress of human consciousness.

Yours for the capital "H" uber alles,
Mr. H.

Published in ONE magazine,
April 1957, 22
[no city published]

Dear Editors of ONE:

Regarding your Dec. 1956 issue: I don't know about Mr. "H" of Los Angeles, but I do not wish to be known as a capital "H" homosexual or a capital "L" lesbian. While I am not ashamed of being either of these sometimes-epithets—a small "h" or "l" will do, thank you.

I do not consider my sexual activity or preference to be the most important single aspect of my being. I should think being a PERSON and a RESPONSIBLE CITIZEN would come first on any man's list of idealistic objectives.

In closing—would suggest that I am suspicious of any who consider themselves capital-anythings except for the personal pronoun "I" or their personal names. All else is adjectival to that.

Miss S.

∽

Published in *ONE* magazine,
January 1958, 30
New York, New York

Dear ONE:
For whatever my opinion is worth, you get better and better with each issue—except poetically. I do protest your choice of poems as not being poetry for the most part. I would rather see you publish a good poem that had no homosexual implications than a non-poem, laid out on the page to resemble poetic form, that suggests a homosexual interpretation.

I know you are not a literary magazine primarily and are in need of manuscripts by your constant appeals for them, but please, there is a great difference between using modern verse as a medium and writing that which can be called a poem. If I thought you had actually picked your choices as the best poems—but oh, your articles are so intelligent, your whole magazine of such a high caliber, I cannot do you the intellectual disservice of such a thought. You are obviously far too intelligent a group of people for me to say—and believe—well they don't know anything about poetry. So you probably try to pick the best of what you get that will be meaningful to your readers.

I do believe in you, support you, talk about you, defend you (when necessary) and try to sell, give subscriptions—so my criticism does not come from one who completely sits on her rear and just finds fault.

Miss H.

∽

Published in *ONE* magazine,
June 1958, 29
Brooklyn, New York

Dear Editor:
You were downright cruel to Miss S., of Sidney, Australia and Mr. B., of Hartford, Conn. You were downright cruel! Don't you realize

that these are two lonely, unhappy kids? Shame on you ONE! Why can't you run a series of human-interest articles that would bring some kind of help to them? Your articles are very nice, very ethical, and very informative, but they are cold as hell! (If it is cold there . . . I don't exactly know—yet). You speak with great authority, from great heights . . . and of course we read and nod our old grey heads in agreement . . . but what about the frustrated, lonely teen-ager, or twenty-ager? The kids want warmth, and ONE hasn't got it. ONE has facts. (God, you must be a well-disciplined bunch out there!)

You are advancing our "cause" as nothing else ever has been able to do. You are showing us that we are not alone, and that others have the same problems. However, your magazine is aimed specifically at people who think, not people who feel. And I don't believe the human brain really begins to operate before the age of forty. The kids are emoting, not thinking. Of course you are correct in saying that letter exchange cannot be permitted, but cannot something be done?

When you do emote you give the already forlorn kids something like: "Rest shall I Never . . . Hunted forever . . . Pitied, a pest . . ." Does this HELP? Let's have some courageous writing. Let's have some chin-up stuff. I certainly would like to see a note of optimism in ONE. I see homosexuality as a wonderful way of life. I certainly rest; I am not hunted; I hope I am not a pest!

Miss W.

Notes

At the time I conducted my research, there were two separate collections of ONE, Inc., correspondence at the ONE National Gay and Lesbian Archives in Los Angeles, California. One collection contained letters exclusively from 1953 to 1965, and a larger collection contained letters from 1953 to the 1990s (after the magazine folded in 1967, ONE, Inc., continued to exist as an educational institution). Aside from the letters published in *ONE* magazine, this book contains letters only from the smaller collection, which contains three subsets: General Correspondence, Social Service Correspondence, and Regional Correspondence. General Correspondence letters were organized alphabetically by last name at the archive. These letters included subscription renewals, comments about the magazine, personal narratives, and general observations about gay life. Social Service Correspondence letters were organized by date at the archive. These letters usually requested specific kinds of help from ONE, Inc.'s "Social Service," which was advertised in the magazine. Regional Correspondence letters were organized by state or country at the archive and included letters about *ONE* magazine's distribution as well as international correspondence.

Below is a chapter-by-chapter breakdown indicating which subset each letter in this book came from. The dates of the letters are listed in the order they appear in each chapter. Letters published in *ONE* magazine are not included here.

Chapter 1: Biography and Self-Analysis

Social Service Correspondence: 15 February 1965, 24 April 1955, 26 June 1960, 7 August 1961, 16 November 1964
General Correspondence: 18 March 1958, 27 November 1958, 5 July 1959, 22 April 1962, 2 August 1963, 26 February 1964, 8 March 1960, 22 March 1961, 24 November 1961, 16 January 1962, 31 July 1960, 2 July 1962, 3 November 1962, 3 March 1963

Chapter 2: Love, Sex, and Relationships

Social Service Correspondence: 26 February 1962, 7 April 1958, 31 October 1962, 13 December 1957, 14 April 1958, 24 January 1964, 4 March 1965, 11 July 1956
General Correspondence: 3 March 1963, 21 March 1965, 8 March 1962, 29 July 1962, 15 June 1963, 22 November 1964, 10 February 1957, 14 February 1957, 26 December 1957, 8 August 1955, 7 June 1963, 27 October 1964, 17 September 1959, 19 September 1959, 7 October 1960, 25 September 1963
Regional Correspondence: 18 September 1958

Chapter 3: Repression and Defiance

Social Service Correspondence: 25 May 1957, 5 July 1957, 8 April 1961
General Correspondence: 31 October 1960, 6 January 1961, 1 August 1960, 26 August 1962, 23 May 1963, 26 November 1963, 29 January 1961, 27 August 1960, 22 December 1960, 24 March 1963, 22 October 1961, 9 January 1958, 27 October 1958, 23 August 1964, 3 April 1954, 3 June 1964
Regional Correspondence: 30 October 1954, 16 September 1954, 29 April 1958, 22 May 1958, 31 May 1957, 28 June 1957, 15 June 1956

Chapter 4: Incarceration

Social Service Correspondence: 8 June 1964, 25 August 1964, 20 March 1961, 24 June 1961, 2 July 1961, 23 August 1960, 23 June 1964, 22 November 1964, 29 January 1964
General Correspondence: 3 April 1955, 23 August 1964
The letter dated 19 January 1955 is stored in a subject file folder separate from the other letters.

Chapter 5: Representations and Stereotypes

General Correspondence: 24 May 1955, 6 September 1959, 14 April 1961, 11 November 1962, 12 June 1963, 29 June 1964, 12 August 1964
Regional Correspondence: 20 February 1956

Introduction

1. John D'Emilio, *Sexual Politics, Sexual Communities: The Making of a Homosexual Minority in the United States* (Chicago: University of Chicago Press, 1983); Marcia M. Gallo, *Different Daughters: A History of the Daughters of Bilitis and the Rise of the Lesbian Rights Movement* (New York: Carroll and Graf, 2006); James T. Sears, *Behind the Mask of the Mattachine: The Hal Call Chronicles and the Early Movement for Homosexual Emancipation* (New York: Harrington Park

Press, 2006); C. Todd White, *Pre-Gay L.A.: A Social History of the Movement for Homosexual Rights* (Urbana: University of Illinois Press, 2009).

2. Ray to *ONE*, 26 February 1964. Letter is reprinted in chap. 1. See p. 221 for further explanation of the archival collections used for this book.

3. Some of the letters in this book were cited or quoted in Craig Loftin, *Masked Voices: Gay Men and Lesbians in Cold War America* (Albany: SUNY Press, 2012). All names have been changed to protect the anonymity of the letter writers. The letters have been reprinted in this book exactly as they were received by *ONE* with minor exceptions for clarification or readability. Many letters thus include spelling and grammatical mistakes.

4. The terms "midsize town" and "small town" in this volume are intended only to provide a relative sense of proportion and are not a rigidly accurate population estimate. The phrase "small town" describes a town with a population less than 10,000 and "midsize town" for those with a population between 10,000 and 150,000 (1960 data). The name of the city is provided for cities with more than 150,000 people (as well as a few distinctive midsize towns). For all of the small towns and most of the midsize towns, more general geographical descriptions, such as a "small town in Western Illinois" or a "midsize town in Northeastern Texas," have been used in order to maintain the anonymity of the letter writers.

5. On the growth of post–World War II gay communication networks, see Martin D. Meeker, *Contacts Desired: Connecting to the Gay Male and Lesbian World from the 1940s into the 1970s* (Chicago: University of Chicago Press, 2006).

6. Allan Bérubé, *Coming Out under Fire: The History of Gay Men and Women in World War Two* (New York: Plume, 1991), 279.

7. Alfred Kinsey, Wardell Pomeroy, and Clyde Martin, *Sexual Behavior in the Human Male* (Philadelphia: Saunders, 1948); Alfred Kinsey, Wardell Pomeroy, and Clyde Martin, *Sexual Behavior in the Human Female* (Philadelphia: Saunders, 1953); Jonathan Gathorne-Hardy, *Sex the Measure of All Things: A Life of Alfred C. Kinsey* (Bloomington: Indiana University Press, 1998).

8. Elizabeth Lalo, "Din," *ONE* I, 12 (December 1953), 18.

9. David K. Johnson, *The Lavender Scare: The Cold War Persecution of Gays and Lesbians in the Federal Government* (Chicago: University of Chicago Press, 2004).

10. Data derived from a survey distributed in 1960 and 1961 in *ONE* magazine. Surveys on file at the ONE National Gay and Lesbian Archives, Los Angeles, California.

11. Ronald Bayer, *Homosexuality and American Psychiatry: The Politics of Diagnosis* (Princeton, NJ: Princeton University Press, 1987).

12. Craig Loftin, "Unacceptable Mannerisms: Gender Anxieties, Homosexual Activism, and Swish in the United States, 1945-65," *Journal of Social History* XL, 3 (Spring 2007).

13. This estimate is based on a sample of approximately 1,000 letters to *ONE*.

14. Tina Fetner, *How the Religious Right Shaped Lesbian and Gay Activism* (Minneapolis: University of Minnesota Press, 2008).

15. Thaddeus Russell, "The Color of Discipline: Civil Rights and Black Sexuality," *American Quarterly* LX, 1 (March 2008), 101-128.

16. Alex to *ONE*, 10 February 1957. Letter is reprinted in chap. 2.

17. On homosexuality and the criminal justice system, see William N. Eskridge Jr., *Gaylaw: Challenging the Apartheid of the Closet* (Cambridge, MA: Harvard University Press, 1999); Joyce Murdoch and Deb Price, *Courting Justice: Gay Men and Lesbians v. the Supreme Court* (New York: Basic Books, 2001); Susan Mezey, *Queers in Court: Gay Rights Law and Public Policy* (Lanham, MD: Rowman and Littlefield, 2007).

18. *ONE* was available at newsstands and bookstores in most large American cities, including San Diego; Long Beach; Los Angeles; San Jose; San Francisco; Berkeley; Portland, Oregon; Seattle; Salt Lake City; Denver; Detroit; Chicago; Toledo; Cleveland; Kansas City; Omaha; Tulsa; Oklahoma City; San Antonio; Dallas; Houston; New Orleans; Baton Rouge; Mobile; Fayetteville; Sarasota; Miami; Atlanta; Knoxville; Baltimore; Washington, DC; Philadelphia; Pittsburg; New York City; Boston; and Portland, Maine. Internationally, it was available in Mexico City, Buenos Aires, Amsterdam, Copenhagen, Hamburg, and Vienna. This list is compiled from various issues' "Where to purchase *ONE*" page as well as ONE, Inc., internal documents located in ONE Regional Correspondence files, ONE Archives.

19. Murdoch and Price, *Courting Justice*, 27–50.

20. Dorr Legg to International Committee for Sexual Equality (Holland), 22 February 1955, Holland Folder, ONE Regional Correspondence.

21. Ronald to *ONE*, 15 February 1965. Letter is reprinted in chap. 1.

22. Vito Russo, *The Celluloid Closet: Homosexuality in the Movies* (New York: Harper and Row, 1981); Richard Barrios, *Screened Out: Playing Gay in Hollywood from Edison to Stonewall* (New York: Routledge, 2005).

23. Paul to *ONE*, 12 August 1964. Letter is reprinted in chap. 5.

24. The long list of books, essays, and films that use the word "Stonewall" in their titles accompanied by such words as "before," "after," "since," or "toward," indicates the extent to which the Stonewall Riots are viewed as the key watershed moment between two dramatically distinct historical periods. Examples include *Before Stonewall* [feature film], directors Greta Schiller and Robert Rosenberg, 1984; Peter Nardi, David Sanders, and Judd Marmor, *Growing Up before Stonewall: Life Stories of Some Gay Men* (London: Routledge, 1994); Byrne Fone, *A Road to Stonewall: Male Homosexuality and Homophobia in English and American Literature* (New York: Twayne Publishers, 1994); David Deitcher, ed., *The Question of Equality: Lesbian and Gay Politics Since Stonewall* (New York: Scribner, 1995); *After Stonewall* [feature film], director John Scagliotti, 1999; Christopher Nealon, *Foundlings: Lesbian and Gay Historical Emotion before Stonewall* (Durham, NC: Duke University Press, 2001); Vern Bullough, ed., *Before Stonewall: Activists for Gay and Lesbian Rights in Historical Context* (New York: Harrington Park Press, 2002); Thomas Waugh, *Out/Lines: Underground Gay Graphics from before Stonewall* (Vancouver, BC: Arsenal Pulp Press, 2002); Nicholas C. Edsall, *Toward Stonewall: Homosexuality and Society in the Modern Western World* (Charlottesville: University of Virginia Press, 2003); Barrios, *Screened Out*; Alan Helms, *Young Man from the Provinces: A Gay Life before Stonewall* (Minneapolis: University of Minnesota Press, 2003); Thomas Foster, *Long before Stonewall: Histories of Same-Sex Sexuality in Early America* (New York: New York University Press, 2007); Felice Picano, *Art*

and Sex in Greenwich Village: A Memoir of Gay Literary Life after Stonewall (New York: Basic Books, 2007); Les Brookes, *Gay Male Fiction since Stonewall: Ideology, Conflict, and Aesthetics* (New York: Routledge, 2009).

25. A few scholars have emphasized continuities before and after 1969, such as Martin B. Duberman, *Stonewall* (New York: Dutton, 1993), xv; Daniel Harris, *The Rise and Fall of Gay Culture* (New York: Hyperion, 1997), 244; John Grube, "'No More Shit': The Struggle for Democratic Gay Space in Toronto," in Gordon Brent Ingram, Anne-Marie Bouthillette, and Yolanda Retter, eds., *Queers in Space: Communities, Public Places, Sites of Resistance* (Seattle: Bay Press, 1997), 127.

26. Among the thousands of letters to *ONE* I read, only one letter used the word "closet," and its usage was more general than the contemporary idea of the closet. A man from Northern California wrote, "Perhaps if everyone would take sex out of the dark closet into which the word [sic] has flung it, we would all be better human beings." Dwayne to *ONE*, 10 August 1960, 1960 Folder, ONE Social Service Correspondence.

27. Homophile publications made frequent use of mask metaphors. For examples, *The Ladder* II, 1 (October 1957); *ONE* VII, 2 (February 1959); Boston Area Mattachine Newsletter, May 1959.

Chapter 1: Biography and Self-Analysis

1. Word is illegible due to smudging.

2. Jim Schneider was a *ONE* activist during the 1960s. He played an important role in the magazine's distribution.

3. "D.O." refers to Doctor of Osteopathic medicine. The letter "O" is handwritten in a way that it could be an "A," thus changing the meaning to District Attorney. Because the correspondent makes no references to the criminal justice system in his letter, I believe D.O. is correct.

4. Paul Petersen is an actor best known for playing the teenaged son on *The Donna Reed Show*.

5. Blanche Baker was a psychologist who wrote an advice column for *ONE* magazine from 1959 to 1961.

6. These paragraphs have not been altered or deleted for this book because of their general, unspecific character.

7. The Mattachine Foundation created the "Citizens' Committee to Outlaw Entrapment" in 1952 to help Mattachine member Dale Jennings fight a homosexual arrest in court. According to Edward Alwood, "Jennings became the first gay person in California history to successfully challenge police entrapment." Jennings also briefly served as a *ONE* magazine editor in 1953. Edward Alwood, *Straight News: Gays, Lesbians, and the News Media* (New York: Columbia University Press, 1996), 28-29; Marvin Cutler, ed., *Homosexuals Today, 1956* (Los Angeles: ONE, Inc., 1956), 22-29.

8. City Lights Bookstore was a focal point of the 1950s Beat movement and one of the first businesses in San Francisco to sell *ONE* magazine.

9. "Grand Inquisitor from Wisconsin" refers to Senator Joseph McCarthy.

10. The correspondent is most likely referring to Karl-Heinrich Ulrichs, a German writer who advocated gay legal rights in the mid-nineteenth century. Writing before the advent of the word "homosexual," Ulrichs referred to men attracted to other men as "Urnings." This was often translated into English as "Uranians."

11. Published in *ONE* III, 4 (April 1955), 9–12.

12. "DOB" refers to the lesbian organization "Daughters of Bilitis." The Daughters opposed ONE, Inc.'s efforts in 1961 to construct a Homosexual Bill of Rights because the proposed rights focused on gay men and ignored lesbians.

13. William Lambert, also known as Dorr Legg, was ONE, Inc.'s business manager as well as a frequent contributor to the magazine. His actual name was William Lambert Dorr Legg.

14. William Edward "Billy" Glover served as *ONE*'s office manager during the 1950s and 1960s.

15. The correspondent refers to Jess Stearn, *The Sixth Man* (New York: MacFadden Books, 1961).

16. Don Slater served as *ONE's* editor from 1958 to 1965.

Chapter 2: Love, Sex, and Relationships

1. "Bill" most likely refers to Billy Glover or William Lambert [Dorr Legg].

2. Rudolph Burckhardt and Karl Meier (alias "Rolf") were a gay male couple who shared duties running the Swiss-based homophile organization Der Kreis.

3. "H.L.R.S." refers to Homosexual Law Reform Society, the United Kingdom's first gay rights organization, founded in 1958.

4. Geraldine Jackson was a regular *ONE* contributor.

5. The letter was addressed to a member of *ONE*'s staff.

6. In 1961 Illinois became the first state in the United States to legalize consensual homosexual behavior.

7. "T-room" refers to a public restroom where men routinely engage in discreet sex with one another.

8. James Barr Fugaté was a writer who used the pen name James Barr. *ONE* magazine published several of Barr's essays in 1954 and 1955. His best-known work is the 1950 gay novel *Quatrefoil*. In 1954, ONE, Inc.'s fledgling book press published exclusive limited edition copies of Barr's play *Game of Fools*.

9. "Ann Carll Reid" [Irma "Corky" Wolf] served as *ONE*'s editor from 1954 through 1957.

10. "Robert Gregory" was a pseudonym used by many *ONE* contributors.

11. Lyn Pedersen [Jim Kepner], "Why Not a Pen Pal Club?" and William Lambert [Dorr Legg], "Sick Sick Sick," *ONE* VII, 9 (September 1959), 5–13.

Chapter 3: Repression and Defiance

1. Marquis Childs was a syndicated newspaper columnist. His editorial on Lester Hunt's suicide appeared in various newspapers on 1 July 1954.

2. George Kennan was the architect of the U.S. government's cold war "containment" policy against the spread of communism.

3. In the Soviet Union, there was a brief period of tolerance toward gay people during the 1920s "New Economic Policy," but under Stalin, homosexuals were arrested and sent to labor camps by the thousands. Daniel Schluter, *Gay Life in the Former USSR: Fraternity without Community* (New York and London: Routledge, 2002).

4. The correspondent refers to the 1960 defection of two National Security Agency employees, Bernon Mitchell and William Martin, to the Soviet Union. They were rumored to have been lovers at the time. "Security Practices in the National Security Agency (Defection of Bernon F. Mitchell and William H. Martin): Report by the Committee on Un-American Activities House of Representatives, 87th Congress, 2nd Session, 13 August 1962 (Washington, DC: U.S. Printing Office, 1962).

5. "Alison Hunter" was a pseudonym used by several members of *ONE's* staff.

6. Lyn Pedersen, "Miami Hurricane," *ONE* II, 9 (November 1954), 8.

7. Subscription request deleted. Letter writer is female.

8. "O., l., or f." is an abbreviation of "obscene, lewd, and filthy." The more common legal term was "obscene, lewd, and lascivious."

9. The correspondent was referring to the Swiss homophile organization Der Kreis.

10. Guy Burgess and Donald Maclean were British government workers who defected to the Soviet Union in 1951 after serving as spies for many years. They were part of a Soviet spy network in Britain called the Cambridge Five.

11. The correspondent refers to *Homosexuality: A Cross Cultural Approach* by Donald Webster Cory (New York: Julian Press, 1956).

12. Karl Menninger was a prominent psychiatrist and author.

13. On the Society for Human Rights, see Jonathan Ned Katz, ed., *Gay American History: Lesbians and Gay Men in the U.S.A.* (New York: Harper Colophon, 1976), 385–397.

14. Psychiatrist Robert Lindner wrote several popular books, including *Rebel without a Cause, The Fifty-Minute Hour*, and *Must You Conform?* Lindner died in 1956.

Chapter 4: Incarceration

1. I came across no letters in the *ONE* collection from women who had been incarcerated because of homosexual offenses. Women were occasionally arrested in gay bar raids at the time, but gay men disproportionately suffered the wrath of the criminal justice system.

2. Criminal psychiatrist J. Paul de River worked as a sex crime consultant for the Los Angeles Police Department during the 1950s. In his book *The Sexual Criminal: A Psychoanalytical Study* (Springfield, IL: Charles C. Thomas Publisher, 1950), de River argued that homosexuality could be eradicated through "Spartan living, hard work, educational methods, suggestive therapy, and last but not least, electric shock therapy" (276).

3. "Norwalk" refers to a state mental hospital in Norwalk, California, near Los Angeles.

4. This letter is analyzed in greater depth in Craig Loftin, *Masked Voices: Gay Men and Lesbians in Cold War America* (Albany: SUNY Press, 2012), chap. 9.

Chapter 5: Representations and Stereotypes

1. The 1953 Broadway stage hit *Tea and Sympathy* featured an effeminate male prep school student suffering harassment from peers and faculty who suspect he is gay.

2. Donald Webster Cory wrote the groundbreaking 1951 nonfiction book *The Homosexual in America* and operated a homosexual-themed book service in the 1950s.

3. Lee Mortimer was a tabloid-style journalist best known for co-authoring a series of "Confidential" books in the 1950s, such as *Chicago Confidential, Washington Confidential, New York Confidential, U.S.A. Confidential, Around the World Confidential,* and *Women Confidential.*

4. Unrelated material deleted.

5. Paul Welch, "Homosexuality in America," *Life*, 26 June 1964, 66–74.

Index

Adler, Alfred, 85
African-Americans, 7, 82, 137, 152, 211, 212; letter from, 187-95. *See also* black civil rights movement
Agee, James, 179
Alaska, 162
Albany, NY, 204-05
alcoholism, 38
Alexander, Franz, 115
Allegro (Philadelphia), 109
"All-Queens-Day," 16
Alwood, Edward, 225n7
American Legion, 45
American Medical Association, 46
am Main, 144
Amsterdam, Netherlands, 143; letter from, 144-47
Anchorage, AK, 162
Andersen-Rosendal, Jorgen, 204
Anger, Kenneth, 182
Arcadie, 68, 92
"Are Homosexuals Necessarily Neurotic?" 39
Argentina, 92, 210. *See also* Buenos Aires
Arkansas. *See* Little Rock
Arlington, VA, 211
Army. *See* United States Army
arrests, 8, 108, 151; descriptions of, 154-55, 164-65, 184; gay activism and, 134; gay bars and, 109; lesbians and, 227n1; obscenity, 198; police tactics, 112; psychiatry and, 40. *See also* attorneys, courts, law

Asheville, NC, 47
Atascadero, CA, 174-75; letter from, 170-83
Atlanta, GA, 46; letter from, 47
Atlantic City, NJ, 110, 188
Atlantic House, The, (Provincetown), 109
attorneys: gay arrests and, 134, 160, 165-66, 170-71, 174; *ONE* magazine and, 123; requests for, 154-56, 184, 187
Austin, TX: letters from, 107-08, 205-07
Australia, 99
Austria, 66, 145

Baker, Blanche, 40, 43, 225n5
Bali, Indonesia, 64
Baltimore, MD, 48, 54; letters from, 53-55, 105-06
Barker Hotel (Los Angeles), 16
Barney's Beanery (Los Angeles/West Hollywood), 212
Barr, James. *See* James Barr Fugaté
bars. *See* gay bars
bathhouses, 73-74, 77
Baudry, André, 92
Beach Bums, 45
Belgium, 129, 145. *See also* Brussels
berdache, 45
Bérubé, Allan, 4
Bible, The, 58, 81
bisexuality, 37, 46, 134, 162
black civil rights movement, 5-6, 212

blackmail, 74-75, 126-27
Blick, Roy, 104
Blue Angels, 163
Bowers, Faubion, 50
Bowman, Karl, 35
Boy Scouts, 45
Brave New World, 175, 206
Bremen, Germany, 144
Bridgeport, CN, 198
British Journal of Delinquency, 68
Brooklyn, New York City, NY: letters from, 41-42, 55-58, 68-71, 86-87, 98-99, 109-110, 203, 207-08, 219-20
Brussels, Belgium, 73, 143
Bryant, Anita, 116
Buenos Aires, Argentina: letter from, 92-93
Burchfield, Charles, 178
Burckhardt, Rudolph, 67-68, 147-48, 226n2
Burgess, Glenn, 127, 227n10
Burns, John Horne, 85

Calcutta, India: letter from, 64
Calgary, Canada, 73
California, 3, 44, 85, 177. *See also* Atascadero, Los Angeles, Norwalk State Hospital, Oakland, Pasadena, Sacramento, San Diego, San Francisco, Santa Barbara, Santa Monica
California State Department of Mental Hygiene, 35
Canada, 3, 68, 73; *ONE* magazine and, 122-24. *See also* Calgary, Hamilton, Montreal, Toronto, Vancouver
Carson, Johnny, 10, 208-09
Catholicism, 57, 78, 83, 108, 112, 118, 169, 184, 217
Cezanne, Paul, 178
Charlotte, NC, 152-53
Chasin, Abram, 49-50
Chattanooga, TN, 46
Chicago, IL, 124, 134-35, 184; letters from, 124-25, 186-87
Childs, Marquis, 104, 226n1(ch3)

Christ and the Homosexual, 20
Christian Conference of the Relevance of Religious Belief to Problems of Everyday Living, 105
Cicero's (Baltimore), 54
circumcision, 83
City Lights Bookstore (San Francisco), 36, 225n8
civil rights. *See* black civil rights movement, homophile movement
civil rights impulse, 6, 9, 103, 133-49
class, 173-74
classical music, 49-50
Cleveland, OH, 77
"closet," 11-12, 225n26
Coast Guard. *See* United States Coast Guard
Cocteau, Jean, 176-77, 182
cold war, 5, 103-07
college students: letters from, 14, 16-17
Columbus, OH: letter from, 65-66
coming out, 10, 11, 14-34, 42, 69
Committee to Outlaw Entrapment, 35, 225n7
communism, 37, 106-07, 136, 137, 211-12
computers, 55-57
Concord Café (Pittsburgh), 77
Confidential Flash, 210
Connecticut, 3, 8, 198; letter from, 20-22
Cooper, Ben, 179
Copenhagen, Denmark, 143-44
Cork and Bottle (Pittsburgh), 77
Cork Room (San Antonio), 110
Cornet, 46
Cory, Donald Webster, 130, 199, 228n2
courts, 164-66, 170-71, 174, 180, 184, 187, 225n7
Cowles, Fleur, 179
Crane, Hart, 178-79
criminal sexual psychopath, 35, 183
Cromwell, Oliver, 128

cruising, 72-77, 79. *See also* gay bars, parks, restrooms, theaters
Cultuur-en Ontspanningscentrum (COC), 141-42, 145-46

Dallas, TX, 110
Dance Magazine, 50
Dante, 85
Daughters of Bilitis, 2, 42, 226n12
Daytona, FL, 96
Delaware, 3, 158-60. *See also* Wilmington
Democrats, 107
Denmark, 112, 145. *See also* Copenhagen
Derby, CN, 198
de River, J. Paul, 171-72
Der Kreis, 67-68, 92, 146-47, 226n2, 227n9
Der Kreis, 92
Derricks, 84-85
Detroit, MI: letter from (including suburbs), 58-60
Dewey, John, 178
Dickens, Charles, 138
Dig, 20
Divine Comedy, The, 85
Donna Reed Show, The, 225n4
drugs, 89-90, 113
Dulles, John Foster, 131
Dynamite, 198

Eastern Airlines, 116
East Orange, NJ, 192
effeminacy: gay men and, 37, 46, 69, 84, 113, 161, 228n1
Eisenhower, Dwight, 131, 217-18
electroconvulsive therapy (ECT), 45, 171, 195, 227n2(ch4)
Eliot, T.S., 179
Ellis, Albert, 39, 206
employment, 19, 25, 129-33, 153; arrests and, 155, 184; discrimination and, 5; government and, 33-34, 120-21, 135, 139-40, 213; lesbians and, 54, 130, 132-33; military discharges and, 33-34, 120-21; nursing, 128; prison and, 156-61; teaching, 73-74, 133
England. *See* United Kingdom
entrapment, 104, 108, 112, 225n7
Eos, 92
epilepsy, 38
Esoteric Side of Love and Marriage, The, 63

family, 52-53; anxiety and, 43-44, 91, 96, 188, 190-95; arrests and, 155; coming out to, 42-43, 70, 193. *See also* marriage
Federal Bureau of Investigation (FBI), 213
female impersonation, 50
"Feminine Viewpoint, The," 47
Fire Island, NY, 69
Firth, Violet, 63
Fitzgerald, Ella, 67
Flair, 179
Florida, 3, 116-21, 133; letter from, 95-96. *See also* Daytona, Fort Lauderdale, Jacksonville, Key West, Miami, Raiford
Florida State University, 157
Fort Dix (New Jersey), 177
Fort Lauderdale, FL: letter from, 117-18
Fort Leavenworth (Kansas), 32, 168
Fortune, Dion, 63
France, 68, 112-13. *See also* Nice, Paris
Frankfurt, Germany, 144
Franklin, Benjamin, 37
Freud, Sigmund, 41, 45, 85
Friends-Club, 144
Friendship and Freedom, 134
Fugaté, James Barr, 84-85, 226n8

Gabor, Eva, 207-08
Gallery, The, 85
Galveston, TX, 47

Game of Fools, 226n8
Ganymedes, 144
gay bars, 69–70, 98, 136, 161, 168, 204–05; coming out and, 42; disapproval of, 86, 87–88, 162, 215–16; lesbians and, 54, 203, 227n1; police harassment of, 8, 76–77, 108–110, 115; relationships and, 23, 83, 86–88; specific bars, 45, 54, 77, 109–10
gay civil rights movement. *See* homophile movement
gender: effeminacy, 37, 46, 69, 84, 113, 161, 215, 228n1; female impersonation, 50; masculinity, 24, 51, 54, 84, 93, 157, 215; roles, 45, 84, 188, 204; sexuality and, 7, 24, 46–58
Generation of Vipers, 46
Gene's Music Bar (Dallas), 110
Genet, Jean, 176, 179, 181–82
Georgia, 3. *See also* Atlanta
Germany, 89, 112, 134, 143, 145–47, 211–12. *See also* Bremen, Frankfurt
Gide, André, 84
glee clubs, 30–31
Glover, William, 82, 226n14
Gothenburg, Sweden, 144
government, 127, 142, 211; crackdown on homosexuals, 5, 103, 105–08; employment and, 33–34, 120–21, 135–36, 139–40, 213. *See also* United States House of Representatives, United States Senate, United States State Department, United States Supreme Court
Greco, Marshall Charles, 198
Greece, 84
Gregory, Robert, 226n10
Group Life, 198
Guillardo, Gene, 76

Hamburg, Germany, 143
Hamilton, Canada: letters from, 122–24
Han Temple Organisation, 148–49
Hard Candy, 179

Harvey, Herman, 173
Havemann, Ernest, 209
Hawaii, 148
Hellas, 144
heterosexuals, 52; letters from, 34–36, 47, 62–63, 149
Hirschfeld, Magnus, 115
Hitler, Adolph, 211–12
homophile movement, 1–2, 19, 225n27; activist strategies, 133–49, 213–20; black civil rights movement and, 5–6; lesbians and, 7, 216–17
Homosexuality: A Cross Cultural Approach, 130
Homosexual Law Reform Society, 68, 226n3
Homosexual League of New York, 80
Homosexual World Organization, 148–49
Hong Kong, 148
hospitals, 130–32, 161, 163–65. *See also* mental hospitals
Houston Chronicle, 115
Houston, TX, 115; letter from, 114–15
Hungary, 100
Hunt, Lester, 104, 226n1(ch3)
Hunter, Alison, 227
Hush-Hush, 10, 197–98, 212
Huxley, Aldous, 63, 175, 206

I am a Camera, 179
I.F.O., 144
Illinois, 3, 8, 60, 76, 134, 160, 187, 226n6; letters from, 78–80, 89, 158–67, 209–10. *See also* Chicago
India, 64. *See also* Calcutta
Indiana, 3. *See also* Norman Beatty State Hospital, Westville
Indiana University, 4
Indonesia, 148
Inside Story, 212
International Committee for Sexual Equality (ICSE), 143–48
Internationalt Forbund for Sexual Lighed, 144
Italy, 94. *See also* Naples, Novara

Jackson, Evrett Lee, 45
Jackson, Geraldine, 226n4
Jacksonville, FL, 157
jail. *See* prisons
James, Henry, 97
James, William, 85
Janus Society, 80, 156
Japan, 50, 204
Jenkin's Arcade (Pittsburgh), 77
Jennings, Dale, 139, 225n7
Jews, 33, 81, 99, 112, 211
Jorgenson, Christine, 46
Jung, Carl, 85

kabuki, 50
Kafka, Franz, 180
Kama Sutra, 64
Kansas, 3; letter from, 15–16. *See also* Fort Leavenworth, Kansas City, Wichita
Kansas City, KS: letter from, 139–41
Kansas City, MO, 199; letter from, 199–203
Kansas City Star-Times, 199–203
Kennan, George, 103, 105–06, 227n2(ch3)
Kennedy, John F., 107–08
Kennedy, Robert, 107
Kentucky. *See* Louisville
Kepner, James (pseud. Lyn Pedersen), 170; pen pals and, 96–98
Keval, The, 99
Key West, FL, 117, 158–60, 161–67; letter from, 117
Kilgallen, Dorothy, 212
Kingman, Dong, 178
Kinsey, Alfred, 4–5, 13, 23, 37, 171–73, 207
Kinsey Reports, 4–5, 7, 13, 23
Knoxville, TN: letters from, 44–46, 76
Korean War, 44, 168

Lady Chatterly's Lover, 129
Lafayette Park (Washington, D.C.), 104
Lambert, William. *See* Dorr Legg
Lancaster, Burt, 179

Langley-Porter Clinic (San Francisco), 171
Last of the Vikings, The, 207–08
Latinos, 48, 82, 191; letters from, 48–53, 92–93
law, 8, 59, 91, 93, 121, 151, 169, 226n6; blackmail and, 126–27; courts, 164–66, 170–71, 174, 180, 184, 187, 225n7; gay activism and, 134–35, 214; legal crackdowns, 108–17; *ONE* magazine and, 104; psychiatry and psychology and, 32, 34–36, 38, 40, 168, 171–73, 177, 227n2(ch4); solicitation, 154–56. *See also* attorneys, police
Lawrence v Texas, 8
lawyers. *See* attorneys
Legg, Dorr, 2, 92, 138–43, 226n13; pen pals and, 96–98
lesbians, 47; arrests and, 227n1; bars, 54, 77, 203; homophile movement and, 7, 216–17; letters from, 39–40, 48, 53–55, 89, 101–02, 111, 130, 132–33, 143–44, 203, 216–20; novels by, 203; *ONE* magazine and, 216–17; visibility and, 48, 89
Liberace, 10, 208–09
libraries, 46
Life, 187, 209–10
Lindner, Robert, 148, 171–73, 175, 227n14
Little Rock, AR, 131
London, United Kingdom, 73, 99, 100; letter from, 100–01
loneliness, 14, 21, 54, 70, 83, 87–93, 98, 130, 188
Los Angeles, CA, 15, 19, 65–66, 104, 184; gay life in, 16, 45, 89, 120; homophile organization in, 2, 71, 93; letters from (including suburbs), 14–15, 34–36, 62–63, 71–72, 93–94, 106–07, 119–21, 130, 134, 137–38, 141–43, 214–16, 217–18; police, 112–13; Post Office, 9
Los Angeles Police Department, 227n2(ch4)

Louisville, KY, 46
loyalty oaths, 135–36
Luxemburg, 145

Macao, China, 148
MacLean, Donald, 127, 227n10
Magnini, Anna, 179
Malaysia, 148
ManAlive, 168
Manchester, United Kingdom, 129; letter from, 126–29
Marine Room (San Antonio), 110
Marines. *See* United States Marines
marriage, 52–53, 54, 101; opposite-sex, 40, 42–43, 91, 95, 101–02, 134, 159, 162, 191; same-sex, 69, 84, 100, 108, 163, 189–90
Martin and Mitchell defection scandal, 107, 227n4
Marxism, 107
Maryland, 3. *See also* Baltimore
Massachusetts, 3, 14; letter from, 118–119
Massacre, The, 207–08
Masters, R.E.L., 21
Mattachine Review, 75, 80, 217
Mattachine Society, 2, 36, 46, 117, 135–36, 198, 217, 225n7
McCarthy, Joseph, 5, 37, 104, 128, 212, 225n9
McCarthyism, 121, 127, 130, 151
McCrea, Joel, 208
media: homosexuals and, 10–11, 84, 165, 197–220
Meier, Karl, (psued. Rolf), 67–68, 147–48, 226n2
Mellon Square (Pittsburgh), 77
Memphis, TN, 46
Menninger, Karl, 131, 227n12
mental hospitals, 10, 19, 43, 44, 169–77, 183–86, 195; letters from, 169–86. *See also* Atascadero, Norwalk
mental illness: homosexuality as, 6–7, 20, 39–40, 169. *See also* neurosis, psychiatry, psychology

Mexicans, Mexican-Americans. *See* Latinos
Mexico, 210
Miami, FL, 60, 116–20, 162–64, 166–67; letters from 22–34, 116–17
Michigan, 3; letter from, 19–20. *See also* Detroit
midsize towns: letters from, 16–18, 20–22, 43–44, 78–80, 89–90, 96–97, 101–02, 110, 113, 125–26, 132–33, 152–53, 155–56, 158–67, 187–95, 197–98, 208–10
military, 73, 76, 164, 204–05; discharges, 40, 44–45, 120–21, 167–68. *See also* Blue Angels, United States Army, United States Coast Guard, United States Marines, United States Navy
Milo's (Los Angeles), 45
Miltown, 89–90
ministers: gay, 58–60, 89, 163, 165, 188, 190–95; letters from, 58–61
Missouri, 3, 111; letter from, 125–26. *See also* Kansas City
Montana, 3; letter from, 83–85
Montreal, Canada, 101
Moon of Beauty, The, 204
Mortimer, Lee, 204, 228n3(ch5)
movies, 58, 115, 179, 205–06

Naked Truth, 212
Naples, Italy, 149
Nashville, TN, 46
National Council for African Affairs, 218
National Informer, 210
national security: homosexuals and, 5, 37, 108, 127, 135–36
National Star-Chronicle, 210
Native Americans, 45
Navy. *See* United States Navy
Nazis, 36, 112, 114, 143, 210–12
Nebraska, 3. *See also* Omaha
Netherlands, 92, 141–42, 145, 148. *See also* Amsterdam

neurosis, 39–40, 73, 97, 214–16
Nevada, 3. *See also* Reno
New Jersey, 3, 38, 110; letters from, 187–95, 197–98. *See also* Perth Amboy
newsstands, 14, 103–05, 224n18
Newsweek, 76
New York, 3; letters from, 16–18, 132–33. *See also* Albany, Fire Island, New York City
New York City, 21–22, 87, 191–92, 199; gay life in, 17, 69–70, 97, 110, 189; letters from (including Brooklyn), 41–42, 48–53, 55–58, 68–71, 86–88, 90–91, 94, 98–99, 101, 109–110, 138, 149, 203–05, 207–08, 219–20; New Yorkers, 48–52, 113; police and, 112; press, 108, 204; Times Square, 14, 17
New York News, 204
New York Times, 49–50
New Zealand: letter from, 91
Nice, France, 145
1984, 175
Norfolk, VA, 76
"normality:" homosexuals and, 13, 15, 17, 25, 36, 48, 59, 71, 100–01, 168, 171–72, 211–12, 214
Norman Beatty State Hospital (Indiana), 183–87
North Carolina, 3; letter from, 152–53. *See also* Asheville
Norwalk State Hospital (California), 35, 172, 174
Norway. *See* Oslo
Novara, Italy: letter from, 148–49
nude photographs, 41, 79–80, 93, 168–69
nudism, 102, 104

Oakland, CA: letter from (including suburbs), 81–83
obscenity, 128, 198; *ONE* magazine and, 8–9, 111, 124–25; Post Office and, 124–26, 135
occultism, 63
Ohio, 3, 66, 77; letter from, 42–43. *See also* Cleveland, Columbus, Youngstown
Oklahoma, 3, 45. *See also* Oklahoma City, Tulsa
Oklahoma City, OK, 38; letter from, 61
Omaha, NE, 19; letter from, 18–19
ONE Confidential, 78, 82
ONE, Inc., 1–2
ONE letters, 1–4; anonymity of, 223n3; collections of, 221–22; geographic breakdown, 3; occupational data, 5; selection of, 2–3; women and, 7
ONE magazine, 1–3, 5; attorneys and, 123; Canada and, 122–24; civil rights and, 9; law and, 104; lesbians and, 216–17; letters published in, 34–36, 39–40, 47–48, 61–64, 87–88, 105–06, 107, 115–16, 117, 134–38, 143–44, 149, 203, 213–20; newsstands and, 14, 103–05, 224n18; obscenity and, 8–9, 111, 124–25; pen pals and, 96–101; psychiatry, psychology, 39–40; representations of homosexuals and, 213–20; secrecy and, 10, 96; subscription anxieties, 36, 84, 121–29, 213; teenagers and, 20–22, 220; volunteers, 71, 169
ONE National Gay and Lesbian Archives, 2, 221
Orwell, George, 175
Oslo, Norway, 143
Otis, Harry, 99
Owen, Jack, 45

Paar, Jack, 209, 212
Paris, France, 113, 143
Parisienne, 198
parks, 77, 104, 108
Pasadena, CA, 10; letters from, 39–40, 121–22, 210–13
Pedersen, Lyn. *See* Kepner, James

Pennsylvania, 3, 168; letters from, 113, 155-56, 167-69. *See also* Philadelphia, Pittsburgh, West Chester
pen pals, 8, 20, 70, 92, 96-101
Perennial Philosophy, The, 63
Perth Amboy, NJ: letter from, 216-17
Peru, 111
Petersen, Paul, 20, 225n4
Philadelphia, PA, 109, 154, 156, 168, 212; letters from, 80-81, 143-44
photographs: nude, 41, 79-80, 93, 168-69; physique, 79
Photo News, 210
physical culture, 15, 25
physique magazines, 45, 93
physique photos, 79
Picnic, 179
Picture Detective Publishing Company, The, 198
Pittsburgh, PA, 77, 168; letter from, 76-78
police, 8, 81, 214; arrests of homosexuals, 154-55, 159-60, 164, 184, 186-87; Canada, 74; Dallas, 110; defense of, 114; gay bar raids, 109-10; Key West, 117, 159-60; Houston, 115; Los Angeles, 112-13, 227n2(ch4); Memphis, 46; newsstands and, 104, 198; obscenity, 198; plainclothesmen, 77, 112; Washington, D.C., 104
politics, 103-08, 141-42
Pomeroy, Wardell, 172
Porcelain, Sidney, 99
Post Office, 80, 121-29, 133, 212; obscenity and, 8-9, 48, 124-26, 135
Pound, Ezra, 179
Prescription for Rebellion, 172, 175
Preston Bradley People's Church (Chicago), 184
Princeton University, 105
prisons, 10, 78, 174-75; experiences in, 32, 157, 164-67, 184; fear of, 29-30, 95; homosexuality in, 24, 32; letters from, 152-55; military, 168-69

Problem of Purity, The, 63
prostitution, 184, 188, 195, 211
Proust, Marcel, 179
Provincetown, MA, 109
psychiatry, psychology, 17-18, 19, 23, 210; "curing" homosexuality, 40, 81, 171, 185; experiences with, 21, 41-42, 43, 90, 195; Freud, Sigmund, 41, 45, 85; law and, 32, 34-36, 38, 40, 168, 171-74; *ONE* magazine and, 39-40; theories of homosexuality, 38. *See also* neurosis
Psychic Self-defence, 63
Puerto Ricans, 48

Quatrefoil, 84, 226n8
Quebec, Canada, 102
Queen of Outer Space, The, 207-08
Quemoy-Matsu crisis, 131

Rabelais, François, 138
Raiford, FL, 156, 166
Reader's Digest, 205-06
Reid, Ann Carll, 47, 226n9
relationships (same-sex), 65-102; falling in love, 65-72, 84; long-term, 8, 83-88; sex and, 7-8. *See also* sexual behavior
religion, 7, 81, 138; Bible, 58, 81; conflicts with, 16-17, 61, 93, 109, 113; gay crackdowns and, 105-06; letters from ministers, 58-61; religious counseling, 21, 32, 59; Unitarians, 118-19, 184. *See also* Catholicism, Jews, ministers
Reno, NV: letter from, 136-37
restrooms, 77, 226n7
Richmond, VA, 188
Rise and Fall of the Third Reich, The, 211-12
Rittenhouse Square (Philadelphia), 212
Riva, Maria, 199-200
River, J. Paul de, 171-72, 227n2(ch4)
Rockwell, George, 211-12
Rockwell Report, 210-12
Roehm, Ernest, 211-12

Rolf. *See* Meier, Karl
Romeo and Juliet, 179
Rose Tattoo, The, 179
Rover, Leo, 104
Rudolph. *See* Burckhardt, Rudolph

Sacramento Bee, 40
Sacramento, CA: letter from, 40–41
sadomasochism, 82–83
Samfundet, 144
San Antonio, TX, 110
San Diego, CA: letter from, 85–86
Sane Occultism, 63
San Francisco, CA: letters from (including suburbs), 36–38, 48
Santa Barbara, CA: letter from, 47
Santa Monica, CA: letters from, 130–32, 135–36
Sartre, Jean-Paul, 181–82
Saturday Review, The, 97, 140
"Scavengers, The," 42
Schenley Park (Pittsburgh), 77
Schneider, Jim, 225n2
Schune's (Pittsburgh), 77
Scott, Larry, 45
Seattle, WA: letter from, 88
Sesso e Liberta, 149
sex education, 52–53
Sexology, 115
sexual behavior: cruising, 72–77, 79; preferences, 38, 79, 81–83, 93, 94, 100, 115–16
Sexual Behavior in the Human Female, 4–5, 7, 13, 23
Sexual Behavior in the Human Male, 4–5, 7, 13, 23
Sexual Criminal, The, 227n2(ch4)
Sexual Frigidity in the Male, 38
Shakespeare, William, 128, 138
Shaw, George Bernard, 138
Shirer, William, 211
shock therapy. *See* electroconvulsive therapy
showers, 73, 79, 93–95
Sinclair, Ed, 197
Singapore, 148

Sixth Man, The, 18
Slater, Don, 71, 81–83, 99, 210, 226n16
small towns, 79; letters from, 15–16, 19–20, 42–43, 83–85, 89, 95–96, 118–19, 167–69
socialism, 106–07
Society for Human Rights, 134
South Africa, 218
Soviet Union, 5, 103, 106–07, 218, 227n3
Spain, 66
Star-Chronicle. See *National Star-Chronicle*
State of California Department of Mental Hygiene, 35
Stearn, Jess, 45, 226n15
stereotypes, 138, 214, 215
Steuart, James, 41, 206
Stockholm, Sweden, 143, 147
Stockhomsavdelningen av Förbundet av 1948, 147
Stonewall Riots, 11, 224n24
Stone Walls and Men, 171
suburbs: letters from, 36–38, 58–60, 81–83, 93–94, 106–07, 141–43
suicidality, 14, 54, 87, 90, 134, 188, 193–95
Sunshine and Health, 104
Sweden. *See* Gothenburg, Stockholm
Switzerland, 112, 147. *See also* Zurich

Tea and Sympathy, 84, 199–202, 228n1
teachers, 73–74, 133
teenagers: experiences of, 26–31, 42, 69, 94; lesbian bars and, 203; letters from, 14, 19–20, 86–87, 93–94; *ONE* magazine and, 20–22, 220; pen-pals and, 97
television, 208–09, 212
Tennessee, 3. *See also* Chattanooga, Knoxville, Nashville, Memphis
Texas, 3, 86, 207; letters from, 43–44, 96–97, 110, 208–09. *See also* Austin, Dallas, Galveston, Houston, San Antonio

Texas Christian University, 85
Thailand, 148
theaters, 115
Times Square (New York City), 14
Tonight Show, The, 10, 208–09
Top Secret, 198
Toronto, Canada: letter from, 62
Townhouse, The, (Provincetown), 109
transgender. *See* female impersonation, gender, transvestitism
transvestitism, 45
"Trial, The," 180
T-rooms, 77
Truman, Harry, 44, 121
Tulsa, OK: letter from, 61–62
Two, 20

Ulrichs, Karl, 226n10
Uncensored, 212
United Kingdom, 60, 68, 99–100, 127, 227n10; letter from, 66–68. *See also* London, Manchester
United States Army, 31–33, 38, 94, 135, 152, 167–68
United States Coast Guard, 163
United States House of Representatives: letter from, 107
United States Marines, 163, 164
United States Navy, 33, 44–45, 66, 76, 85–86, 161–65
United States Post Office. *See* Post Office
United States Senate, 5, 135–36
United States State Department, 105, 211, 212
United States Supreme Court, 8, 9, 78, 111–12, 122
Unitarianism, 118–19, 184
University Grill (Pittsburgh), 77
University of California, Los Angeles (UCLA), 34–35, 172
University of Delaware, 158
University of Missouri, 125
University of Southern California (USC), 153, 173

USSR. *See* Soviet Union

Vancouver, Canada, 73; letter from, 73–75
venereal disease, 53, 73
Vienna, Austria, 66–67
Villa Fontana (Dallas), 110
violence, 154
Virginia. *See* Arlington, Norfolk
Vriendshap, 92

Ward, Stephen, 212
Washington, 3. *See also* Seattle
Washington, D.C., 3, 33, 103–04, 168; letters from, 103–05, 115–16, 134–35
Washington, D.C., Metropolitan Police Department, 104
Weathering Heights (Provincetown), 109
West Chester, PA: letter from, 153–55
West Hollywood, CA, 212
West Side Story, 49
Westville, IN: letters from, 183–86
West Virginia, 77
Whitman, Walt, 179, 201
Wichita, KS, 16; letter from, 111
Wilde, Oscar, 201
Williams, Tennessee, 179
Wilmington, DE, 158; letters from, 99–100, 156–58
Winchell, Walter, 87, 211, 212
Wisconsin, 3; letter from, 89–90
women, heterosexual, 50–53; letters from, 47, 62–63. *See also* lesbians
World War II, 4, 5, 31, 152, 168
WQXR, 49–50
Wylie, Philip, 46

YMCAs, 46, 57, 73, 76, 77
Young, Chuck, 45
Youngstown, OH, 76

Zurich, Switzerland, 92, 126; letter from, 147–48

Made in the USA
Las Vegas, NV
13 November 2020